OSCAR WILDE

MELISSA KNOX

OSCAR WILDE

A LONG AND LOVELY SUICIDE

YALE UNIVERSITY PRESS NEW HAVEN AND LONDON

Published with assistance from the foundation established in memory
of Philip Hamilton McMillan of the Class of 1894, Yale College.

Designed by Nancy Ovedovitz. Set in Berkeley Medium type by
The Composing Room of Michigan. Printed in the United States of
America by Vail-Ballou Press, Binghamton, New York.

Library of Congress Cataloging-in-Publication Data

Knox, Melissa, 1957–
    Oscar Wilde : a long and lovely suicide / Melissa Knox.
        p.   cm.
    Includes bibliographical references and index.
    ISBN 0-300-05905-1
    1. Wilde, Oscar, 1854–1900.   2. Authors, Irish—19th century—
Biography.   3. Psychoanalysis and literature.   I. Title.
PR5823.K65   1994
828'.809—dc20   94-276
[B]   CIP

A catalogue record for this book is available from the British Library.

The paper in this book meets the guidelines for permanence and
durability of the Committee on Production Guidelines for Book
Longevity of the Council on Library Resources.

10   9   8   7   6   5   4   3   2   1

For Oscar Sternbach, mentor and teacher

The true artist is a man who believes absolutely in himself, because he is absolutely himself.
    —*Oscar Wilde, "The Soul of Man under Socialism"*

Our most fiery moments of ecstasy are merely shadows of what somewhere else we have felt, or of what we long some day to feel. So at least it seems to me. And, strangely enough, what comes of all this is a curious mixture of ardour and indifference. I myself would sacrifice everything for a new experience, and I know there is no such thing as a new experience at all. I think I would more readily die for what I do not believe in than for what I hold to be true. I would go to the stake for a sensation and be a sceptic to the last! Only one thing remains infinitely fascinating to me, the mystery of moods. To be master of these moods is exquisite, to be mastered by them more exquisite still. Sometimes I think that the artistic life is a long and lovely suicide, and am not sorry that it is so.

—*Oscar Wilde, letter to H. C. Marillier, ca. early 1886*

CONTENTS

ACKNOWLEDGMENTS

Without the support of my mother, Sylvia Maynard, this project could not have been possible. For her deep understanding of the importance of the book to me and for her great generosity I am very thankful.

I wish to thank Oscar Sternbach, who encouraged me every step of the way, challenged my assumptions, and helped me to think. Without his kindness, his many questions, and his important ideas about ways to approach Wilde, this book would never have been written. I am grateful to Steven Marcus for the example of his scholarship and for the great care, patience, and tact he showed in helping me shape this manuscript. George Stade offered continual support by reading the manuscript carefully, making many valuable suggestions, lending me books, listening, and giving friendly advice. Doris Getzler's wit, humor, common sense, and sanity sustained me throughout my years at Columbia. Elsie O'Donoghue helped me greatly during my stay in Ireland. Elena Aguilar usually disagreed with me and was therefore one of my best readers. And many thanks to Neal Steigbigel for his patience, understanding, and sympathetic listening.

I owe a great deal to the many libraries whose collections I consulted: the Bodleian Library at Oxford, the British Library, the National Library of Ireland, the Royal Irish Academy, and the William Andrews Clark Memorial Library, University of California, Los Angeles. The director, Thomas Wright, the librarians, and the staff at the Clark, whom I relied upon for most of my sources, were never too busy to help. Suzanne Tatian and Michael Halls were always willing to stop and assist me in deciphering handwriting. John Bidwell patiently researched queries and provided me with useful microfilms.

Hal Gladfelder, Deborah Kearney, Sergio Takeo Morita, and Keith Owens kept me provided with manuscripts and kept my spirits up.

A generous fellowship from the William Andrews Clark Memorial Library enabled me to study their extensive Oscar Wilde collection for two months.

INTRODUCTION

E very great man nowadays has his disciples, and it is always Judas who writes the biography," Oscar Wilde remarked in 1890.[1] Five years later he quipped in a letter: "Treachery is inseparable from faith."[2] If this paradox has meaning, then Wilde has revealed its message in his epigram "Children begin by loving their parents; as they grow older they judge them. Rarely, if ever, do they forgive them."[3]

The rare children who forgive their parents resemble the rare biographers who forgive their subjects.[4] The more one knows, the more one relinquishes the joy of hagiography or the delight of character assassination. What one loses in idealizing—or in demonizing—gets replaced by the ability to integrate conscious and unconscious motives in the contradictory feelings, behavior, and thinking of the subject. The psychoanalytic biographer does more than analyze personality and expose motives and unconscious wishes. To resurrect Oscar Wilde it becomes necessary to fit each of the images that he created of himself into the mosaic of his life.

Wilde, who tried to show the contradictions in every truth, deserves a biographical study that reveals them and attempts to show their purposes in his total personality. In "Notes on the Uses of Psychoanalysis for Biography," Bernard C. Meyer begins with reflections on the instability of truth: "The clear show of truth flickers and falters, which suggests that, like beauty, it may reside mainly in the eye of the beholder, rendering its definition illusory and its attainment a chimera."[5] This is in the spirit of Wilde, who wrote, "What is truth? . . . It is . . . one's last mood" (CW, 1047).

A psychobiographic study of Wilde is therefore particularly appropriate. He was very much a part of the revolution in human consciousness that began in England with William Wordsworth's discovery and poetic exploration of the unconscious, one of the new perceptions of the mind that flowered at the turn of the century with Sigmund Freud's *Interpretation of Dreams*. Wilde, who lived as though he wanted to prove the truth of Freud's remark that fate is not a blow from the outside but an expression of character, has surprisingly not attracted much interest from psychoanalysts or psychoanalytically oriented biographers. Perhaps his pathology seems too obvious, although its sources, as well as their final contributions to his work, are not obvious.

The psychoanalytic biographer tries to enhance the understanding of a person's life and work by investigating and analyzing the genetic aspects of that life, including sexuality and its transformations—the instincts and all their vicissitudes—as if the body and the mind of the subject could become transparent: ideally, one sees not just the outside actions but whence they originate. Psychoanalysis, though it can tell us nothing about the origins of a particular talent and genius, can identify the unconscious conflicts that determine the forms Wilde's creative genius took, as well as choices of subject and approach—genre, theme, style, plot. The disturbances of creativity, because they are usually unconscious, cannot be mapped without psychoanalytic theory. Writer's block is oppressive in part because to the sufferer its sources seem invisible or nonexistent.

Standard biography focuses on the well-known life experiences of a person and on the conscious mind as revealed in letters, literary works, or public and family life. The psychoanalytic biographer, however, feels justified in examining more than just the conscious mind when unconscious conflicts of the subject are expressed in his or her art or can be deduced from life experiences, particularly those of early childhood. Wilde himself remarked that "consciousness, indeed, is quite inadequate to explain the contents of personality. It is Art, and Art only, that reveals us to ourselves" (*CW*, 1194). He always felt that the unconscious mind of the artist had to be understood in order to explain personality, motives, and the development of style.

And, indeed, efforts to attribute events in Wilde's life to his conscious decisions leave us with unsatisfactory conclusions. It is impossible to believe that he was completely unaware of the dangers caused by his flamboyant, public homosexual conduct. His decision to remain in London when he knew that he could avoid imprisonment by escaping to France was irrational, particularly because he knew that the judge who sentenced him to two years of hard labor deliberately had left him plenty of time before his arrest to catch the last train to Dover. Something drove him to put himself in a position that would destroy his career, his fame, his family, and himself. To ignore the unconscious conflicts beneath his show of self-assured bravado is to miss an opportunity to understand not just Wilde's personality but some of the deepest influences on the development of his many literary styles.

The psychoanalytic critic or biographer tries, of course, to look at the work of art objectively, to understand what the artist wants to express, and to see the work as a representation of the artist's thinking and feeling. Reconstructing the life experiences and the thinking that appear to have gone into the artist's work, critics react with their own feeling and thinking: projective identification is inevitable. The observers, the appreciators, the recipients of an artistic communication transform and remodel it in their own image, projecting the self into the art. That is the only possible way to enjoy art, and Wilde knew this: "It has been said by one whose gracious memory we all revere [Matthew Arnold] . . . that the proper aim of Criticism is to see the object as in itself it really is. But this is a very serious error, and takes no cognizance of Criticism's most perfect form, which is in its essence purely subjective, and seeks to reveal its own secret and not the secret of another. For the highest Criticism deals with art not as expressive but as impressive purely" (*CW*, 1028).

The influence of the critic's personality is therefore just as important in nonpsychoanalytic biography and literary criticism as the personality of the psychoanalyst is when treating a patient. The psychoanalytic biographer, like the analyst, has an agenda, though it may encompass general interest in a personality or, in the case of a therapist, interest in helping a personality develop and free itself from conflicts. The objective of the psychoanalytic biographer may vary, but it is probably always imbued with introspective self-interest, that is, with interest in understanding the self through understanding another person. Wilde summed up this approach in the essay "The Critic as Artist": "To know anything about oneself one must know all about others. There must be no mood with which one cannot sympathise, no dead mode of life that one cannot make alive" (*CW*, 1040).

In this passionate discussion of the critic's emotional investment in the work, Wilde argues that the critic's personality, far from being "a disturbing element," is "an element of revelation." It is the ability of critics to project their personalities into the subject that makes understanding possible; without the projective identification with the artist no real understanding is possible:

The critic will certainly be an interpreter, but he will not treat Art as a riddling Sphinx, whose shallow secret may be guessed and revealed by one whose feet are wounded and who knows not his name. . . . The critic will indeed be an interpreter, but he will not be an interpreter in the sense of one who simply repeats in another form a message that has been put into his lips to say. For, just as it is only by contact with the art of foreign nations that the art of a country gains that individual and separate life that we call nationality, so, by curious inversion, it is only by intensifying his own personality that the critic can interpret the personality and work of others, and the more strongly this personality enters into the interpretation, the more real the interpretation becomes, the more satisfying, the more convincing, and the more true. . . . As art springs from personality, so it is only to personality that it can be revealed, and from the meeting of the two comes right interpretive criticism. (*CW*, 1033–34)

With these remarks, Wilde virtually defined psychoanalytic literary criticism.

In the article "Freud and Literary Biography," Richard Ellmann, Wilde's latest and most thorough biographer, sums up some of the differences in biographical approach since Freud. Ellmann points to the "heightened sensitivity" of the modern biographer and his awareness of the impact of the unconscious, of the fact that "every motive is a multiplicity of motives, many of them in conflict." But he deplores the idea that the "tracing of ultimate causes"—by which he means unconscious causes—"may reduce differentiation." He feels that identifying universal unconscious patterns in authors may tell us nothing, because if the patterns are common to all, poet and peasant alike, they may say little about the uniqueness, the individuality, of the writer's style: "The biographies of Woodrow Wilson by Freud and Bullitt, of Martin Luther by Erikson, and of Flaubert by Sartre, all make so much of their Oedipal complexes and their relation to God the Father, that the president, the religious reformer, and the writer might almost be confused with one another. The unconscious is a great melting pot."[6]

True, unearthing unconscious motives is never enough. Wilde himself pointed out that our motives can be boringly alike. "It is a humiliating confession, but we are all of us made out of the same stuff. In Falstaff there is something of Hamlet, in Hamlet there is not a little of Falstaff. . . . The more one analyses people, the more all reasons for analysis disappear. Sooner or later one comes to that dreadful universal thing called human nature" (*CW*, 975). What we come to sooner or later is unconscious sexuality and aggression, which are not the sources of genius. The sources of genius and the nature of creativity cannot be described by psychoanalysis; as Freud admitted, "Before the problem of the creative artist analysis must, alas, lay down its arms."[7]

In fact, Wilde's assertion that we are all alike, alluring as it may be, is not the whole story. There are fortunately so many individual variations on common themes of experience, so many differences in drive endowment, ability, and talent, that the expected conflicts look quite different from one personality to the next.

But the old problem of idealizing or demonizing lingers. "It is difficult not to be unjust to what one loves," lamented Wilde in "The Critic as Artist." As a biographer he had faced this problem in "The Portrait of Mr. W. H.," a fanciful literary foray into Shakespeare's life. In it Wilde speaks of being "almost afraid to turn the key that unlocks the mystery of the poet's heart" (*CW*, 1155–56).

Ellmann's biography of Wilde, published in 1988, highlighted the need for a thorough psychoanalytic investigation of Wilde's life story and literary styles. In many ways, my scope is much more limited than Ellmann's: I do not discuss every event in Wilde's life or every work he wrote. But I do reveal, through the use of psychoanalysis, new facets of Wilde's life and integrate material that remained untouched in Ellmann's interpretation. Although Ellmann's biography is the most complete one to date, he deals in only a limited way with the influence of Wilde's childhood on his artistic and personal development. My study is selective: I examine Wilde's personal and artistic growth by tracing the integration of conscious purposes and unconscious needs in his life and work. The time seems ripe to attempt a biographic study of Wilde that traces the connections between Wilde's psychological development, sexual orientation, and changing styles as a writer and personality.

Focusing on the early life of Oscar Wilde, I explore his relationship with his parents and especially with his younger sister, Isola, whose early death deeply saddened him and determined the course of his life and art. My study of his childhood experiences and the lifelong inner conflicts that resulted from them yielded new insight into his most important life choices and the development of his diverse literary styles.

One of the most trenchant criticisms of psychoanalysis as a technique in literary biography is that the biographer lacks the psychoanalyst's direct access to essential early childhood material. Again, Wilde answers this criticism in "The Critic as Artist." Presenting us with a virtually Freudian view of the literary critic as a detective of the mind unearthing mental artifacts from the dawn of human consciousness, Wilde writes: "Where there is no record, and history is either lost, or was never written, Criticism can re-create the past for us from the very smallest fragments of language or art, just as surely as the man of science can from some tiny bone, or the mere impress of a foot upon a rock, re-create the winged dragon or Titan lizard that once made the earth shake. . . . Prehistoric history belongs to the philological and archaeological critic. It is to him that the origins of things are revealed" (*CW*, 1056).

Plenty of Wilde's own history is lost, or was never written. By applying psychoanalytic principles and by examining his writings for the screen memories and wishes that they contain, as well as for their formal and literary structure, I hope to supply some of the missing history and to demonstrate its influence on the development of Wilde's styles. Such an approach seems particularly applicable to an author whose writings are filled with psychological remarks and whose wit largely illuminates psychological observations of inner conflict.

To understand Wilde I felt it necessary to explore Wilde's childhood, to seek out the buried and forgotten experiences that shaped his sexuality in adulthood, and particularly to reconstruct hypothetically the seductions he experienced as a child, which transformed him into a hypnotically seductive artist. Only in early childhood is the mind open to the unconscious, for education inevitably distances the mind from the unconscious, the source of creativity. The foundation of Wilde's art is the ease with which the unconscious fights its way through the resistances of his conscious mind into his art. He could not have become Oscar Wilde the artist without remaining Oscar the young child who is always saying no, or Oscar the young child feeling seduced by his adored mother.

There has never been any question in my mind that Jokanaan, who senses the highly active and dangerous sexuality of the girl-child Salome and excitedly rejects her, must represent a conflict from the author's past. Like Wilde, Jokanaan feels no sexual attraction to women. Unlike Wilde, he easily resists any temptation. Wilde, who boasted with typical bravado, "I can resist anything—except temptation," admired the ability of Jokanaan to say no to Salome. The play then began to look to me possibly like an early screen memory of the author, masking a disturbing memory of his family. I wanted to know what conflict or conflicts *Salome* may cover up.

The result of my search is this psychobiographic study of Oscar Wilde. As one might expect, this undertaking took me through concentric circles far removed from their starting point. Yet I always seemed to return to Oscar the child, a boy whose adoring, gifted, somewhat bizarre, and very self-centered mother made demands that might have crushed someone less talented but that finally made him seek death, in spite of his genius. A boy who suffered under the degradation of a beloved father, a father who lowered his status publicly and in the eyes of his sons by leading a scandalous life. And a boy who at the age of eleven lost his beloved younger sister but whose image he carried in his heart and imagination all his life.

In Salome's kiss of Jokanaan, John the Baptist, Wilde reveals the plan of his life. His quip "I often betray myself with a kiss" is a hint that helps unravel one of the secrets of the play. Jokanaan, blazing the trail for Christ, became for Wilde the virtual representative of a new sexuality, a new psychology, a new philosophy, and a new politics—of ideas also developed by Friedrich Nietzsche, Karl Marx, and later by Freud. Wilde thought literary critics should be "unpractical people who can see beyond the moment and look beyond the mob"; he asserted that "it is through the voice of one crying in the wilderness that the ways of the gods must be prepared" (*CW*, 1043). He had been trying to become such a voice all his life. "Shall I tell you what is my greatest ambition—more even than an ambition—the dream of my life?" he asked Coulson Kernahan, a journalist, author, and adviser to his publisher.

Not to be remembered hereafter as an artist, poet, thinker or playwright, but as the man who reclothed the sublimest conception which the world has ever known—the Salvation of Humanity, the Sacrifice of Himself upon the Cross by Christ—with new and burning words, with new and illuminating symbols, with new and divine vision, free from the accretions which the centuries have gathered around it. I should thereby be giving the world back again the greatest gift ever given to mankind since Christ himself gave it, peerless and pure two thousand years ago—the gift of Christianity as taught by Christ. . . . I hope before I die to write the Epic of the Cross, the Iliad of Christianity, which shall live for all time."[8]

But Wilde could not be the trailblazing philosopher himself. Trying to find new paths in literature and literary criticism, art criticism, social criticism, and especially psychology, Wilde was unable to continue in one intellectual direction. Each choice eliminated the possibility of the others. "It seemed to me that I was always on the brink of absolute verification, but that I could never really attain to it" (*CW*, 1178). In September 1900, a month before he died, he summed up himself and his life: "I am in my usual state, drifting along. I wish I had . . . concentration of purpose, and controlled intellect" (*L*, 834).

The story of *Salome* is in part the story of why he did not. But he was never simply a storyteller. What he said and wrote also had an underlying thought. In *Salome* he complains about "the Jews, always arguing about their religion," who are Jokanaan's critics. Some are positive, because they feel that the Messiah (that is, Oscar Wilde) has come; others are negative: the Messiah has not come. They are, in fact, an echo of Wilde's own mind, of his ambivalence: the need, so much a defining element of his intellectual character, to say no to any of his own new ideas. ("Antithesis is the accompaniment of every movement in life," he remarked, consciously or unconsciously quoting Hegel, to the writer A. H. Cooper-Prichard.)[9] Altogether the Jews in the play do not understand Jokanaan-Wilde's idealized vision of himself—any more than Wilde understands he cannot become Jokanaan, as much as he would like to be him. The Jews do not realize that he has to put his own head under the ax in a defiant gesture, as a way out of his dilemmas, a way of asserting his belief in himself against the world—a belief that fails at the heroic moment of death: "A thing is not necessarily true because a man dies for it. . . . Martyrdom was to me merely a tragic form of scepticism, an attempt to realise by fire what one had failed to do by faith. No man dies for what he knows to be true. Men die for what they want to be true, for what some terror in their hearts tells them is not true," he wrote in "The Portrait of Mr. W. H." (*CW*, 1161–1201).

The Jews are also behind the figure of Judas, the biographer. Judas is a Jew who betrays himself by betraying his Lord. Wilde seized the privilege of self-betrayal, which he did not want to entrust to biographers, "the mere body-snatchers of literature." Reminiscing in *De Profundis* about his conviction, Wilde compared the solicitor-general's denunciation of him to "a thing out of Tacitus . . . a passage in Dante . . . one of Savanarola's indictments of the Popes at Rome." He felt "sickened with horror at what I had heard," not because he had been betrayed as an immoral lecher, but because he hadn't betrayed himself. The prosecution had stolen his thunder: "How splendid it would be if I was saying all this about myself!" (*L*, 502). Unless he condemned himself, he feared being seen as just another Pagliaccio hiding his Canio, a desperate human being. In *De Profundis*, Wilde called himself a clown whose heart was broken, a zany of sorrow.

The surreal Middle Eastern world of *Salome* seems far removed from the middle-class Dublin of the 1850s in which Wilde grew up. This exotic piece of theater nonetheless reveals, in distorted symbols and dreamlike disguises, the boyhood loves and terrors of Oscar Wilde and the family problems that contributed to his development as a wit, dramatist, and highly public personality. The drama, bizarre as such, is an attempt to resolve a childhood conflict between giving in to his urge to seduce openly as a homosexual or forgoing the urge, which might cost him his head. The conflict about seduction runs like a thread through his life and art. Thirty-five years after Wilde's death in November 1900, one of his oldest friends, Reginald Turner, who took care of Wilde in his last days, remarked in a letter: "It was his theory that it was always the young who seduce the old. . . . One of the most serious conversations I had with Oscar was on that subject when he said that no one had any real influence on anyone else. At the time I ventured strongly to deny that, but when I began to think that he was perhaps rather arguing with himself than trying to convince me I desisted."[10] Wilde himself invites us to recognize the autobiographical elements of his art, to recognize that we cannot understand it without interpreting its hidden depths: "Art . . . shows us . . . our own soul, the one world of which we have any real cognizance. And the soul itself, the soul of each one of us, is to each one of us a mystery. It hides in

the dark and broods, and consciousness cannot tell us of its workings" (CW,
1194). Wilde went on to make it clear that his unconscious could be discovered through an examination of his art.

The idea of the biographer as a traitorous Judas is hardly novel; it is
perhaps too ordinary, too simple for Oscar Wilde. Indeed, Judas had always
been a rather contradictory figure whose role as a traitor was periodically
disputed and whose motivations and meanings were, like Wilde's, difficult to
second-guess.[11] I love Oscar Wilde, and yet as his biographer I betray his
conflicts, his weaknesses, his childishness, his fears, and his deep shames and
secrets—in order to make it possible for the reader to love him.

The image of an ambivalent Apostle kissing his Lord and by this act of love
betraying Him is an appropriate one for Oscar Wilde, who according to many
of his closest friends contracted syphilis from a female prostitute while an
undergraduate at Oxford and lived a life of carefree promiscuity without
much regard for the health of those whom he may have infected. He seems to
joke about a Judas kiss in a letter of 1 February 1894: "Indeed, everyone in the
world should be either killed or kissed" (L, 351). In De Profundis, he writes,
"Desire, at the end, was a malady, or a madness, or both. I grew careless of the
lives of others. I took pleasure where it pleased me and passed on" (L, 466).[12]

Arthur Ransome, in Oscar Wilde: A Critical Study, seems to have been the
first biographer to state that Wilde had syphilis. I believe that he was right. In
the first (1912) edition of his biography, he states that Wilde's "death was
hurried by his inability to give up the drinking to which he had been accus-
tomed. It was directly due to meningitis, the legacy of an attack of tertiary
syphilis." The form of meningitis from which Wilde died was the result of a
chronic middle ear infection and is not the type of central nervous system
involvement typically seen in tertiary syphilis, so that the immediate cause of
his death was not syphilis, as Macdonald Critchley, a British neurologist, has
documented in his 1990 article "Oscar Wilde's Fatal Illness: The Mystery
Unshrouded." In any case, Ransome, whose information came from Robert
Ross, Wilde's dear friend, literary executor, and former lover, removed the
reference to syphilis in the second (1913) edition of his book and included in
his preface the remark that "in bringing out this new edition I have considered the question of reprinting in its original form, as I have perfect right to
do, but as I do not consider the passages complained of are essential to the
critical purpose of my book I have decided, in order to spare the feelings of
those who might be pained by the further publication of those passages, to
omit them from this edition." The phrase "as I have a perfect right to do"
probably refers to the unsuccessful libel action against Ransome taken by
Lord Alfred Douglas in April 1913. Ransome had referred in his book to

Wilde's scathing accusations of Lord Alfred in *De Profundis*—a letter that Douglas claims not to have known about until the Ransome trial and that remained unpublished (apart from a very abridged version) until 1962.[13]

But why take out the part about syphilis? Was Ransome afraid of hurting the feelings of Wilde's children, who had certainly suffered enough under the shadow of a homosexual father without the added onus of syphilis? We shall never know. Many of Wilde's biographers—including Richard Ellmann and H. Montgomery Hyde—accept the theory that Wilde had syphilis. Considerable circumstantial evidence suggests that Wilde suffered from the disease. Letters from close friends like Robert Sherard alluded to Wilde's supposed infection, and remarks attributed to Robert Ross and Reginald Turner reveal that his friends worried about the effect of the disease on his mental and physical health.

For my purpose it is not so important that Wilde had contracted this dread disease as that he appears to have believed he had: he behaves as though he were living under the shadow of the horror, the uncertainty, the guilt of feeling that he had committed a crime against himself by contracting the disease and of having bestowed it again and again with a kiss. "Each man kills the thing he loves," he wrote repeatedly in his last poem, *The Ballad of Reading Gaol,* and his wife, Constance, may have been one of his victims. After 1886 he apparently stopped having sexual relations with her, in part because he developed syphilitic symptoms. His reaction was typical: attempting to deny distress, guilt, and pain, he protested too much his guiltlessness and innocence. His writings, and as I shall show, the transformations of his style, reveal his efforts to stem the despair that overwhelmed him in the face of the disease.

Evidence of his fear of the disease exists in a number of his writings, especially *The Picture of Dorian Gray* and several of his short stories. He was influenced by the work of the Belgian writer Joris-Karl Huysmans, who in *A rebours*—a novel many critics believe is a blueprint for *The Picture of Dorian Gray*—includes this revealing insight into the depression of the main character, Des Esseintes: "'Dammit, I'm going crazy,' Des Esseintes said to himself. 'My dread of the disease will bring on the disease itself if I keep this up.'" Later in the novel, Des Esseintes stares at his collection of hothouse flowers and remarks: "Most of them, as if ravaged by syphilis or leprosy, displayed livid patches of flesh mottled with roseola. . . . Others had the bright pink colour of a scar that is healing or the brown tint of a scab that is forming." Satisfied with his collection, he adds: "It all comes down to syphilis in the end." At this point he has a "sudden vision of the unceasing torments inflicted on humanity by the virus of distant ages. Ever since the beginning of the world, from

generation to generation, all living creatures had handed down the inex-
haustible heritage, the everlasting disease that ravaged the ancestors of men
and even ate into the bones of the old fossils that were being dug up at the
present time."[14] A doctor's son, Wilde knew the truth of this. In Wilde's
novel, Dorian reads a mysterious book (never identified) that Wilde referred
to in a letter of about 12 February 1894 as the "book that poisoned, or made
perfect, Dorian Gray." He goes on to claim that the book "does not exist," but
in an earlier letter of 15 April 1892 he had revealed that the book was "partly
suggested by Huysmans's *A rebours* (L, 352, 313).

Although initially I thought that my interest in Wilde was rather isolated, I
was not surprised to learn of Ellmann's biography, the first serious biography
of Oscar Wilde in many years. While I had been working on my research,
homosexuals were proclaiming their sexual identities in ever-greater numbers. A world that had been cautiously hidden from attention now began to
use the power of its numbers in contemporary Western democracy. Homosexuals campaigned to be understood and accepted, not just tolerated.[15]
Behind that campaign were both the political push of civil liberties and the
force of psychoanalysis.

The current interest in the homosexual artist, or the artist as a homosexual, and the rise within the past ten years of gay and gender studies in
academic departments are due in part to the ongoing battle of the gay rights
movement for acceptance.[16] Wilde is the martyr and mascot of this movement. His fate arouses sympathy, admiration, and anger. His superb irony, the
beautiful humor that sustained him through preparations for and reactions to
disaster, seems distinctly modern. Always "improbable, not impossible," he
styled himself an absurdist. In their meaningful absurdity and pointed social
criticism, Wilde's life and wit are related to expressionist literature, dadaism,
and stream-of-consciousness writers.

Praised in his day as a brilliant playwright and conversationalist and stig-
matized as a dangerous seducer of youth, he has fared somewhat better in our
time. He has been recognized as more than a hanger-on of the aesthetic
movement, a stylish echo of Walter Pater and John Ruskin. Although Wilde
liked to project the image of a dilettante and dandy, he was, in fact, a serious
social critic. His perceptions, so deeply rooted in the philosophy and psychology of his time, have led us from one fin de siècle to the next.

OSCAR WILDE: A BRIEF CHRONOLOGY

1854	Born on 16 October in Dublin.
1864–71	Student at Portora Royal School, Enniskillen.
1867	Death of Isola Wilde, his beloved younger sister (b. 2 April 1857).
1871–74	Student at Trinity College, Dublin.
1874–79	Scholarship at Magdalen College, Oxford.
1876	Death of Sir William Wilde on 19 April.
ca. 1878	Reportedly contracts syphilis at Oxford from female prostitute.
1880	Publication of *Vera, or the Nihilists*.
1881	Publication of first collection of his poems.
1882	Lecture tour of the United States.
1884	Marriage to Constance Lloyd on 29 May.
1885	Birth of first son, Cyril.
1886	Birth of second son, Vyvyan.
1887	Publication of "The Canterville Ghost" and "Lord Arthur Savile's Crime" in *Court and Society Review*.
1887–89	Editor of *Woman's World*.
1888	Beginning of intense literary activity. Publication of *The Happy Prince and Other Tales*.
1889	Publication of "The Decay of Lying" in *The Nineteenth Century*; "Pen, Pencil and Poison" in *Fortnightly Review*; "The Birthday of the Infanta" in *Paris Illustré*; and "The Portrait of Mr. W. H." in *Blackwood's*.
1890	Publication of *The Picture of Dorian Gray* in *Lippincott's*.

1891   Publication of *Intentions; A House of Pomegranates; The Picture of Dorian Gray* in book form; and "The Soul of Man under Socialism."

ca. 1891   Meets Lord Alfred Bruce Douglas (1870–1945), known as "Bosie," son of the eighth Marquess of Queensberry. Writes *Salome* in Paris (published in French in 1894).

1892   *Lady Windermere's Fan* produced at St. James Theatre (published 1893). Writes *A Woman of No Importance* (produced 1893; published 1894).

1893   Writes *An Ideal Husband* (produced 1895; published 1899).

1894   Writes *The Importance of Being Earnest* (produced 1895; published 1899).

1895   Brings libel suit against the Marquess of Queensberry. Queensberry acquitted; Wilde arrested. After two trials, found guilty of "indecent acts" and sentenced to two years of hard labor. Imprisoned in Pentonville; later transferred to Wandsworth and Reading prisons.

1896   Death of his mother on 3 February. *Salome* produced in Paris.

1897   Writes *De Profundis* while in prison (published in full in 1962).

1897   Released from Reading Prison on 9 May. Goes to Berneval, France. In June begins *The Ballad of Reading Gaol* (published 1898).

1898   Death of his wife on 7 April following surgery. Wilde goes to Paris.

1900   Visits Sicily and Rome. Dies in Paris on 30 November at age forty-six.

OSCAR WILDE

CHAPTER 1 *SALOME:* IN HIS END, HIS BEGINNING

O scar Wilde once said that he "lived in terror of not being misunderstood" (*CW,* 1016). In typical Wildean fashion, he formulated even this sentence so that he might be easily misunderstood. Such eminent literary figures as Richard Ellmann, Hesketh Pearson, André Gide, and Jorge Luis Borges have described Wilde as an essentially contradictory figure.[1] Indeed, his aim in life was to be contradictory. Moreover, although he was deeply introspective, he failed to understand himself throughout his life: "If one tells the truth one is sure, sooner or later, to be found out," he said, although finding out about himself was the last thing he really wanted (*CW,* 1205). His endless quips might eventually betray him. He remarked that "nowadays, to be intelligible is to be found out" (*CW,* 390).

"How his moods varied and how he revelled in inconsistency! The whim of the moment he openly acknowledged as his dictator," commented an Oxford classmate.[2] Once, Wilde justified his admiration of the moon because "to look at anything that is inconstant is charming nowadays" (*CW,* 465). Almost every story about him reveals provocation as well as charm directed in one and the same attack on an audience. When he was required to take an exam in divinity at Oxford, he showed his contempt for it by sleeping late, claiming to have forgotten the day on which it was to be given. The clerk of the schools roused him, and Wilde contemptuously remarked, "You must excuse me! I have no experience of these 'pass' examinations"—that is, exams one had only to pass in order to receive one's degree. As punishment he was asked to translate a difficult passage of Saint Paul from the Greek testament. So attentive and assiduous did he appear to his examiners as he wrote that they relented, instructing him to stop; he ignored them, however, and continued the exam. When they interrupted him again, he vented his anger for being

1

Passionate

treated like a little boy by feigning innocence: "I was so interested in what I was copying that I could not leave off. It was all about a man named Paul, who went on a voyage and was caught in a terrible storm, and I was afraid that he would be drowned. But, do you know, Mr. Spooner, he was saved? And when I found out that he was saved, I thought of coming to tell you." Mr. W. H. Spooner, a university lecturer in divinity and a nephew by marriage of the archbishop of Canterbury, was not amused. Whatever pleasure he may have taken in Oscar's perfect translation evaporated, and he flunked him on the spot.[3]

Wilde had not changed some twenty years later, when the opening night audience of *Lady Windermere's Fan* shouted for the author to appear. Known by that time as the wittiest and most successful society dramatist, Wilde stepped out on stage, a cigarette in his gloved hand, and said: "Ladies and gentlemen, I have enjoyed this evening *immensely*. The actors have given us a *charming* rendition of a *delightful* play, and your appreciation has been most intelligent. I congratulate you on the *great* success of your performance, which persuades me that you think *almost* as highly of the play as I do myself."[4] Flattered by his covert appeal, the audience laughingly accepted his outrageous behavior. He built his career on such alluring provocations, once going into a florist's and asking him to remove several bunches of primroses from the window. "With pleasure, sir. How many would you like to have?" asked the florist, allowing Wilde to croon, "Oh, I don't want any, thank you. I only asked to have them removed from the window because I thought that they looked tired." On another occasion, upon hearing a passerby say, "There goes that bloody fool, Oscar Wilde," he remarked, "It's extraordinary how soon one gets known in London."[5] How did it happen that his almost deliberately childlike exhibition of his invincible importance stirred up delight as much as anger, so that he is now fondly remembered as "a great, almost legendary victim . . . the foremost homosexual in the English mind"?[6]

"Would you like to know the great drama of my life?" Wilde remarked to André Gide in 1895, before returning from Algiers to London for the start of the disastrous trials that ruined him: "It's that I've put my genius into my life; I've put only my talent into my works."[7] The life into which Wilde put his genius was not comedy but the great tragedy he never wrote about a martyred prophet. Where did Wilde see the genius in suing for libel the Marquess of Queensberry, a very prominent and powerful man, who had publicly accused Wilde of posing as a sodomite? How did Wilde summon the nerve to sue him? Wilde and the marquess' son, Lord Alfred Douglas ("Bosie"), publicly displayed their affection every chance they got, especially in the most fashionable London watering holes. Considering his flagrant encounters with various male prostitutes, as well as with Bosie, Wilde would never have expected to win the case. One senses an intention in shaping his own life that was more important to him than his work. It can be shown that, indeed, he reserved all his inventiveness and intelligence to fashion this life, that his work was a rehearsal or dry run to plan meticulously the crucial events of his life. In a scene that his producer cut from *The Importance of Being Earnest* because of constraints of time, a young dandy narrowly escapes arrest and imprisonment in Holloway for refusing to pay outstanding debts to the Savoy Hotel. Wilde in fact owed the Savoy a considerable sum of money, which contributed to his bankruptcy, and his first incarceration was in Holloway. In *An Ideal Husband,* his third great comedy, he imagines what it will be like for a character whose scandal is exposed, especially after the newspapermen get hold of it: "Think of their loathsome joy, of the delight they would have in dragging you down, of the mud and mire they would plunge you in. Think of the hypocrite with his greasy smile, penning his leading article, and arranging the foulness of the public placard" (*CW,* 498). He was savoring his disgrace ahead of time.

Alongside his brilliant wit, his "fatal and idiotic step," as he later wrote, of ensnaring himself in a hopeless legal tangle still provokes astonishment (*ML,* 138). Sir Travers Humphreys, junior counsel for Wilde, wrote: "Wilde was given every opportunity to leave the country if he so desired. He elected to stay; or more accurately, he could not make up his mind to go, though he drew money from his bank and had his bag half-packed when arrested late in the afternoon."[8] Humphreys goes on to relate that the magistrate in charge of arresting Wilde was "careful to inquire the time of the boat-train's departure" to Calais and to have "fixed the time of the application" for Wilde's arrest "a quarter of an hour later."[9] When a friend of Wilde's who had repeatedly urged him to leave town during the trials finally exclaimed, "Oh, you're impossible!" Wilde chuckled. "No, not impossible, my dear fellow. Improbable, yes . . . I grant you improbable."[10] It was indeed improbable that a man given the chance to escape from the humiliation of two years at hard labor in an English prison could remain at the Cadogan Hotel, drinking hock and seltzer, waiting for the police to arrest him, instead of catching the first ferry to Calais. Improbable unless there was an intention behind his remaining. Every charming provocation was a flirtation with self-sacrifice: his divinity exam, his sentiments about fatigued primroses, his fun at the expense of the audience of *Lady Windermere's Fan,* for which the press criticized him severely, the various jokes he told to ridicule and inflame the prosecution at his trials—all part of this dangerous lifelong flirtation—originated in his relationship to his parents.

In the Dublin of his childhood, his well-known parents were loved and revered but also judged rather harshly. Famous as "Speranza," a writer of fervidly nationalistic verse, Jane Francesca Elgee Wilde gave birth to Oscar on 16 October 1854. A Junoesque woman, who George Bernard Shaw thought might have been the victim of a pituitary disorder known as pathological gigantism,[11] she towered over her short, notoriously unkempt husband. Behind her back people called her "a walking burlesque of motherhood" and remarked that her husband "resembled a monkey."[12] "Why are Sir William Wilde's nails black?" asked a popular Dublin joke. "Because he scratches himself."[13] Shaw, recalling his boyhood impression of Sir William, remembered him "dressed in snuffy brown; and as he had the sort of skin that never looks clean, he produced a dramatic effect beside Lady Wilde (in full fig) of being, like Frederick the Great, Beyond Soap and Water, as his Nietzschean son was beyond Good and Evil."[14] A fellow of Trinity College, Dublin, classified Sir William with the apes, as "a pithecoid personality of extraordinary sensuality and cowardice."[15]

Even so, Sir William was more than the intellectual equal of his writer wife. A successful eye-and-ear specialist known later as the father of modern otology, he was, around the time of Oscar's birth, appointed "Surgeon-Oculist in Ordinary to the Queen," a post created for him.[16] Wilde's son, Vyvyan Holland, writes that Sir William "invented the operation for cataract and performed it on King Oscar of Sweden, for which he received the Order of the Polar Star" (*CW*, 9). Sir William was also widely acclaimed for his travel books, archaeological researches, knowledge of Irish folklore, statistical work on the Irish census, and a study of Jonathan Swift (in which he tried to prove that Swift was not mad in his last days). In recognition of his many accomplishments, he was knighted in 1864. His extremely busy professional life did not, however, get in the way of his private escapades; he is rumored to have done his share in raising the Irish birthrate, leaving, as Shaw said, "a family in every farmhouse" (though only three such children are actually known).[17] Years later, Oscar was to justify his father's absence from the home, remarking dryly, "Fathers should be neither seen nor heard. That is the only proper basis for family life" (*CW*, 538). He grew up in an eccentric home that was "dirty and daring, disorderly and picturesque," conditions he accepted with ironic equanimity. "I want to introduce you to my mother," he told a college friend; "we have founded a Society for the Suppression of Virtue."[18]

At birth he was given the name of a warrior-bard: Oscar Fingal O'Flahertie Wills Wilde. The O'Flaherties, warlike relatives of Sir William, were known as the "ferocious O'Flaherties of Galway"; the Wills, his cousins, were known to have some literary and artistic ability.[19] The other names, taken from

heroes of Celtic mythology, reveal the dreams of his mother's youth. While
still a young woman, she had joined the radical Young Ireland movement,
which had been inspired by the disastrous potato crop failure and subsequent
famine of the 1840s. This genocidal experience for the Irish was, as Robert
Kee writes, "sometimes seen as comparable in its impact on popular national
consciousness to that of the German 'final solution' on the Jews."[20] Blaming
the British for their failure to provide adequate relief and prevent the deaths
of approximately one million Irish peasants, Oscar's mother took up the
sword by taking up the pen. Assuming the "nom de guerre, or rather nom de
vers" of Speranza, she saw herself as the hope of Ireland in troubled times.[21]
As one of her letters reveals, she longed for a thrilling, heroic fate, like the one
she later envisioned for her son: "I want excitement, excitement is my genius.
I have none without it and Dublin is bleak of the divine inspirer as a Polar
icefield—I should like to rage through life—this Orthodox creeping is too
tame for me—ah, this wild rebellious ambitious nature of mine. I wish I
could satiate it with Empires, though a St. Helena were the end. . . . Is it my
fault if I was born first cousin to Aetna and half-sister to Vesuvius?"[22]

   Unfortunately for her dreams, the Young Ireland movement fizzled out,
and she retreated into marriage and motherhood. Following the arrest of
several of her associates for sedition, she confessed in a letter, "I shall never
write sedition again. The responsibility is more awful than I imagined or
thought of."[23] Years later, Oscar wrote in a melodrama about a Russian
revolution a line that sounds like a comment on his mother's revolutionary
activities: "Reforms in Russia are very tragic, but they always end in a farce"
(CW, 683). This was Lady Wilde's own view. In a letter written shortly after
Oscar's brother, Willie, was born and two years before Oscar's birth, she
complained,

> I never read now, as someone said seeing me over little saucepans in the nursery.
>> Alas! the Fates are cruel
>> Behold Speranza making gruel![24]

But she had not really relinquished her revolutionary cause, for she was
determined to raise seditious sons. The same letter closes with a promise:
"Well, I will rear him a Hero perhaps and President of the future Irish
Republic. Chi sa? I have not fulfilled my destiny yet. Gruel and the nursery
cannot end me." By living their lives according to her dreams, her sons were
to give her the vicarious thrill of being a "wild rebellious ambitious" warrior.
   She seems to have called herself Speranza as a defense against depression.
Apparently devoid of hope, she liked to pretend she embodied it. She threw
herself into motherhood to escape from the chronic depression she had been

coping with for years. As she wrote in a letter of 1850, "[There are] the depressed days when I am miserable. I don't know why. Would be glad even for the society of a cat. I could do nothing on these days but drown myself. They are very frequent, too. Black, bleak and unutterably desolate, isolation, gloom, a horrible sense of loneliness, a despairing feel [fact?] as if all the world were standing in sunlight, I alone condemned to darkness."[25] A woman so exhausted by depression and fending off thoughts of suicide would have had little energy to devote to her children's emotional needs.[26] Like her famous son later on, she "tended to lie long abed, stirring herself only to entertain guests at afternoon soirées, or to sit with the children in the nursery."[27] She felt abandoned by her husband: "He envelopes himself . . . in a black pall and is grave, stern, mournful and silent as the grave itself."[28] At her soirées she could at least be the center of attention, decked out in exotic costumes and delivering suggestive remarks. These moments in the limelight lifted the depression temporarily, as did her flight into frenzied activity for the Young Ireland movement. Her instantaneous identification with this movement, which went entirely against the religion and politics of her family, shows a certain desperation. For a while the joys of caring for her children rescued her: in a letter of November 1852, written when Willie was seven weeks old, she enjoys the "enchanting richness and fullness these young (children) give to one's life. It is like the return of a second youth. Hope, energy, purpose, all awake again." Up to this point she may sound like any young mother, but the same letter is full of ambivalence about her role and about all the ambitions she has had to relinquish in order to fill it: "How is it that I am enthralled by these tiny hands? Was there a woman's nature in me after all? Oh Patriotism, oh Glory, Freedom, Conquest, the rush, the strife, the battle and the crown, ye Eidolons of my youth, where are you?" She is full of doubt, and the depression inevitably returns: "Was I nobler then? Perhaps so, but the present is the truer life. A mere woman, nothing more. Such as I am now. The other was an abnormal state."[29]

Her solution to this dilemma was an attempt to merge emotionally with her children: "Well, after all it is a satisfaction to have been through the whole circle of human emotion, literature, ambition, love, motherhood, till my wings fall from me at last beside an infant's cradle. How many lives we live in life! We need not die to lose our identity; every phase of circumstance seems to bring its corresponding soul along with it."[30]

She lost and found and lost again her identity in motherhood. She loves it, but she laments: "Genius should never wed. You cannot serve two masters."[31] She feels "bound heart and soul to the home hearth by the tiny hands of my little Willie," and she gloats over the child she is rocking in the cradle as she writes, "my second son—a babe of one month old . . . and as large and fine and handsome and healthy as if he were three months." Poor Oscar had to appear bigger and better even at the tender age of one month. And that was not all: "He is to be called Oscar Fingal Wilde. Is not that grand, misty, Ossianic?"[32]

Her campaign seems to have begun very early in Oscar's life. She recognized his literary talents when he was quite young; and because she believed in him, it was easy for her to imagine his growing up to be a hero-martyr. She needed her sons to remain a part of her; any attempt by either boy to strike out on his own would have been regarded as a cruel abandonment. No wonder Oscar struggled so torturously with the idea of who he was and who he should be. The stage was set for tragedy. As John Lahr wrote, "[Speranza's] overweening sense of family destiny . . . undid both her sons: Willie could not live up to the challenge of greatness, became a feckless journalist; Oscar fulfilled her every dream, and it killed him."[33] He would be another Ossian, the ancient Irish warrior-bard. She applied pressure consistently: a letter of 5 March 1883 urges him "to war and *conquer* as you always do."[34] And she always praised him when he did: "Truly you are a startling celebrity!!! I must now pose as 'The Mother of Oscar'!" she effuses in a letter of about 1895.[35]

Oscar's adolescent letters from boarding school, which he began to attend in 1864 at age nine, so delighted his mother that she described them as "wonderful and often real literature."[36] She unfavorably compared her eldest son, Willie, to his talented little brother: "Oh, Willie is all right—he has a first-class brain—but as for Oscar, he will turn out something wonderful."[37] By the time Willie was in his last year, Oscar had indeed outstripped him. During this period others besides his mother noticed Oscar's abilities. A schoolmate remembered him as "an excellent talker" with "descriptive powers far above the average." His "exaggerations of school occurrences were always highly amusing."[38] On the occasion of his father's knighthood, Oscar's mother published her poems with the dedication "To my sons Willie and Oscar Wilde" and an unidentified quotation, possibly written by her:

> I made them indeed
> Speak plain the word COUNTRY. I taught them, no doubt
> That a country's a thing men should die for at need![39]

No wonder Oscar later wrote, "A mother's love is very touching, of course, but it is often selfish. I mean, there is a good deal of selfishness in it" (*CW,* 459). Her ideals, so insistently expressed, had made their imprint.

She drove home her message, writing articles in which she exalted Irish history as "an endless martyrology written in tears and blood" and asserted that "the Irish must search for the names of their heroes on the walls of a prison."[40] She brought up her boys among contemporary martyrs to Irish nationalism. Oscar was often in the company of his mother's revolutionary colleagues, some of whom were poets whose patriotic ideals had originally inspired her to write. He later remembered one of them as "the earliest hero of my childhood." In a lecture on Irish poets that he gave in San Francisco when he was twenty-eight, he spoke of looking on their work with "peculiar reverence and love" and confessed, "I was indeed trained by my mother to love and reverence them as a Catholic child is the Saints of the Calendar." He felt that not just their work but their lives were "noble poems also"; they were for him "men who had not merely written about the sword, but were ready to bear it, who could not only rhyme to Liberty, but could die for her also, if need had been."[41] He had grown up to be Speranza's son.

What he admired most about these men was their making noble poems of their lives in addition to writing them. He saw his mother as having made her life into a noble poem, too; he spoke of her reverently as having been "a young girl who had been brought up in an atmosphere of alien English thought, among people high in bench and senate, and far removed from any love or knowledge of those wrongs of the people to which she afterwards gave such passionate expression." He then adds the story of her conversion to patriotism: "One day in 1845, standing at the window of her lordly home, she saw a great funeral pass in its solemn trappings of sorrow down the street. . . . She . . . learned the dead man was a poet . . . and knew for the first time the meaning of the word country."[42]

This is an impressive encomium, but none of it is quite true. The atmosphere of English thought was not alien to the Wilde family, since both parents came from an old Anglo-Irish family. His mother's family included several dignitaries of the Church of England, and her grandfather had been the archdeacon of Wexford.[43] Her home was not a lordly one, as Oscar claims, but half a house in Lower Leeson Street, a modest, middle-class neighborhood. Apparently Oscar's later concept of his life as a "work of art" was the continuation of a dream that his mother had inspired and required.

Oscar's ostentatious self-confidence as an adult was probably the result of her enormous confidence in him when he was quite young. As Freud suggested, "If a man has been his mother's indisputed darling he retains throughout life the triumphant feeling, the confidence in success, which not seldom brings actual success with it."[44] Even in later life, Oscar was his mother's favorite, owing to his phenomenal success and ability to support her when the parasitic, alcoholic Willie continued to ask for handouts. At the time of

Willie's disastrous second marriage in 1893, Lady Wilde wrote to Oscar, "You have always been my *best and dearest hope in every misery.*"[45] She was even more effusive about his work. When Oscar won the prestigious Newdigate prize for poetry at Oxford, she wrote to him, "Oh, Gloria! Gloria! . . . It is the first throb of joy I have had. . . . Well, after all, we have *genius.*" Years later, shortly before the opening of *A Woman of No Importance,* she wrote, "I believe in you and your genius."[46]

Oscar's self-confidence might also have been strengthened by an identification with his father's feeling of omnipotence. Like many a young doctor, Sir William had often taken chances that only a person imbued with a sense of invulnerability would have dared. He treated a cholera patient no one else would touch, fumigated the house when the man died, and buried the corpse almost single-handedly. He saved a child who was choking on a potato by slicing open its neck with the nearest pair of scissors. While traveling in Jerusalem Sir William heard about a recently discovered tomb and, at considerable risk, stole several skulls from it. He also stopped at Tenerife to have "the opportunity of ascending the peak" and there decided to test "the poisonous properties of the *euphorbium canariensis* by laying its juice for an instant on his tongue from off the top of his penknife."[47] Apparently the thrill or the dare was worth the agony of being "scarcely able to crawl back to town as a result."

Along with his parents, Wilde's younger sister, Isola, played a crucial role in his life. In 1867, when Wilde was twelve, nine-year-old Isola died after a brief illness, possibly scarlet fever. Her death was of immense consequence to him. It is possible to discover, from quite convincing circumstantial evidence, that the relationship between this young boy and his younger sister was central to the course of his life and art. The younger of Wilde's two sons, Vyvyan Holland, whose name was changed by his mother's family after the trauma of Oscar's trials, said that Isola had been "the pivot around which the family affections of the Wildes revolved." The longed-for daughter after two sons, she was "idolised by the whole family" and "frankly worshipped" by her brothers.[48] The doctor attending Isola during her final days described her as "the most gifted and lovable child" he had ever seen. He reported that "Ossie" was then "an affectionate, gentle, retiring, dreamy boy" whose "lonely and inconsolable grief" was expressed "in long and frequent visits to his sister's grave in the village cemetery."[49] Years later, as Wilde strolled through Paris with a journalist friend, he spoke of little Isola "dancing like a golden sunbeam about the house." He then recited a memorial poem composed for her when he was twenty. The friend later remarked that Wilde "drew nearer to sensibility" when speaking of Isola than he did "on any other topic."[50]

The poem, "Requiescat," is a graceful expression of profound loss:

> Tread lightly, she is near
> Under the snow,
> Speak gently, she can hear
> The daisies grow.
>
> All her bright golden hair
> Tarnished with rust,
> She that was young and fair
> Fallen to dust. (*CW,* 724)

The rather uncommon meter of parts of the poem (dactylic trimeter with an extra stress) has been thought to bear a deliberate resemblance to the meter of Thomas Hood's "Bridge of Sighs," which concerns the death of a young prostitute. The relevant portion of Hood's poem reads,

> Take her up tenderly,
> Lift her with care;
> Fashion'd so slenderly,
> Young, and so fair!
>
> Still, for all slips of hers,
> One of Eve's family—
> Wipe those poor lips of her
> Oozing so clammily.[51]

In *The Aesthetic Movement in England* (1882), Walter Hamilton dismissed Wilde's "Requiescat" with the caustic question: "Is there anything sweeter or more pathetic in Tom Hood than these few lines? I think not."[52] In his introductory remarks to *Parodies of the Works of English and American Authors* Hamilton quotes from a letter he received from George Augustus Sala in August 1882:

I have not read Oscar Wilde's poems, but in the very sweet stanzas (*Requiescat*) which you quote—I mark a single passage:

> All her bright golden hair
> Tarnished with rust.

Golden hair (*experto credo*) does not tarnish in the tomb. Read the last paragraph in Zola's *Nana* which physiologically is astoundingly accurate.[53]

In this passage the prostitute Nana has died of smallpox, after which, because "the pustules had invaded her whole face," she was recognizable only by "the hair, the beautiful hair" which "blazed like sunlight and flowed downwards in rippling gold."[54] With this sarcastic reference to Nana's revolting death, Sala senses a motive for Wilde's borrowing of Hood's meter, namely, that Isola reminded Wilde of Hood's prostitute.

This is such a sad revelation that one might be inclined to object that not enough evidence exists for it and that Wilde may have been interested in imitating Hood's unusual meter only, not his subject matter. Yet Hood chose to express a fantasy about a prostitute in this particular meter, and the two became inextricably woven in Wilde's mind. Oscar would not have been inclined to think of Isola as a prostitute unless there had been a sexual current flowing between them.[55]

It is not easy to accept the idea that the brother of the "darling child" saw her as an "impure" seductress. Considering this problem, one should first examine the romantic ideas about prostitutes in the nineteenth century—the heroines of *La Traviata* and *La Dame aux camélias,* Manon, and others, even as portrayed in Hood's poem. It seems to me historically wrong to interpret Wilde's probably unconscious thought of his sister while he thinks of a prostitute as a condemnation of Isola. On the contrary, this was probably a romanticizing of her. In *Fallen Women,* Martin Seymour-Smith suggests that "Camille is a representative of a male fantasy-figure, the 'tart with the heart,' that was created by nineteenth century public morality. When tarts were, by and large, taken for granted, there had been less need to endow them with hearts of gold. But the triumph of public morality caused what was in fact indulged in as much as ever to become 'forbidden,' so that forbidden fruit guiltily needed to be endowed with impossibly sentimental qualities of self-sacrifice and nobility. This was one of the main reasons for the nineteenth century . . . sentimentalization of the whole concept of prostitution."[56]

Wilde's poem "The Harlot's House" echoes the hidden meaning of "Requi-escat" by describing prostitutes as "strange mechanical grotesques," "skeletons," and "phantoms." I think that the seductive little sister comes alive in these phrases:

> Like wire-pulled automatons,
> Slim-silhouetted skeletons
> Went sliding through the slow quadrille
>
> . . . .
>
> Sometimes a clockwork puppet pressed
> A phantom lover to her breast,
> Sometimes they seemed to try to sing.
>
> Sometimes, a horrible marionette
> Came out, and smoked its cigarette
> Upon the steps like a live thing. (*CW,* 789)

The rest of the poem concerns the seduction of a girl, the narrator's beloved, by the prostitutes, her betrayal of him, and the emerging of the dawn as a young girl:

> Then, turning to my love, I said,
> "The dead are dancing with the dead,
> The dust is whirling with the dust."
>
> But she—she heard the violin
> And left my side, and entered in:
> Love passed into the house of lust
>
> . . . .
>
> And down the long and silent street
> The dawn, with silver-sandalled feet
> Crept like a frightened girl. (*CW,* 789–90)

What can be discovered here is the memory of a frightened but erotically eager little girl. In the poem Wilde transforms this memory of a seductive girl into a morbid fantasy, like the drug-induced dreams of decadent writers fashionable at the time. Turning the prostitutes into machines, automatons, or skeletons is, because automatons and dead creatures have no feelings, an effort to diminish the memory of his sexual passion for Isola—a defense against remembering it. The thought of his buried sister conjures up "the dead . . . dancing with the dead" and "a frightened girl." Even "Requiescat," his chaste memorial poem, is, through the associative bridge of Hood's meter, a monument to Isola's seductiveness.

The meter of "The Harlot's House," though not the rhyme scheme, is the same as much of Alfred Tennyson's "In Memoriam." Tennyson wrote this long poem after the sudden death of his dear friend Arthur Henry Hallam, who died just before he was to marry Tennyson's sister. Tennyson devoted years to writing "In Memoriam" and even named one of his sons Hallam. Tennyson so identified with both his sister and Hallam that twice in the poem he imagines himself as a grieving widower. In one verse he sees "two partners of a married life" and, reminded of Hallam, thinks "of my spirit as a wife." The wish to have Hallam marry his sister is gradually replaced in the poem by the idea of being married to Hallam himself:

> I feel it, when I sorrow most,
> 'Tis better to have loved and lost
> Than never to have loved at all.[57]

The themes of incest, suppressed homosexual yearning, and tender love for the departed apparently struck a chord in Wilde, whose love for Bosie was, as I shall show, in many ways a recapitulation of his love for Isola. The tender, suppressed eroticism of Tennyson's poem can be sensed only in the final line of Wilde's "Harlot's House," which compares the dawn to "a frightened girl," and in the meter borrowed from Tennyson. The meter hints at a deeply suppressed tenderness beneath Wilde's cold vision of the harlots as "strange mechanical grotesques," just as the vision of Isola as a prostitute lingers in the meter of "Requiescat," well hidden beneath the overtly expressed sorrow. It seems that Wilde could not feel tenderness and lust at once, that he was among the psychically impotent, of whom Freud wrote: "They are incapable of giving physical expression to their tenderest feelings towards the opposite sex, while towards less loved objects they may perhaps have every reaction at their command."[58] Wilde's love for Bosie was apparently not as physical as is often imagined; rather, his love for Bosie perhaps inhibited his sexual desire. Both Oscar and Bosie preferred younger men, especially those from the lower classes, and anonymous sex. / Can it leave anyone ?

The thought of his little sister in her grave never left Oscar. When he was near death, he fearfully recounted a horrible dream: "I was supping with the dead." He laughed hysterically at the correct interpretation of a friend, whose remark touched Wilde's wish to dine with the dead: "My dear Oscar, you were probably the life and soul of the party."[59] An early poem, "Ballade de Marguerite," which concerns a forester's love for a princess far beyond his reach, concludes with Wilde's thinly disguised wish to lie down beside his sister in the grave:

> O mother, you know I loved her true:
> ✓ O mother, hath one grave room for two? (*CW*, 774)

Wilde also almost certainly got the title of "Requiescat" from Matthew Arnold's poem of the same name, which includes the lines,

> In quiet she reposes;
> Ah, would that I did, too![60]

Through imitating the meter of Hood's poem, borrowing Arnold's title, and producing a number of erotically charged poems concerning young girls and, often, their deaths, such as "Charmides," "Madonna-Mia," "The Burden of Itys," and "The Dole of the King's Daughter," Wilde expresses obsessive erotic fantasies about his sister. He reveals not just that he had incestuous desires but that he found her behavior seductive. There is of course nothing out of the ordinary in a four-year-old girl seducing her six-year-old brother; younger children are, we can assume, less inhibited, and erotic play among children of the same family is anything but abnormal.

Besides, the background of the Wilde family at this time suggests that the parents were too preoccupied to give their children enough care and affection. Oscar and Isola probably had to turn increasingly to each other for love and emotional support, which would have quickly ripened into the pregenital type of intimacy found in these situations. This kind of erotic activity, when later practiced by adults, has the flavor of perversion; in the case of Wilde this eroticism is glorified in *Salome*.

Lady Wilde's depression depleted her energies so that she could never have met the exhausting demands of young children. Her husband was also depressed, as shown by his frenetic, incessant work habits, which frequently drove him to exhaustion. His apparently boundless energy and ability to take on enormous tasks, for instance, single-handedly doing the medical portion of the Irish census, were legendary. The compulsive quality of his thrill seeking and his reputation as a Don Juan also suggest an underlying depressive strain, as does his habitually sloppy dress and personal uncleanliness. In 1852, quite early in the marriage and two years before Oscar's birth, his mother was already uneasy about her husband's mental state. In a letter, she portrays herself as a warrior tired out by her husband's invincible despair: "Although naturally I have my high spirit and long warred bravely against his gloom, yet at length his despondency has infected me and I am now nearly as gloomy as himself. This is bad. . . . When I ask him what could make him happy he answers *death* and yet the next hour if any excitement arouses him he will throw himself into the rush of life as if life were eternal here." She seems to sense that his manic activity fails to protect him from increased depression: "His whole existence is one of unceasing mental activity, and this has made the peculiarities of his nature—for myself I died long ago. . . . I love and suffer. . . . Nothing interests me beyond the desire to make *him* happy—for this I could kill myself."[61] It seems that his depressions deepened her own. As an old woman she was to reflect, "Literary men are often very irritating. . . . In the fatal intimacy of daily life illusions soon vanish, and [a wife] finds that, except in moments of inspiration, her divinity is weaker than even an ordinary mortal. . . . So she resents the knowledge that her idol is only made of clay, and her feelings alternate between contempt and dislike."[62] Apparently, the union did not improve with time.

The marriage underwent another strain, further distracting both parents from their children, when Mary Travers, the lover now spurned by Dr. Wilde, began harassing the entire family for revenge. She put garlic in the soap dishes of his waiting room to annoy his patients, wrote a pamphlet implying that he had raped her (signing it Speranza), hired newsboys to sell copies of his love letters in front of a hall where he was giving a lecture, and printed doggerel verse insulting his illegitimate brood in the local papers. She also came repeatedly to the Wilde home, though she was no longer admitted, and once broke into Lady Wilde's boudoir, from which she was summarily dismissed. So distressing was Mary's behavior that Lady Wilde took the children to Bray, a nearby seaside resort, to get away from further harassments. But

Mary followed them and even recruited local newsboys to sell at Lady Wilde's door more copies of the scandalous pamphlet about Dr. Wilde's supposed rape. Lady Wilde seized the newsboy's placard advertising the pamphlets, and Mary took out a summons against her in the Bray petty sessions court, charging her with abusing the newsboy and taking his placard without paying for it. Before the case was heard, Isola, then seven years old, came to her mother's bedroom one morning to report that a boy in the hall was selling pamphlets with "Speranza" written on them. How did that boy know her mother's name, she wondered. In a rage, Lady Wilde wrote a letter of complaint to Mary's father, and Mary, after stealing it from his drawer, sued her for libel.[63]

The trial was the biggest sensation Dublin had seen in a long while; even the London papers devoted several editorials to it.[64] Mary ended up winning, in the sense that Lady Wilde's letter was deemed "not true in substance and fact," but Mary received only one farthing in damages. Unfortunately, because she had technically won, the Wildes had to pay the crippling court costs, which nearly ruined them. After the trial Dr. Wilde, having lost prestige and heart, was to spend more and more time away from home at his fishing lodge in Moytura. The trials made a definite impact on Oscar. The ten-year-old boy had just been sent to boarding school, where a schoolmate remembered that during a boyish discussion about a current ecclesiastical prosecution, Oscar seemed to know all about the Court of the Arches, the English ecclesiastical court of appeal, and showed great interest in the case: "He told us there was nothing he would like better in life than to be the hero of such a cause célèbre and to go down to posterity as the defendant in such a case as *Regina* vs. *Wilde*" (the queen of England versus himself).[65]

In a home dominated by such parents the increasingly tender and fateful attachment between Oscar and Isola blossomed. When he died, a curiously decorated envelope containing a lock of her hair was found in his possession.[66] On it is written: "She is not dead but sleepeth." The drawing on the envelope, on which he inscribed "My Isola's Hair," seems to indicate a fantasy of being united in the grave with her. Above the inscription are two wreaths linked by a garland. One wreath surrounds an initial O for Oscar, the other I for Isola. On either side of the inscription are identical graves, each bearing a cross with the letters I and O written on either side, in mirror image of the other. The final lines of "Requiescat,"

> All my life's buried here,
> Heap earth upon it (*CW*, 724),

sum up the meaning of the artwork on the envelope.

On the eve of his sentencing years later, when Wilde knew he would be going to prison, he wrote passionately to his lover, Alfred Douglas, the young lord whom he called "the supreme, the perfect love of my life": "My sweet rose, my delicate flower, my lily of lilies . . . even covered with mud I shall praise you, from the deepest abysses I shall cry to you. In my solitude, you will be with me. I am determined not to revolt, but to accept every outrage through devotion to love, to let my body be dishonoured so long as my soul may keep always the image of you. . . . To keep you in my soul, such is the goal of this pain which men call life. . . . My soul clings to your soul, my life is your life, and in all the worlds of pain and pleasure you are my ideal of admiration and joy" (L, 397–98). Such words, such intense worshipful love as this, are reminiscent of the feeling expressed on the envelope containing Isola's hair. Wilde's love for Bosie Douglas was really a revival of his love for Isola. In *Dorian Gray* he wrote: "Romance lives by repetition. . . . Each time that one loves is the only time that one has ever loved. . . . We can have in life but one great experience at best, and the secret of life is to reproduce that experience as often as possible" (*CW*, 149). Wilde was fond of calling Bosie— a blond, like Isola—his "honey-haired boy," a phrase borrowed from Walter Pater, who had been Wilde's Oxford tutor; Pater used the phrase "honey-like hair" in describing a dying child, another fact that may have given the phrase particular appeal for Wilde.[67] Going to prison must have meant for Wilde being buried, "covered with mud," as he says in the letter to Bosie, in the grave beside his sister. In *The Ballad of Reading Gaol,* written after he emerged from prison in 1897, he refers to his cell as "my numbered tomb" (*CW*, 849).

Some of the imagery of this last poem by Wilde strongly resembles that of "The Harlot's House." In the earlier poem he describes "mechanical" prostitutes who resemble "automatons." In *The Ballad of Reading Goal*, his elegiac rendering of an execution in the prison, and his reaction to it, he describes "crooked shapes of Terror" (phantoms that appear the night before the condemned man's execution) as having "the pirouettes of marionettes." He adds:

> Some wheeled in smirking pairs
> With the mincing step of a demirep. (*CW*, 850–51)

This recalls his effort in "The Harlot's House" to distance himself from memories of his passionate love for Isola by evoking it through the actions of automatons and marionettes, creatures that have no feeling. The ghost of his sister, his guilt over his sexual interest in her, and his fear that her death was a consequence of that interest haunt him. This fear would have been especially strong if Oscar and Isola's sexual play continued up to the time of her final illness. In the beginning of *The Ballad of Reading Gaol*, Wilde says of the condemned man,

> . . . they found him with the dead
> The poor dead woman whom he loved
> And murdered in her bed.

Describing the night before the execution, he remarks,

> Alas! it is a fearful thing
> To feel another's guilt!
> For, right within, the Sword of Sin
> Pierced to its poisoned hilt. (*CW*, 850)

The lines that follow make no sense in the narrative of the poem and so must have a private meaning for Wilde:

> For he who sins a second time *, 2nd "bad" act*
> Wakes a dead soul to pain, / *wakes his sister in pain*
> And draws it from its spotted shroud / *After such a long-time*
> And makes it bleed again. (*CW*, 854)
> *suffers yet again for same sin*

Evidently, Wilde is thinking of himself sinning "a second time" with Bosie, who is a constant reminder of Wilde's earlier "sins" with Isola and his "killing" of her; by loving Bosie he "wakes a dead soul"—his sleeping memories of Isola and their relationship.

Other lines in *The Ballad* are strikingly similar to some lines of Samuel Coleridge in "The Rime of the Ancient Mariner," which could amplify Wilde's meaning. The lines Wilde writes in imitation of Coleridge contain nothing that could be interpreted as a direct reference to Isola; the full meaning becomes evident only when one realizes that they are associatively connected to Coleridge's poem in meter as well as imagery. Coleridge's poem is, in the portion not imitated by Wilde, full of images that would evoke in Wilde his erotic attachment to Isola. Wilde's imitative lines, concerning the marionette-phantoms haunting the prisoner, are:

> About, about, in ghostly rout
> They trod a saraband:
> And the damned grotesques made arabesques
> Like the wind upon the sand! (*CW*, 851)

Coleridge's lines, concerning a curse put on the Ancient Mariner for killing a harmless bird, the albatross, are:

> About, about, in reel and rout
> The death-fires danced at night;
> The water, like a witch's oils,
> Burnt green, and blue and white.[68]

Several stanzas after his depiction of the ghostly death-fires, Coleridge introduces a grisly couple, Death and his "Spectre-Woman" companion, called
"Life-in-Death"; they are casting dice for the crew of the Ancient Mariner's
ship, and Life-in-Death wins the Ancient Mariner. "His ship-mates drop
down dead," explains Coleridge in his marginal gloss to the poem, "But Life-
in-Death begins her work on the Ancient Mariner." All their souls "did from
their bodies fly," but the Ancient Mariner lives on in the power of "Life-in-
Death." Later the dead crew are "inspirited . . . by a blessed troop of angelic
spirits."[69] Naturally this bizarre fantasy would evoke in Wilde his own fantasies of seeing the dead brought to life and of being in the power of his dead
sister. His use of Coleridge's poem does more than that: it suggests all Wilde's
ambivalence about Isola; she is simultaneously dead and alive.

Wilde's description in *The Ballad* of the condemned man's death indirectly
aligns the two great love affairs of his life:

> And all the woe that moved him so
> That he gave that bitter cry,
> And the wild regrets, and the bloody sweats
> None knew so well as I:
> For he who lives more lives than one
> More deaths than one must die. (*CW*, 853)

Bosie/Isola

The riddle of "he who lives more lives than one" points clearly to Wilde. He
loved more loves than one, and each of these was a life. On 20 May 1895, a few
days before he was sentenced, he wrote to Bosie, "I feel that my love for you,
your love for me, are the two signs of my life, the divine sentiments which
make all bitterness bearable. Never has anyone in my life been dearer than
you, never has any love been greater, more sacred, more beautiful" (*L*, 397).
But Wilde had in 1886 described the "most fiery moments of ecstasy" as
"merely shadows of what we have felt" (*L*, 185), expressing lyrically the same
idea scientifically captured by Freud in the concept of the return of the
repressed. There is enough evidence to suggest that Wilde's love for Bosie
revived his love for Isola; the end of the love for Bosie brought back the death
of Isola; Wilde was dying "more deaths than one."

-- love, I suppose, can do that --

In this context I assume that *The Ballad* expresses emotions that welled up
through the following associations in Wilde's mind: while Wilde was in
prison, a man was executed for killing his beloved wife. The killing of this
woman aroused Wilde's guilt about sinful memories—the erotic play with
his sister, who died soon after. Wilde himself connected his poem with Bosie.
Robert Ross, Wilde's friend and literary executor, reports his remark that the
poem described not his prison life but life at Naples with Bosie following

prison, and that all the best stanzas were the immediate result of his existence there (L, 730n). Wilde apparently meant that his dirty, humiliating life in prison resembled his homosexual orgies with Bosie at Naples, a homosexual colony.

Bosie's autobiography indirectly confirms this: "[Wilde] told me that he had composed certain of the stanzas of [Reading Gaol] in prison and he added to them at Berneval. But there can be no question that the poem was completed at Naples. He laboured over it in a manner which I had never known him to labour before. Every word had to be considered; every rhyme and every cadence carefully pondered. I had Ballad of Reading Gaol for breakfast, dinner, and tea, and for many weeks it was our sole topic of conversation." Bosie goes on to claim that Wilde wrote three of his comedies, A Woman of No Importance, The Importance of Being Earnest, and An Ideal Husband, in his presence and with his assistance, adding that "there are passages in Reading Gaol which he lifted holus-bolus from a poem of my own."[70] In any case, Oscar's need to talk over the poem constantly with Bosie and to write it in his presence suggests the unconscious connection between Bosie's presence and the covert theme of the poem—Wilde's incestuous love for Isola and its revival in his relationship with Bosie.

Wilde's use of Coleridge again brings up the problem of Wilde's tendency toward an openly imitative style. In such cases I believe that his style revealed his hidden incestuous love for Isola. Wilde's imitative tendency had, however, a much broader base. As Edward Shanks, one of the early critics of Wilde's poems, wrote in 1924, his work was "exceedingly like a volume of serious parodies."[71] Much of his work is flagrantly derivative. In his early poems Wilde borrowed so heavily from Milton, Keats, Tennyson, Coleridge, Arnold, Thomas Hood, Rossetti, and others that a contemporary Punch reviewer commented: "Mr. Wilde may be aesthetic, but he is not original. This is a volume of echoes, it is Swinburne and water."[72] W. H. Auden, similarly, comments in Forewords and Afterwords that "of his poems not one has survived, for he was totally lacking in a poetic voice of his own; what he wrote was an imitation of poetry-in-general."[73] In his recent study entitled "'Literary Petty Larceny': Plagiarism in Oscar Wilde's Early Poetry," Averil Gardner identifies much outright appropriation, especially from romantic and pre-Raphaelite poets, and finds self-accusation in Wilde's sarcastic condemnation of other authors' "literary petty larceny."[74]

When Wilde sent the Oxford Union, the debating society to which he had belonged as an undergraduate, a copy of his poems, a member named Oliver Elton argued that the book should be returned to the author: "It is not that these poems are thin, and they are thin; it is not that they are immoral, and

[handwritten annotation:] So is his love for of Bosie merely a Freude and/or make-up for his love of Isola?

they are immoral; it is not that they are this or that, and they are this or that; it is that they are for the most part not by their putative father at all, but by a number of better known and more deservedly reputed authors. They are in fact by William Shakespeare, by Philip Sidney, by John Donne, by Lord Byron, by William Morris, by Algernon Swinburne, and by sixty more. . . . The Union Library already contains better and fuller editions of these poets."[75] These remarks have a curiously Wildean ring, as though Elton were imitating Wilde in spite of himself. In any case, the members voted to carry out Elton's suggestion.

As Elton made quite clear, it is often obvious whom Wilde imitates in his art; it is less obvious why Wilde chose to imitate so many writers so deliberately—why a man with a brilliant sense of style prided himself on being an imitator, seeing it as "the privilege of the appreciative man" and as a demonstration of his ability to distinguish a good author from a bad. His mother is believed to have hoped for a girl when she was pregnant with Oscar and to have dressed him in female garb and ornaments "like a little Hindoo idol" long past the age when little boys were customarily dolled up in feminine attire.[76] Despite her dreams of Ossianic glory for him, she must also have passed on her wish that he be a girl. This longing of hers may have stimulated in Wilde a desire to imitate others whom he appreciated and admired, especially Isola, the family favorite so valued by his mother.

His relationship with his mother was conducive to establishing this tendency in more than one way. His first identifications with her created his propensity to be a borrower. Lady Wilde borrowed styles to glorify her presence; Oscar used them to mask, and, perversely, to display, his homosexuality and feminine identification. His mother seems to have exhibited similarly conflicting images of self. She made it clear in an early letter to her editor, during her involvement with Young Ireland, that she needed a mask or disguise to impart her revolutionary message successfully, because no one would listen to a woman: "If a page of the *Nation* [the radical newspaper of the movement] were devoted to feminine contributions it would probably be the only page left unread. If Women teach or preach politics, they should probably do so masked to produce any Effect. . . . No one puts *faith* in the opinions of women."[77]

So strong was her longing to be an Ossianic warrior and so great her disdain for women that she scornfully rejected "this redundant female population," commenting, "Oh, Henry! Eight of England and First of Ireland, that you murdered your wives is little—(women are too numerous as it is)."[78] Shortly after Oscar was born, she fumed in a letter, "A Joan of Arc was never meant for marriage."[79] The plethora of feminine accessories in Lady Wilde's costumes, including at least two crinolines, topped by "flounces of limerick lace," an oriental scarf about her waist, battalions of brooches across her chest and, literally, a mask of stagy caked-on makeup—makes it seem that the lady protested too much.[80] She apparently adorned herself excessively to conceal, perhaps even from herself, her wish to be a man. The quantity of embellishment substituted for the "hundred thousand shining muskets glittering brightly in the light of heaven" that she, in her seditious article "Jacta Alea Est" (The Die Is Cast) had imagined pointing at England.[81] It is difficult to overlook the symbolic meaning of those "hundred thousand shining muskets." In one of her poems, "Historic Women," which Wilde included in an 1888 issue of the *Woman's World*, a periodical he edited, she praised women who were

> Strong, splendid souls that chafed at human wrong,
> And tyranny and servile servitude,
> And bonds that strangle nations to the death;
> So flung their lives down with a passionate waste,
> As incense upon altar sacrifice,
> For glory, country, love, or some great cause;
> For a whole people merged in nationhood,
> Or one, more loved than nations or the world
> Annihilating even womanhood. . . .

The last line is most revealing. The other lines read like a prescription for the life of her famous son, who certainly flung down his life "with a passionate waste."

Lady Wilde goes on to declare:

> This must at least be granted to the sex,
> That Woman is no coward fronting fate.
> Sublime in love, in suffering, in death,
> She treads all terrors down with calm disdain,
> As stars tread out the blackness of the sky,
> In silent Grandeur. Such the Roman wife
> Who drew the dagger from her husband's hand
> And stabbed herself, to teach him how to die;
> Then, smiling, said, "It is not painful, Paetus;"
> Such the proud queen, who would have flung away
> A kingdom for her lover, like a pearl
> Yet scorned to wear the Victor's gilded chain.[82]

If she wanted to teach her son how to die, she succeeded.

At the height of his conquest of the English in the 1890s, when they had come to revere him as a playwright and brilliant talker, his attire revealed a compromise between his longing to express a feminine identification and his wish to appear as the Ossianic epitome of virility. He overdid his dress as an English gentleman through exaggerated attention to detail, decorating his lapel with a large bouquet of Parma violets or, alternatively, sporting the green carnation that was, among Parisian homosexuals, a symbol of sexual inversion. In doing so, he was in part making fun of the English gentleman; there could be no mistake that his dress and movements were among other things a caricature. Max Beerbohm summed up the effect of Wilde's style, describing the opening night of *A Woman of No Importance*: "When little Oscar came on to make his bow there was a slight mingling of hoots and hisses, though he looked very sweet in a new white waistcoat and a large bunch of little lilies in his coat."[83] Wilde's overdoing of details suggested femininity. His ostentatious way of dressing, together with his pomp and wit at social gatherings, became for him a means to attack and undermine the attitudes of the English upper classes and at the same time covertly make homosexuality socially acceptable.

Wilde's homosexuality is of course important in any attempt to understand his life, style, and literary work. The cause of homosexuality has been approached from various points of view, none of which is altogether satisfactory.[84] But if one thinks of Freud's model of the etiology and development of homosexuality in his paper on Leonardo da Vinci, the scenario in the Wilde household seems to fit. Oscar lacked a strong father figure, since Sir William was always traveling, seeing patients, flinging himself into scholarly quests, or pursuing amorous encounters. The Herodias-like Lady Wilde, whose seductive nature Oscar hints at, dominated the home. The element of anality, well known as having an important role in homosexuality, is striking in Oscar's personality and was demonstrably a family characteristic. The home was always unkempt; Oscar's mother is said to have admonished a servant with "Why do you put the plates in the coalscuttle? What are chairs meant for?"[85] One thinks, too, of his unwashed father. Oscar's brother, Willie, took after their father and, as Max Beerbohm put it, was "very vulgar and unwashed and inferior."[86]

Oscar's anality is visible in his style and choices of subject matter; many of his works show a preoccupation with smell, particularly perfumes. The opening of *The Picture of Dorian Gray* is typical: "The studio was filled with the rich odour of roses, and when the light summer wind stirred amidst the trees of the garden, there came through the open door the heavy scent of the lilac, or the more delicate perfume of the pink-flowering thorn" (*CW*, 18). To give a more obvious example, he expressed special glee at having been able to work the word *latrine* into *The Ballad of Reading Gaol*, using it to round out his description of his cell. Exulting to Robert Ross in a letter, Wilde wrote: "I have got in 'latrine:' it looks beautiful" (*L*, 635). The passage reads:

> Each narrow cell in which we dwell
>   Is a foul and dark latrine,
> And the fetid breath of living Death
>   Chokes up each grated screen,
> And all, but Lust, is turned to dust
>   In Humanity's machine. (*CW*, 858)

Wilde's preoccupation with gold, silver, and precious stones in *Dorian Gray* and *Salome* is another expression of anal interests. Freud remarked: "After a person's own faeces, his excrement, has lost its value for him, this instinctual interest derived from the anal source passes over into objects that can be presented as *gifts*. And this is rightly so, for faeces were the first gift that an infant could make. . . . This ancient interest in faeces is transformed into the high valuation of *gold* and *money*."[87] Hence in *Salome* one finds Herod's litany of jewels in his attempt to bribe *Salome* with gifts: "I have an emerald, a great round emerald. . . . You would like that, would you not? . . . I have jewels hidden in this place—jewels that your mother even has never seen; jewels that are marvellous. I have a collar of pearls. . . . I have amethysts of two kinds, one that is black like wine, and one that is red like wine which has been coloured with water. I have topazes. . . . I have opals that burn always with an ice-like flame. . . . I have moonstones. . . . I have sapphires. . . . and I will give them all to you, all, and other things I will add to them" (*CW*, 571–72).

Sir Edmund Trelawny Backhouse, who as an Oxford undergraduate had sexual encounters with numerous people, including Lord Alfred Douglas's brother, and who had previously had encounters with Bosie in boarding school, claims to have enjoyed intimate encounters with Wilde: "The unbiassed reader will not be astonished to hear that sexual relations were frequently commemorated between us; although Oscar admitted to me that he derived greater pleasure from association with the type of laquais, 'la canaille et la lie du peuple,' because their passion was all body and no soul!" Backhouse discussed Wilde's sexual tastes in his memoirs: "Incidents repeated themselves when he left behind ocular proofs of his orgies in hotel bedrooms: horrible proof of a most painstaking 'pedicatio' were found on the sheets and meticulously preserved by the management to be produced at the third 'process' [trial] with the medical analysis of human semen, human excrements, 'et de la vaseline': like Messalina (except for the homosexuality) he performed a mock marriage in the Hotel Bristol with a catamite in female attire from the gutter and the results of their union were concrete and visible (as formerly at the Savoy hotel) on the drapery of the nuptial couch." Backhouse reports that Aubrey Beardsley told him: "One night at the Savoy when a lot of us were having an after-theatre supper, he boasted of having had five love affairs and resultant copulations with telegraph and district messenger boys in one night." Boasting of kissing each one "in every part of their bodies," Oscar asserted that "they were all dirty and appealed to me just for that reason."[88] Although H. Montgomery Hyde has called Backhouse's memoirs scabrous and has suggested that they be "regarded with considerable caution," testimony given at Wilde's trial bears out the truth of these stories.[89] At one point his lawyer desperately tried to explain the stains on Wilde's sheets by claiming that his client "had been suffering from attacks of diarrhoea at the time."[90]

Both Wilde's homosexuality and his childhood love for Isola became a breeding ground for other important artistic developments in his career, the most monumental of them being *Salome*. This play, more than any of his other works, illuminates the history of his earliest and most hidden emotional investment in martyrdom. A treasure trove of significant wishes and attempts at conflict resolution, *Salome* decodes many mysterious turns of his life. The strange symbolism and surrealism of *Salome* seem closer to his unconscious mind than his other writings. Like a dream, *Salome* seems impossible to understand without seeking the symbols beneath the surface, the distortions of persons, places, and affects that one finds in dreams.

I was introduced to *Salome* through Richard Strauss's opera, which premiered in 1905, five years after Wilde's death. The journalist Richard Le Gallienne, reviewing *Salome* in February 1893, prophetically remarked, "It seems built to music. Its gradual growth is exactly like the development of a theme in music." Wilde gratefully responded to Le Gallienne: "You have got into the secret chamber of the house in which *Salome* was fashioned, and I rejoice to think that to you has my secret been revealed" (*ML,* 120–21). What was that secret? Quoting Walter Pater, Wilde wrote in "The Critic as Artist" that music was the "perfect type of art. Music can never *reveal* its ultimate secret" (*CW,* 1031, my emphasis). Music has the curious quality of revealing and defending against revelation. Revealing emotion in sounds, it keeps the sources of emotion from being verbalized. Music is closer to the unconscious, which distances the mind from reality. Consciousness requires verbalization; music does not. Wilde sensed the structural similarity between the work of art and the dream. One thinks of Freud's remark in *The Interpretation of Dreams*: "There is at least one spot in every dream at which it is unplumbable—a navel, as it were, that is its point of contact with the unknown."[91]

Salome is indeed a dreamlike play, a symbolist play in the French sense, fashionable for its atmosphere of opiated decadence and Aestheticism. The eerie, frightening music first called my attention to the work, but the story proved even more enigmatic. What purpose could Wilde have had in portraying a teenage voluptuary, an allegedly fourteen- or fifteen-year-old girl who orders the decapitation of a man to relish the taste of blood as she kisses the lips of the severed head? And why set this strange story in biblical times and, on top of that, write the whole thing in a foreign language? Was Wilde trying to interpret the ambience into which the newly arrived Messiah, Jesus Christ, had stepped? Was he trying to explain the arrival of the Savior? Or was he just attempting to make money and get publicity by writing a modish Baudelairean or Maeterlinckian play that would, moreover, exhibit his worldliness because it was written in French? Did he hope to attract Sarah Bernhardt, the Parisian diva, to act in one of his plays? Wilde being the publicity seeker that he was, the last explanation might be reasonable.

What all the critics of the play stressed, but could not make sense of, was the perverse desire of this young girl. Perhaps for the operagoer the difficulty in understanding what is going on is made greater because the role of Salome is usually sung by a Brünnhilde type—huge, full-bosomed, statuesque—the antithesis of all that Salome represents. Visually, the Salome of Strauss's opera could be of no help to critics trying to understand her personality.

The lustful gazing of this adolescent, her exhibitionism in the dance of the seven veils, her longing for Jokanaan to look at her, and her almost cannibalistic attraction to the severed head of Jokanaan have always stirred confusion in critics. They waver between taking Wilde seriously and feeling that he was making a grotesque joke. W. Graham Robertson, one of Wilde's friends, inadvertently offended him by laughing. "One was ill prepared for Wilde's serious moods, they were so rare: as I listened I decided that this could not be the result of one of them." Describing Wilde "chanting the phrases with great satisfaction," Robertson cautiously decided that Wilde had written a burlesque of Maeterlinck. "I thought I was safe and laughed approvingly. . . . 'That's a funny bit,' said I with a complimentary chuckle." Wilde reacted with great disappointment.[92]

The tone of the drama has been difficult to understand because Salome's sexuality appears bizarre. When Jokanaan refuses her advances, she asks, with what seems to be chilling cruelty, that his head be brought to her on a silver platter. When she gets it on a silver platter, she responds with a taunt: "Ah! thou wouldst not suffer me to kiss thy mouth. Well! I will kiss it now. I will bite it with my teeth as one bites a ripe fruit" (*CW*, 753). Her next lines, however, are a clue to the whole character: "But wherefore dost thou not look at me? Art thou afraid of me?" They reveal that she has no understanding of the permanence of death. What seems like cruelty is only a momentary mood, a blow dealt out of infantile frustration, not out of desire to gratify a sadistic impulse. She wants nothing more than to punish Jokanaan for failing to look at her. And how can she fulfill her desire to kiss him unless she has his head in her hands? Holding the bloody head, she still wonders why he will not open his eyes. She expects that he will stand up again and—having learned the error of his ways—finally kiss her. Her persistent demands and her lack of fear of the events she is causing might be frightening in an adult or teenager. But in children's play, behavior like this has quite another meaning. The story that is played out here is that of a three- or four-year-old child. Here the child Oscar speaks through the man he has become.

Salome's childish longing for this strange young prophet and her inability to comprehend that a man who has lost his head is dead shows in her questions. A sadist would experience satisfaction in seeing the blood drip-ping from Jokanaan's neck as proof that he had really suffered. Instead Sa-lome is perplexed because he will not look at her. Her questions betray the pathetic surprise she feels when he does not wake up.

She equates love with looking and being looked at: "If thou hadst looked at me, thou hadst loved me" summarizes her interest in him. Salome expresses all her sexuality through the orality of the child: "I am hungry for thy body; and neither wine nor apples can appease my desire." She never alludes to the sexual organs. Strong emphasis on oral incorporation of the beloved is char-acteristic of early childhood. In *Three Essays on the Theory of Sexuality* Freud describes this early pregenital organization, the "oral, or cannibalistic" phase: "Here sexual activity has not yet been separated from the ingestion of food, nor are opposite currents within the activity differentiated. The sexual aim consists in the incorporation of the object."[93] Salome's desire to kiss and to bite the lips of the head is the natural culmination of the child's love for Jokanaan. The final insult was his not looking at her when she was writhing with impatience for him to do so: "Ah! Ah! wherefore didst thou not look at me, Jokanaan?" (*CW*, 574).

When the severed head of Jokanaan ignores her final threat—to throw it to the dogs and the birds of the air—her true lament begins. She yearns for the beauty of his body and longs to have him look at her again. She feels entirely bewildered: "Well I know that thou wouldst have loved me, and the mystery of love is greater than the mystery of death." The mystery of death is that he does not regain consciousness, a mystery that all children eventually fathom as they grow up and begin to understand reality. The mystery of love is that Jokanaan is not aroused by her, as she is by him. The fact is that because of Wilde's nature, the mystery of love preoccupied him all his life. In one of his comedies, *Lady Windermere's Fan,* a character confesses that he is a mystery to himself, adding: "I am the only person in the world I should like to know thoroughly; but I don't see any chance of it just at present" (*CW,* 413). Wilde did and did not want his homosexuality to remain the mystery that it was to himself. He longed to talk about it, to understand it, and to make it clear to himself—and yet he foresaw the consequences.

The childish, the childlike nature of Salome gave me another clue. Behind the mask of a cosmopolitan roué, Wilde hid a child. Essentially he remained a child throughout his life—a highly educated and sophisticated child, full of the charm, naive kindness, demonstrativeness, and exhibitionism that characterize childhood. His taste for anonymous sex with dirty and dangerous young male prostitutes, the heedlessness with which he pursued harmful encounters, and his contrariness are characteristic of an immature personality, and all are revealed in *Salome.* Both Salome and Wilde possess the qualities he attributed to another young girl in his comedy *An Ideal Husband*: "the fascinating tyranny of youth, and the astonishing courage of innocence" (*CW,* 483). The typical child possesses a megalomaniacal self-confidence as he constantly experiences—but tries to stave off—powerlessness.

All characters emanate from Wilde's personality, each revealing as well his vision of the members of his family. Queen Herodias, "who wears a black mitre sewn with pearls" and other assorted jewels, and "whose hair is powdered with blue dust," dresses no more outlandishly than Oscar's mother (*CW,* 553). One of Lady Wilde's guests remarked on her "white-powdered blue-black head . . . invariably crowned with a gilded laurel wreath."[94] It is reported that "sometimes she would dress in white, her . . . hair hanging down her back, like a Druid priestess. Other times she would be seen in purple brocade, with a towering headdress of velvet decorated with white streamers, or a crown of gilt laurels on her hair, enormous brooches fastening the lace across her chest. She wore long gold ear-rings, huge gold bracelets, and rings on every finger. She moved to a clatter of ornaments."[95]

With many a charming off-color innuendo, Lady Wilde made herself into a Herodias. In her sixties, she remarked to a young man, "When you are as old as I, young man, you will know there is only one thing in the world worth living for, and that is sin."[96] Herodias is a woman who, "having seen the images of men painted on the walls, the images of the Chaldeans limned in colours, gave herself up unto the lust of her eyes . . . gave herself unto the captains of Assyria . . . [and] hath given herself to the young men of Egypt"

(*CW*, 557–58). At her eccentric salon, Lady Wilde "listened to the flood of bawdy talk without turning a hair" and enjoyed contributing to it. Bram Stoker, the creator of Count Dracula and the man who later stole Oscar's first love, Florrie Balcombe, and married her, remembered introducing a girl he described as "half English and half Irish" to Lady Wilde. "Glad to meet you my dear," said Lady Wilde; "your English half is as welcome as your Irish bottom."[97] Another time, someone asked to bring a guest described as "respectable," and Lady Wilde intoned, "Respectable! Never use that word here. It is only tradespeople who are respectable."[98] She was also fond of declaring, "There never has been a woman yet in this world who wouldn't have given the top off the milk jug to some man if she had met the right one." To the daughter of a third-rate novelist, she remarked, "Welcome, my dear. I hear you have a lover. This is a pity, since love puts an end to ambition. But don't on any account bind yourself until you have seen more of men."[99]

She may have substituted sexual talk for sexual actions, but a young boy would not have been able to sense the difference between the two. Her spirit was apparently willing. John Butler Yeats, father of the poet, claims that as a young woman, Speranza enjoyed an affair with a married man. He writes, "When she was Miss Elgee, Mrs. Butt found her with her husband when the circumstances were not doubtful, and told my mother about it."[100]

Lady Wilde's salon, where "'Bohemians preferred' might almost have been on the invitation cards," was the meeting place for all kinds of people. Like her famous son, she was good at attracting celebrities; a visitor said that "the house was a rallying place for all who were eminent in science, art, or literature." Years later, after Oscar became famous and she had moved to London, she was visited by Oliver Wendell Holmes, Henry Ward Beecher, and John Ruskin, all of whom were probably drawn at least as much by Oscar as by her. Ruskin, who had been Wilde's tutor at Oxford, was accosted by a female guest, Mrs. Stannard, whom he did not know but who announced to him, "I'm Bootles, 'Bootles Baby,' you know. Of course I'm really John Strange Winter. You know that, don't you?" Ruskin left swiftly, remarking, "What an extraordinary woman. I wonder if she is right in her head." Asked by a visitor, "How do you manage to get together such a lot of interesting people?" Lady Wilde answered, "It's quite simple. All one has to do is to get all sorts of people—but no dull specimens—and take care to mix them. Don't trouble about their morals. It doesn't matter if they haven't any."[101] With these remarks of Speranza's ringing in the ears, one feels that Oscar did not have to look farther than his mother's parlor for inspiration in his description of the orgiastic banquet of Herod and Herodias: "There are Jews from Jerusalem who are tearing each other in pieces over their foolish ceremonies, and barbarians, who drink and drink, and spill their wine on the pavement, and Greeks from Smyrna with painted eyes and painted cheeks, and frizzed hair curled in twisted coils, and silent, subtle Egyptians, with long nails of jade and russet cloaks, and Romans, brutal and coarse, with their uncouth jargon" (CW, 555).

Speranza's promiscuous husband, who amorously pursued a young patient, Mary Travers, resembles Herod in his pursuit of Salome. The lustful Herod's first words in the play, after inquiring about Salome's whereabouts, are: "The moon has a strange look tonight. . . . She is like a mad woman, a mad woman who is seeking everywhere for lovers. She is naked, too. She is quite naked. The clouds are seeking to clothe her nakedness, but she will not let them. She shows herself naked in the sky. . . . I am sure she is looking for lovers" (CW, 561). Herod's lecherous glances so disturb Salome that she runs away from his banquet hall. Following her, he begs her to sip from his wineglass, to bite a fruit he offers her so he can see the imprint of her teeth in it, and, finally, to dance for him. Dr. Wilde was equally persistent with Mary Travers, who was quite poor, and attempted to entice her with books, theater tickets, dresses, bonnets, and "even warm underclothing."[102] He frequently invited her to the Wilde home when Oscar was growing up and pressed her to accompany him and his children to various events. Eventually she accused him of seducing and raping her in his office.

Regarded in the context of Wilde's life and work, Salome looks like a disguised, symbolic confession. The concrete imagery of the severed head expresses the abstraction "I lost my head" in the sense of losing all control. Freud, describing such imagery in dreams, mentioned a patient who dreamed that "his uncle had given him a kiss in an auto (mobile)," an image conveying the idea of "auto-erotism."[103] Theodor Reik reported the case of an American patient who during his analysis spoke in an odd linguistic mix of German and English and who dreamed, on the night after his girlfriend failed to show up for a tryst, that Prince Metternich arrived in her stead. In part this was a consolation: someone important wanted to see him. But it also meant that he "met her nicht"—he met her not.[104] Similarly, Wilde admits, in the language and style of dreams, that in spite of his resistance he did "lose his head" to Isola.

This dream confession was also clearly stated in De Profundis, his long letter to Bosie from prison; in it he spoke of his relationship with Bosie and of Bosie's father's jealous torment of them: "Between you both I lost my head" (L, 430). With this, Wilde made clear his identification with Jokanaan. The dialogue between the relentlessly seductive Salome and Jokanaan, a man preferring the solitude of his dark, dirty dungeon to the enjoyment of a kiss from a seductive girl, shows unmistakably Wilde's sexual preference. Hearing the voice of Jokanaan from the tomblike cistern where he is imprisoned, as Wilde was later to be, she flirts with the captain of the guard until he reluctantly agrees to bring forth the prophet: "You will do this thing for me, Narraboth," she coaxes, "and tomorrow when I pass in my litter beneath the gateway of the idol sellers I will let fall for you a little flower, a little green flower" (*CW*, 557). (Here Wilde was probably having a chuckle at the green carnation sported by Parisian homosexuals.) When Narraboth gives in, she wounds him so deeply by staring at Jokanaan and continually expressing her desire to kiss his mouth that Narraboth falls on his sword and dies. Perhaps Wilde was thinking of his competitor and older brother, Willie, when he created this short-lived character. Salome is instantly fascinated with Jokanaan: "Jokanaan, I am amorous of thy body! . . . Let me touch thy body. . . . Let me kiss thy mouth. . . . I will kiss thy mouth, Jokanaan, I will kiss thy mouth" (*CW*, 558–59). She teases like a little girl trying to make her older brother play with her.

Christopher Nassaar, an American critic, writes in his study of Wilde that "as Salome woos him, [Jokanaan's] repeated rejections of her are so exaggeratedly violent as to suggest a tremendous effort to prevent his repressed longing from erupting forth into the open."[105] I doubt this interpretation, although Nassaar is correct in noticing Jokanaan's vehemence, which is a sign of Wilde's homosexual disgust with women and fear of them as destroyers of men: "Bid her rise up from the bed of her abominations, from the bed of her incestuousness," Jokanaan howls, reprimanding Herodias. To Salome he says, "Thy mother hath filled the earth with the wine of her iniquities, and the cry of her sins hath come up to the ears of God. . . . By woman came evil into the world." He adamantly refuses each of Salome's invitations: "Never, Daughter of Babylon! Daughter of Sodom! Never" (*CW*, 557–59). This rejection suggests a wish fulfillment rather than a defense: Wilde shows himself proclaiming, "I *do* reject Salome," just as he wishes he had refused Isola.

The ego of the dreamer distorts, and so conceals, the message arising out of the id, and by the same mysterious process, Wilde's *Salome* hides his confession of "losing his head" to Isola and Bosie. Wilde wrote the play in French, as if by distancing himself from the familiarity of the English language he could distance himself from the familiar truth of his subject matter. He also tossed in the usual mixture of gorgeous phrases lifted from the Song of Songs, Isaiah, Maeterlinck, Flaubert, Gautier, and others, causing one critic to write, "Mr. Wilde . . . has shown, not for the first time, that he can mimic, where he might have shown, for the first time, that he can create."[106] Cloaking his story in a foreign language, in exotic literary borrowings, and in a highly ornate, artificial style, Wilde gave the play the unreality of a dream, showing that he wanted it to be interpreted as a message, just as someone recounting a dream hopes that his listener, in decoding it, will accept it.

Because Wilde wrote *Salome* about ten months after meeting Bosie, asked Bosie to translate it when he could have done so more easily—and more artistically—himself, and stated that "Bosie is very gilt-haired and I have bound *Salome* to suit him," the play might be regarded as an unconscious message to Bosie (*L,* 333). The identification of Salome with the dead Isola is clear from the beginning of the play. It opens with a description of Salome as "a woman rising from the tomb . . . like a dead woman. You would fancy she was looking for dead things . . . like a woman who is dead." The cool, inanimate imagery associated with her reinforces her deathlike quality; she is "like a little princess whose feet are of silver . . . [and] so pale . . . like the shadow of a rose in a mirror of silver . . . a little princess whose eyes are of amber" (*CW,* 552–56). As if she were, like Isola, a young child, Salome has "little white doves for feet . . . little white hands fluttering like doves. . . . They are like white butterflies" (*CW,* 552–54). Emotionally, she seems four or five, much younger than Isola, who died at ten. It makes sense that Salome would be the age at which Oscar's strong sexual attachment to Isola was formed. Even when one loses a sibling as an adult, the sometimes surprisingly intense grief for someone to whom we have little current attachment derives from the strength of the attachment during childhood; one mourns the young child, not the adolescent or adult he or she has become. At roughly the same time he was writing the play, Wilde was also writing letters in which he pleaded, "Bosie, you must not make scenes with me. They kill me, they wreck the loveliness of life"; or begged, "I want to see you. It is really absurd. *I can't live without you*" (*L,* 336, 358). The implicit message of Salome was that Bosie's destructive, seductive ways would ruin Wilde, just as Wilde's relationship with Isola had had a disruptive effect on him. Wilde's dissatisfaction with Bosie's "schoolboy" translation of the French text reveals his anger at Bosie's failure to decode the message—and having done so, to change his behavior (*L,* 432).

Wilde sought in Bosie the same aggressively seductive qualities he had experienced in Isola. Backhouse recounts that when he and Bosie were together at Winchester boarding school, Bosie "was usually the ascendent and I the pathic." He further comments: "He has persuaded himself in his old age, perhaps sincerely, that Wilde seduced an innocent pure boy (himself) with 'pedicatio' and its attendant delights. Having seen the two together, I can definitely contradict this admirable, though possibly disingenuous, rehabilitation of his character. Bozie [*sic*] though many years younger, beguiled and seduced Oscar. . . . He (Douglas) was a 'coquet' of the first water, who would leave Paris and Oscar for an unknown address and then telegraph from his temporary sojourn: 'Oscar! If you do not come to me, I shall die.'"[107] Shades of Salome.[108]

Wilde's equation of Salome with Bosie, and of both with Isola, is visible in the language of the play as well as in the characterization of Salome as childlike. In a letter to Bosie, Wilde used the same florid language as he later used to describe Salome, emphasizing Bosie's childlike qualities, addressing him as "my child," and remarking, "From your silken hair to your delicate feet you are perfection to me." Silken hair, delicate feet, and little feet, as Wilde later calls them, are all attributes of small children, so they might have described little Isola as well.

In the same letter, Wilde continues, "O my love, you whom I cherish above all things, white narcissus in an unmown field. . . . I love you, I love you, my heart is a rose which your love has brought to bloom, my life is a desert fanned by the delicious breeze of your breath, and whose cool springs are your eyes; the imprint of your little feet makes valleys of shade for me, the odour of your hair is like myrrh, and wherever you go you exhale the perfumes of the cassia tree. . . . You have been the supreme, the perfect love of my life; there can be no other. . . . O sweetest of all boys, most loved of all loves" (L, 398). Salome, similarly, is "like a dove that has strayed . . . like a narcissus trembling in the wind . . . like a silver flower" (CW, 555). She has the same childish exhibitionism and delight in teasing as Bosie. When her stepfather, Herod, asks her to drink from his wineglass, she says, "I am not thirsty." When he offers her her mother's throne, she replies, "I am not tired" (CW, 562). Finally, she dances her erotic dance of the seven veils, gradually exhibiting more and more of her body, on the condition that he give her whatever she wants. What she wants turns out to be the head of Jokanaan, whom she loves and wants to kiss. Oblivious to Herod's horror, Salome fondles and chats with the grisly, decapitated head and ultimately kisses it on the lips.

Bosie rivaled Salome in self-centered exhibitionism and displayed his friendship with Wilde at every opportunity. Richard Ellmann writes, "To flaunt their roles as 'nature's stepsons,' as he called them, Douglas always insisted that their relationship be as obvious as possible. Although Wilde had his own effrontery, he did venture as their relationship became more obvious to suggest that, so as to create less talk, they should go in the Savoy hotel restaurant by a side entrance. But Douglas insisted, 'I wanted everyone to say, "there goes Oscar Wilde and his boy,"' so they had to march in the front door." They must have been obvious, if not brazen. Backhouse records that

"Max Beerbohm produced a cartoon of Oscar and Bozie [sic] copulating, the expression on the former's face resembling a goat of Pompei, while Douglas the willing pathic was deliciously satirized."[109] Later in life Bosie was to indulge his insatiable exhibitionism by writing three autobiographies and by provoking three highly publicized libel proceedings against himself; once he libeled Winston Churchill and spent six months in Wormwood Scrubs Prison. To the last, Bosie seems to have remained, as Max Beerbohm put it, "a very pretty reflection of Oscar."[110]

Both Salome and Bosie are presented by Wilde as being prone to uncontrolled childish outbursts of rage, followed by equally childish abject penance. Salome pouts like a little girl: "Thou wouldst have none of me, Jokanaan. Thou didst reject me. Thou didst treat me as a harlot, as a wanton, me, Salome, daughter of Herodias, Princess of Judea! Well, Jokanaan, I still live, but thou, thou art dead, and thy head belongs to me. I can do with it what I will. I can throw it to the dogs and the birds of the air. That which the dogs have, the birds of the air shall devour." She talks to the head as though she believed her threats could force it to open its eyes. As soon as her rage is vented, her love resurfaces; she sorrows over him and herself, pleading: "Ah, Jokanaan, Jokanaan, thou wert the only man that I have ever loved. All other men are hateful to me. But thou, thou wert beautiful" (CW, 574). In De Profundis Wilde complains of Bosie's "long resentful moods of sullen silence" and "sudden fits of almost epileptic rage" (L, 429).

On another occasion, when Wilde had resolved to break off with Bosie and had actually left him after a particularly vicious spat, Bosie followed him. They made up, and Wilde described the sight of the tearful Bosie: "Your tears, breaking out again and again all through the evening, and falling over your cheeks like rain. . . . The unfeigned joy you evinced at seeing me, holding my hand whenever you could, as though you were a gentle and penitent child: your contrition, so simple and sincere at the moment, made me consent to renew our friendship" (L, 435). It was obviously the childish aspect of Salome's and Bosie's personalities that most appealed to Wilde, because their childishness reminded him of Isola and helped him re-create in fantasy his early relationship with her. Bosie always thought of himself as a child; according to Mary Hyde, he believed that all great poets had the "spirit of a child" and that "because, according to Thomas à Kempis one could choose one's age in heaven, he would be a child forever."[111] In one of his three autobiographies, Oscar Wilde and Myself, Bosie dwells on his childlike qualities: "When I met Wilde I was very young in years, and still younger in temperament and in experience. I was, in fact, a mere child. . . . Even at the age of twenty-three, I had the appearance of a youth of sixteen."[112] Even his nickname, Bosie, was a contraction of "Boysie," or "Little Boy," his mother's pet name for him.[113]

Besides excavating his relationship with Isola, Wilde also explores in *Salome* his own identity through Jokanaan. The figure of Jokanaan allowed Wilde to identity himself with Christ and even to advertise himself as a Christ figure, since Jokanaan, as the baptizer of Christ, was, according to Wilde, Christ's biggest public relations man: "Every time that my name is mentioned in the papers I write at once to admit that I am the Messiah. Why is Pears' soap successful? Not because it is better or cheaper than any other soap, but because it is more strenuously puffed. The journalist is my 'John the Baptist.'"[114] Wilde identified himself with Christ as a self-sacrificing hero-martyr, like the Ossian his mother had wanted him to become. In a political article entitled "The American Irish" she wrote: "When they say of a man, 'He has died for Ireland,' the voice is low and tender, as if they spoke of the passion of Christ."[115] Wilde's desire to fulfill his mother's ambitions for him gave him compelling reasons to martyr himself. In *Salome* he does so by martyring Jokanaan. Jokanaan, however, is not an Ossianic hero. In him, Wilde's own wishes and inner conflict break through. Jokanaan dies because of his homosexual loathing of women. The cause for which he is martyred is not so much Christian morality as homosexuality.

Having planned his deliberate and obvious martyrdom in the figure of Jokanaan, Wilde made it clear in court that he considered his homosexual cause a noble one. When the prosecution asked him about the meaning of the phrase "the love that dare not speak its name" in an obviously homosexual poem by Bosie, Wilde replied, in a speech that drew cheers,

"The love that dare not speak its name" in this century is such a great affection of an elder for a younger man as there was between David and Jonathan, such as Plato made the very basis of his philosophy, and such as you find in the sonnets of Michelangelo and Shakespeare. It is that deep, spiritual affection that is as pure as it is perfect. It dictates and pervades great works of art like those of Shakespeare and Michelangelo, and those two letters of mine, such as they are [love letters to Bosie that were read aloud in court]. It is in this century misunderstood, so much misunderstood that it may be described as the "Love that dare not speak its name," and on account of it I am placed where I am now. It is beautiful, it is fine, it is the noblest form of affection. There is nothing unnatural about it. It is intellectual, and it repeatedly exists between an elder and a younger man when the elder has intellect, and the younger man has all the joy, hope, and glamour of life before him. That it should be so the world does not understand. The world mocks at it and sometimes puts one in the pillory for it.

Later on at his trials, Wilde showed that he wanted to be convicted. Asked whether he had kissed a certain sixteen-year-old boy, he could have replied no. Instead, he ridiculed the idea that kissing boys was a crime: "Oh, dear no! He was a peculiarly plain boy. He was, unfortunately, extremely ugly. I pitied him for it."[116]

This statement proved to be a turning point—the moment when for the first time he lost the sympathy of the audience he had been entertaining. In front of them, he had finally fulfilled his boyhood dream of being the defendant "in such a case as *Regina* vs. *Wilde*." He was also fulfilling his mother's dearest ambitions for him. Hesketh Pearson records that Lady Wilde, by "some curious process of thought," had "managed to convince herself that Ireland was defying the universe in the person of her second born [Oscar], to whom she said [before he was convicted]: "if you stay [in London] even if you go to prison, you will always be my son; but if you go I will never speak to you again." Oscar's brother said, "Oh, yes, he could escape . . . but he has resolved to stay, to face it out, to stand the music like Christ."[117]

The first of Wilde's attempts to fulfill his mother's aspiration that he become a revolutionary warrior is a melodrama, *Vera, or the Nihilists*, which he wrote at the age of twenty-five.[118] In Russia, revolutionary anarchists known as nihilists had been active since the 1860s, trying to undermine and ultimately to overthrow the imperial government. The political situation was in a way similar to that in Ireland, where his mother's friends in the Young Ireland movement were trying to undermine hated English rule. In fact, so contemporary a phenomenon was Russian nihilism that Wilde had to cancel the London production of the play, which he called "my first attack on Tyranny," for fear of offending the prince and princess of Wales (*ML*, 38). Russian nihilists had just killed Czar Alexander II, and the new czar's wife was a sister of the princess of Wales. As a revolutionary with social pretensions, Wilde, in his typically paradoxical way, did not wish to risk offending anyone in the imperial government that theoretically he found so oppressive.

In *Vera*, Wilde tells the story of a Russian peasant woman who, emulating the ideology of her brother, becomes a nihilist after seeing him in chains on his way to Siberia. As a prisoner of the government, the brother is identified with Wilde, who was imprisoned by the government for his own revolutionary cause, the emancipation of homosexuals. Vera and her prisoner brother can be seen as distorted images of Wilde. He was a nihilist within English society; with his wit he negated the social, political, cultural, and economic institutions that were dear to the English upper and middle classes. Marriage was one of his prime targets: "Men marry because they are tired; women, because they are curious; both are disappointed," he remarked in *Dorian Gray* (*CW*, 48). "The one charm of marriage is that it makes a life of deception absolutely necessary for both parties," he added (*CW,* 20). "How marriage ruins a man! It's as demoralizing as cigarettes, and far more expensive," he says in *Lady Windermere's Fan* (*CW,* 416). He attacked general social customs as well: "The English country-gentleman galloping after a fox—the unspeakable in full pursuit of the uneatable" (*CW,* 437). He dismissed the snobbish disregard of the upper classes for literature: "If the English aristocracy will not read Shakespeare as a poet, they should certainly read him as a sort of early peerage" (*CW,* 1071). The peerage he deemed "the one book a young man about town should know thoroughly, and . . . the best thing in fiction the English have ever done" (*CW,* 461). He lambasted their politics: "In England, a man who can't talk morality twice a week to a large, popular, immoral audience is quite over as a serious politician" (*CW,* 507). He disposed of their economic arrangements: "What between the duties expected of one during one's lifetime and the duties exacted from one after one's death, land has ceased to be either a profit or a pleasure. It gives one position, and prevents one from keeping it up" (*CW,* 332). In "The Soul of Man under Socialism," an essay in which he advocates demolishing the English monarchy and instituting socialism, he comments, "Property not merely has its duties, but so many duties that its possession to any large extent is a bore" (*CW,* 1081).

Typically, he made a point of reversing the significant elements of old clichés, so as to annihilate even the clichés in his criticism of the English: "Divorces are made in heaven," he comments in *The Importance of Being Earnest* (*CW,* 323). "The English have a remarkable power of turning wine into water," he said in conversation.[119] "I remember your name perfectly, but I can't recall your face," he observed blandly to a journalist who had insulted him.[120] "In matters of grave importance, style, not sincerity, is the vital thing," says the aristocratic Gwendolen in *Earnest* (*CW,* 371). Ernest remarks that "it is a terrible thing for a man to find out suddenly that all his life he has been speaking nothing but the truth" (*CW,* 383). Wilde said acidly of one companion, "He is old enough to know worse," advised a second, "Don't be led astray into the paths of virtue," and complained of a third, "He hasn't a single redeeming vice."[121] These quips also show one of his frequently used techniques: by inverting the sense of accepted English homilies he attacked the hypocrisy of English attitudes, customs, and values. If the English upheld the importance of truth and integrity, he would in "The Decay of Lying" praise lying as an art form that deserved to be cultivated.

The plot of *Vera* and the reasons for her nihilism are a bonanza for understanding Wilde. The oath that Vera takes when she joins the nihilists, "To strangle whatever nature is in me; neither to love nor be loved; neither to pity nor be pitied, neither to marry nor be given in marriage," is spoken out of deep love for the prisoner, her brother in the play (*CW,* 653). She fails in her desire to annihilate all emotion, however, by falling in love with a man she refers to as brother; this man, who is not her brother but who resembles him by being a nihilist, happens to be the czarevitch. Her nihilist oath could therefore be seen as a defense against incest, which becomes the means of fulfilling a forbidden incestuous desire.

When Wilde began denying all the accepted tenets of English society with his wit, he was also starting to exhibit his homosexuality more and more ostentatiously, appearing in every fashionable London restaurant with Bosie. Going out in public with a male lover represented an assertion of self-worth. Wilde, however, could not help being influenced by the morality he condemned. There remain many indications that he felt ambivalent about his homosexuality. His need to criticize himself provoked him to blame the English for their intolerance. Telling them that they were wrong about everything, not just homosexuality, camouflaged his conflict from himself. Arthur Schnitzler wrote somewhere in *Der Weg ins Freie* (The Road to Freedom): "Does it ever happen that one is right in an argument? One argues after all only to convince oneself—and never to convince others." Wilde himself said: "It is only the intellectually lost who ever argue." *(Not in all cases)*

His attempts to tell the English that they were wrong about homosexuality, and about much more, show that it was necessary for him to defend his homosexuality. His own condemnation of it broke through in his trials, when he quite consciously martyred himself. The martyrdom made the punishment a triumph, but certainly his later work shows his guilt openly. By annihilating the English with his remarks, he had only temporarily staved off the urge to annihilate himself. Prince Paul, the Russian prime minister in *Vera,* who overflows with Wildean wit, remarked, "I would sooner annihilate than be annihilated" when he joined the nihilists (*CW,* 674). By the time Wilde was on trial, the tide had turned. The magnitude of his self-destructive activity suggests that he agreed with Goethe, whom he is known to have read, that "Dass alles was ensteht ist wert dass es zu Grunde geht" ("Everything that is created is worthy of being destroyed"), in the sense that life has in its inception the seeds of its own deterioration. It almost seems as if Wilde were determined to prove Freud's idea of the death drive. He wanted to destroy the English, he wanted to destroy conventional wisdom and conventional principles, and, to crown it all, he wanted to destroy himself.

After his imprisonment, when he was living in Paris, Wilde confessed to an old acquaintance, Anna, comtesse de Brémont, who asked why he no longer wrote, that he had written "all there was to write. I wrote when I did not know the meaning of life; now that I do know the meaning of life, I have no more to write; life cannot be written, life can only be lived. . . . Would you know my secret? I will tell you. I was happy in prison. I was happy because I found my soul. What I wrote before I wrote without a soul, and what I have written under the guidance of my soul, the world shall one day read, it shall be the message of my soul to the souls of men!"[122] In the success of his gigantic project of destruction through which he found his soul, he had finally fulfilled his wish to be united with Isola. When he was first imprisoned in Holloway, he wrote to a friend, "I am dazed with horror. Life has at last become as real as a dream" (*ML*, 133). A letter of August 1898 written after his release proclaims, "I don't think I shall ever write again. Something is killed in me. I feel no desire to write. I am unconscious of power" (*L*, 760). The path that led to this sad conclusion can be discerned in all his work and will now be traced.

CHAPTER 2 DISEASE AND INSPIRATION

Between 1886 and 1895, Oscar Wilde produced *The Picture of Dorian Gray, Salome,* several provocative essays—among them "The Soul of Man under Socialism," "The Decay of Lying," and "The Critic as Artist"—and his funniest comedy, *The Importance of Being Earnest.* His previous writings, relatively uninspired and blandly imitative, could not begin to match his conversational prowess. He seems to have found his voice as an author only after becoming obsessed with crime, guilt, and moral decay: Dorian Gray's hideous rotting face and "passion for sin, or for what the world calls sin"; Salome's salacious pursuit and murder of John the Baptist; and the snide trivialization of the potentially tragic and the glorification of the trivial in *The Importance of Being Earnest.*

Clearly his fascination with crime, sin, and transgression fueled his creativity. Richard Ellmann has suggested that Wilde first engaged in homosexual activities in 1886, when he was thirty-two. "From late in the year 1886," Ellmann writes, "Wilde was able to think of himself, if he wanted to, as criminal."[1] Ellmann points out that Wilde's preoccupation with the danger and glamour of crimes colored his work after 1886. Wilde's first active participation in a homosexual encounter may indeed have occurred as late as 1886, but long before that he accepted homosexual urges as a matter of course.[2] In a letter of July 1876, written when he was a twenty-year-old Oxford undergraduate, he tells his close friend William Ward how he almost missed an exam: "While lying in bed on Tuesday morning with Swinburne (a copy of) I was woke up by the Clerk of the Schools to know why I did not come up" (*L,* 15). Imagining himself lounging in bed with Swinburne, "the first English poet to sing divinely the song of the flesh," a man who specialized in painting lurid portraits—for instance, of Sappho's sadomasochistic lust for

Anactoria—Wilde coyly invites Ward to approve, or perhaps share, some kind of erotic life.[3]

A few weeks later, on 6 August 1876, he casually questions Ward in another letter: "I want to ask your opinion on this psychological question. In our friend Todd's ethical barometer, at what height is his moral quicksilver?" He continues with an incriminating tale: "Last night I strolled into the theatre at about ten o'clock and to my surprise saw Todd and young Ward the quire boy in a private box together, Todd very much in the background. He saw me so I went round to speak to him for a few minutes. . . . I wonder what young Ward is doing with him." Then he tries to render the scene innocent: "Myself I believe Todd is extremely moral and only mentally spoons the boy, but I think he is foolish to go about with one, if he *is* bringing the boy about with him." Finally, he singles out Ward as "the only one I would tell about it, as you have a philosophical mind," and cautions, "Don't tell anyone about it, like a good boy—it would do neither us nor Todd any good. . . . He (Todd) looked awfully nervous and uncomfortable" (*L*, 23). How much dare he reveal of his own sexual inclinations to William Ward and still protect both their reputations? Incidentally, Wilde's metaphor of the "ethical barometer" with its "moral quicksilver" has a curiously personal slant; as will be seen, Wilde had reasons to worry about quicksilver, or mercury.[4]

Wilde's early poems, first published as a collection in 1881, reveal an erotic preoccupation with male beauty—in particular "Wasted Days," "Endymion," and "Charmides." "Wasted Days," for instance, begins:

> A fair slim boy not made for this world's pain
> > With hair of gold thick clustering round his ears
> > And longing eyes half veiled by foolish tears
> Like bluest water seen through mists of rain;
> > Pale cheeks whereon no kiss hath left its stain,
> > Red under-lip drawn in for fear of love. (*CW*, 732)

And "Endymion" includes this description:

> Ah! thou hast young Endymion,
> Thou hast the lips that should be kissed! (*CW*, 751)

In January 1893 he used similarly florid language in a letter to Bosie: "My Own Boy . . . it is a marvel that those red rose-leaf lips of yours should have been made no less for music of song than for madness of kisses" (*L*, 326). A first physical homosexual encounter in 1886 thus seems unlikely to have been the only event inspiring Dorian Gray's murder of Basil Hallward. Something else of great consequence happened to Wilde in 1886: he discovered

that mercury treatments had not cured the syphilis which he had apparently
contracted from a female prostitute when he was a twenty-year-old Oxford
undergraduate.

In a series of unpublished letters written to A. J. A. Symons between 1931
and 1937, Robert Sherard, Wilde's friend and first biographer, discusses
Wilde's life, including what Sherard remembered and had heard of Wilde's
syphilis. In April 1935, he wrote that the "syphilis he contracted at Oxford
when he was 20, which broke out again in 1886 and destroyed his married
life accounts for most of the rest of the deplorable gesta."[5] (Earlier, on 3
December 1933, Sherard had written to one Douglas William Gray Esq. that
"Oscar . . . knew himself to be syphilitic.") In May 1937, possibly after
Symons requested further information, he wrote, "I cannot remember where
I got the story of the infection of Oscar at Oxford at age 20; but it was after I
had written my attack on Harris. It satisfied me so completely that though I
had it well in mind when last year I revised that m.s. and omitted any
reference to it, I have since regretted this omission."[6]

In the summer of 1935, however, Boris Brasol, another of Wilde's biographers, visited Sherard in London and learned of Wilde's syphilis. He extracted from Sherard a statement based on an authority whose name Sherard did
not disclose:

Oscar Wilde . . . while at Oxford, had contracted syphilis for the cure of which
mercury injections were administered. It was probably due to these treatments that
Wilde's teeth subsequently grew black and became decayed. Before proposing to Miss
Constance Lloyd, Wilde went to see in London a doctor who assured the poet that he
had been completely cured and that there was no pathological obstacle to his marriage. However, shortly after the birth of Vyvyan, Wilde discovered that syphilis,
which apparently had been altogether dormant, had broken out in his system. He
clearly realized that if he were to continue marital intercourse with his wife, a syphilitic child might have been born.[7]

Richard Ellmann considers Wilde's contraction of syphilis from a woman
prostitute "an event . . . that was to alter his whole conception of himself."[5]
Ellmann continues: "My belief that Wilde had syphilis stems from statements
made by Reginald Turner and Robert Ross, Wilde's close friends present at his
death, from the certificate of the doctor in charge at that time . . . and from
the fact that the 1912 edition of Ransome's book on Wilde and Harris's 1916
life (both of which Ross oversaw) give syphilis as the cause of death." He adds
that "perhaps now the parable of Dorian Gray's secret decay began to form in
his mind, as the spirochete began its journey up his spine toward the men-
inges."[8] But because the spirochete was not discovered until 1905, Wilde

could not have had an image of corkscrew-shaped organisms relentlessly destroying his body and brain. He must, however, have been terrified by the threat of physical and mental deterioration from the progressive disease.

In Wilde's day knowledge of the treatment and course of the disease was relatively primitive. Syphilis had been distinguished from gonorrhea only since 1837, and chancroid was not distinguished from syphilis until 1852. The specific organism of gonorrhea was not discovered until 1879. The incubation period of syphilis was not known until 1859, nor was the extreme contagiousness of secondary syphilis. Generally, however, the clinical picture of primary, secondary, and tertiary syphilis had been well described in the first half of the nineteenth century, and physicians had begun to understand the congenital form of the disease.[9] Thus Wilde could easily have learned that the disease had three phases; the first, in which a painless but alarming chancre develops, occasionally with swollen lymph nodes near the lesion, had probably sent him to the doctor. Secondary syphilis, which appears six weeks to several months after infection, can include a rash ("generalized mucocutaneous lesions"), fever, patchy hair loss (a "moth-eaten" look), and malaise. Five to fifteen years after the primary stage, tertiary, or late, syphilitic symptoms can occur. These involve, variously, the brain, spinal cord, heart, aorta, and eyes; and occasionally tumors (gummas) appear in the organs and over the skin. A so-called meningovascular syphilis may develop between the secondary and late phases of the disease.[10] A 1990 standard textbook in the field includes the observation that "it was once an adage of medicine that 'he who knew syphilis knew medicine'"—because of the many forms the illness can take.[11]

The leading authority on syphilis at the time, Dr. Jonathan Hutchinson, insisted "on an interval of two full years between the date of contracting the disease and marriage," during which the patient received mercury treatments.[12] Ellmann therefore speculates that Wilde waited out the two years and then, believing he was no longer infected, married.[13] He may have been mistaken in believing so, however, for although mercury could kill spirochetes, it was no cure for the disease.[14] On 7 April 1898, at the age of forty, his wife, whom he had married in 1884, died of an operation to correct a creeping spinal paralysis, with which she had been afflicted for several years. The paralysis, which was somewhat mysterious, supposedly resulted from a fall down a flight of stairs, but it is not at all impossible that she was suffering from locomotor ataxia—neural degeneration of tertiary syphilis. A long letter of 27 May 1937 from her brother, Otho Holland Lloyd, to A. J. A. Symons includes a striking paragraph that begins: "What follows is told to you in confidence." He goes on to say that apart from a few happy years away from their cruel mother, "my sister's life was in some sense a tragedy, in consequence of her very ill treatment by her mother. . . . Two women cousins still living could testify to what she underwent at her mother's hands, especially from the time of her father's death. I shall always think that her internal tumour was brought about in the first place by what she went through under her mother."[15] Lloyd was apparently speculating that the severe beatings to which their mother subjected his sister caused the growths that put pressure on her spine. Medically this is not feasible: beatings do not cause tumors. But the types of tumors known as gummas are sometimes part of the clinical picture of late syphilis. Robert Sherard recalled seeing a letter Constance wrote to Wilde "just about the time of the scandal reproaching him with the words, 'And you know that you made me ill.'" It is interesting to note that even during their courtship Constance expressed forebodings about the relationship. Her unpublished love letters reveal a passionate attachment to Wilde, whom she calls her hero, but also extreme anxiety and depressive tendencies. In one letter she confesses her fear during a storm at night, remarking that the wind calls to mind death and separation. In another she laments the death of a pet given her by Wilde and wonders whether it is her fault if everything he gives her comes to an "untimely" end. Thanking him for a lily he sent her, she says it reminds her of Paradise.[16]

Sherard, always eager to protect Wilde, adds that although Constance's allusion to illness "at the time made me think the damned thing had come out again while they were cohabiting . . . later information and reflection satisfied me she was referring to the damage to her health caused by his year-long marital neglect of her."[17] Considering Sherard's attempt to explain away Wilde's homosexuality as the result of too much drink, this reflection about Constance Wilde's health may have only been more wishful thinking.[18] She could have had the disease for fourteen years by the time she died—plenty of time for tertiary symptoms to develop. It is also possible that she tripped and fell because the disease had impaired her balance and gait.

Wilde's gait may also have been affected by the disease; his friends knew that he loathed walking, even for short distances. Wilfrid Scawen Blunt recorded that in July 1884 he attended "a brilliant luncheon" at which Wilde was present and that the two of them happened to leave at the same time. Blunt suggested that they walk as far as Grosvenor Square together. "No, no," said Wilde, hailing a passing hansom, "I *never* walk."[19] This was a far cry from his days at Oxford, when he loved the outdoors and enjoyed hunting, shooting, riding, swimming, and lawn tennis, as well as "long chats and walks" with special friends (*L*, 21, 32, 45). His corpulence may account for much of his distaste for walking, but perhaps not for the exaggerated antipathy that he expressed on a visit to a friend, W. Graham Robertson. At an undetermined time after 1887, Wilde was staying with Robertson in the country where, as Robertson writes, "he was like a fish out of water." They had been for what Robertson considered "a short stroll" and "were coming back through a wood, Wilde curiously quiet and toiling along with an expression of deep discomfort." Then "suddenly he brightened":

> "Let's sit down," he said.
> "What for?" I inquired.
> "Well, what do people usually sit down for?"
> "You can't be tired," I said sternly. "We have been no distance, and we can't sit down now. We shall never get home if we do."
> "I shall never get home if we don't," said Oscar, seating himself with an air of finality.[20]

When Wilde was released from prison in May 1897, his friends met him in Dieppe. As he disembarked from the boat, Robert Ross remarked on "that odd elephantine gait which I have never seen in anyone else."[21]

Wilde's terminal illness consisted of ear pain, delirium, and high fever. His attending physician made the reasonable claim that the illness was an "encephalitic meningitis," that his "cerebral disturbances" stemmed "from an old suppuration of the right ear."[22] It is possible, though rare, for syphilis to involve the inner ear and produce a chronic ear infection. A febrile meningitis would be most unusual as a result of third-phase syphilis, the phase in which Wilde is likely to have been by 1895—assuming that he contracted the illness as an undergraduate in approximately 1878.[23] As mentioned, the direct cause of death was not syphilis. If he contracted it much later than 1878, he might well have been experiencing symptoms of secondary syphilis at this time.

Poignant expressions of Wilde's deterioration have been provided by Backhouse in his unpublished memoirs. He recounted that

Aubrey [Beardsley] came to Paris in May, 1897. . . . He and I visited Oscar Wilde (just enlarged from gaol) "au sixième" of a second-rate hotel in the Quartier: we found him surrounded by the "green and yellow" wine (as he called it) i.e. the chartreuse of his predilection, absinthe and fine champagne with baskets of hot-house peaches and grapes at his elbow. "As you see," said he, "I am dying expensively." His physical wreckage (the flotsam and jetsam of an erratic genius), bad as it was, distressed us less than his mental decay. It was clear from his talk with Aubrey, a sad mockery of bygone days and the brilliance of epigram that we remembered, that he was yearning after conversion, though it was not till November 1900, just before his death, that he was actually received into Holy church by an Irish father.[24]

Because syphilis is known as the great imitator of other diseases, it remains impossible at this late date to describe its clinical impact on Wilde during the last years of his life. His mental state from the mid-1890s on seems to me consistent with the degeneration of tertiary syphilis. On 21 September 1895 Wilde's wife wrote a letter to Robert Sherard after visiting Wilde in prison, in which she said: "He has been mad the last three years." This description, though it gives no details, is consistent with syphilitic deterioration.[25] Wilde's increasingly heavy drinking, his corpulence, his frenetic promiscuity, his compulsive exhibitionism, his profligate spending to the point of bankruptcy, and his decision to sue Bosie's father and then to remain in London in spite of the obviously disastrous turn the trials were taking, all of which can be seen as logical extensions of his temperament, could have been exacerbated by the damage the disease was doing to his cerebral cortex.

The impact of Wilde's syphilis on his development as a writer is hard to overestimate. His dread of the disease permeated every aspect of his life and work. The evolution of his style has been attributed to his conception of homosexuality as a "contagion" or as the "dark side" of his life, as Ellmann and Christopher Nassaar suggest, but the contagion was also literal.[26] When in July 1896 the prisoner Wilde petitioned the Home Office for an early release, he referred to homosexuality as "sexual madness" and to his "terrible offenses" as "diseases to be cured by a physician, rather than crimes to be punished by a judge." His terminology suggests syphilis as well as homosexuality, and perhaps a preoccupation with physical ailments that were a result of syphilis, for which he received inadequate medical care in prison. As he mentioned in the petition, he had while incarcerated "almost entirely lost the hearing of his right ear through an abscess that caused a perforation of the drum." He speaks of "ceaseless apprehension" that "this insanity, that displayed itself in monstrous sexual perversions" would overtake "the entire nature and intellect." Deprived of books and conversation, his mind, "forced to think," can contemplate only "thoughts that defile, desecrate, and destroy" and "vices" that are "embedded in his flesh" and spread over him "like a leprosy, feeding on him like a strange disease" (L, 404–05, 403).

His worst fears were only increased by the incompetence of the prison doctors:

The medical officer here has stated that he is unable to offer any assistance, and that the hearing must go entirely. The petitioner, however, feels sure that under the care of a specialist abroad his hearing might be preserved to him. He was assured by Sir William Dalby, the great aurist, that with proper care there was no reason at all why he should lose his hearing. But though the abscess has been running now for the entire time of his imprisonment, and the hearing getting worse every week, nothing has been done in the way even of an attempted cure. The ear has been syringed on three occasions with plain water for the purpose of examination, that is all. The petitioner is naturally apprehensive lest, as often happens, the other ear may be attacked in a similar way, and to the misery of a shattered and debilitated mind be added the horrors of complete deafness. . . . His eyesight . . . has also suffered very much. . . . He is conscious of great weakness and pain in the nerves of the eyes, and objects even at a short distance become blurred.

As the son of the greatest Irish oculist and aurist of the day, Wilde must have had an even keener awareness than most of the extent of his physical deterioration. He pleads repeatedly that his "chief danger is that of madness, his chief terror is that of madness"—a fear quite consistent with fear of paresis— and hopes that his imprisonment will not be "uselessly or vindictively prolonged till insanity has claimed soul as well as body" (L, 404–05).

His extreme anxiety about his health at this time was nothing new. Richard Ellmann suggests that when Wilde contracted the disease at Oxford, "physical sickness . . . perhaps revived his never quelled anxiety about the state of his soul. . . . Upset as he was, Wilde came as close now to becoming Catholic as he ever would until his deathbed." Terror drove him to contemplate conversion, but with typical whimsy, at the very moment he was expected at the Brompton Oratory to be received into the church, a large bunch of lilies arrived in his stead. "It was Wilde's polite way of flowering over his renunciation," observes Ellmann.[27]

From the time Wilde was infected in the mid-1870s, his distress must have invaded his creative imagination. For instance, "Pen, Pencil and Poison," his ironic tribute to a murderer notoriously skilled at lacing his relatives' meals with strychnine, may have had a source in his suspicion that he had "poisoned" his wife and children and in his anticipation that his sexual needs would drive him to "poison" others. Yet "the fact of a man being a poisoner is nothing against his prose," he mutters in the essay (CW, 1007). Each detail in the life of Thomas Griffiths Wainewright, whom Wilde presents as a rather refined, artistic murderer, corresponds to his own: he saw himself in Wainewright and tried to understand himself by understanding Wainewright.

Like Wainewright, the young Wilde had experienced "a severe illness, in which, to use his own words, he was 'broken like a vessel of clay'" and which "prostrated him for a time." Like Wilde, Wainewright's "delicately strung organisation, however indifferent it might have been to inflicting pain on others, was itself most keenly sensitive to pain. He shrank from suffering as a thing that mars and maims human life" (CW, 994). Also like Wilde, Wainewright "determined to startle the town as a dandy, and his beautiful rings, his antique cameo breast-pin, and his pale lemon-coloured kid gloves, were well known and indeed were regarded . . . as being the signs of a new manner in literature." Wilde adds, "This young dandy sought to be somebody, rather than to do something. He recognized that Life itself is an art" (CW, 995). He defends "this strange and fascinating figure that for a few years dazzled literary London" from the "shallow, or at least . . . mistaken" view of his biographer, W. Carew Hazlitt, who sees Wainewright's love of art and nature as "mere pretense and assumption" (CW, 1007).

For Wilde, Wainewright, "a forger of no mean or ordinary capabilities . . . a subtle and secret poisoner almost without rival in this or any age," qualifies as an artist by virtue of his creativity as a poisoner and his finesse as a poseur (CW, 993). Poisoning becomes an art ranked with writing and painting: "Indeed painting was the first art that fascinated him. It was not till much later that he sought to find expression by pen or poison," as though pen and poison were metaphors for each other (CW, 994).

In an almost "Christian" spirit, he loves Wainewright as he loves himself and in the same spirit is fascinated by Wainewright's self-crucifixion. Wilde recounts that in 1837 Wainewright returned as a convicted felon to England, with the full realization that he was thereby "imperilling his life." He was brought back by "some strange mad passion. . . . He followed a woman whom he loved. . . . It was said that the woman was very beautiful. Besides, she did not love him." Wainewright was of course discovered and punished: "The sentence now passed on him was," like Wilde's own, "to a man of his culture a form of death" (CW, 1004–05). He was transported to Van Dieman's Land, a prison colony in Australia, and forever separated from the art and culture that made life worthwhile for him. Wilde comments: "His crimes seem to have had an important effect upon his art. They gave a strong personality to his style, a quality that his early work certainly lacked" (CW, 1007). This sounds like a proud eulogy to himself. The title of his next essay, "The Decay of Lying," an elegiac satire on the death of lying as an art form, allows another glimpse of his obsessive concern with his deteriorating condition.

Wilde's defense against the despair brought on by his illness was his humor—the characteristic wit that dazzled the 1890s. The Importance of Being Earnest, for instance, was probably one of many attempts to minimize his disease by ridiculing it—to cheer himself up as he felt or feared that he was rotting away. He claimed that this brilliant comedy was "exquisitely trivial, a delicate bubble of fancy that has its philosophy . . . that we should treat all the trivial things of life very seriously, and all the serious things of life with a sincere and studied triviality."[28] Denial in the face of terror becomes his strategy. He appeals to his contemporaries to adopt this attitude and so give him support. He experiences their applause and laughter as an approval of his strategy of defense.

At the same time, his laughter often reveals not just acceptance of a terrible situation but an impish delight in outwitting fate by enjoying the worst blows that fall. When Wilde was standing in prisoner's garb, drenched by rain, handcuffed to two other convicts, on a railway platform en route to bankruptcy court, he turned to one of his warders and said: "Sir, if this is the way Queen Victoria treats her convicts, she doesn't deserve to have any."[29] When in 1900 Robert Sherard visited Wilde's "small and gloomy" bedroom in a squalid Paris hotel and encouraged his literary efforts, Wilde said, "One has to do something. I have no taste for it now, but as was said of torture, it always helps one to pass an hour or two." During his final illness he sighed, "I am dying beyond my means" (*L*, 848);[30] shortly before expiring he complained, "My wallpaper and I are fighting a duel to the death. One or the other of us has got to go."[31] Freud described this kind of "liberating" humor in "On Humour" (1927) as having "something of grandeur and elevation . . . in the triumph of narcissism, and the victorious assertion of the ego's invulnerability. The ego refuses to be distressed by the provocation of reality, to let itself be compelled to suffer. It insists that it cannot be affected by the traumas of the external world; it shows, in fact, that such traumas are no more than occasions for it to gain pleasure."[32]

When Wilde was not joking, however, his preoccupation with disease and degeneration in general betrayed itself. He describes the minute details of Dorian Gray's face as it slowly rots in the portrait: "still loathesome—more loathesome, if possible, than before—and the scarlet dew that spotted the hand seemed brighter, and more like blood newly spilt. . . . And why was the red stain larger than it had been? It seemed to have crept like a horrible disease over the wrinkled fingers" (*CW*, 166). Dorian keeps the portrait, with its "horrible disease," locked in a hidden room and shows only his handsome, youthful face to the world; Wilde's style reflects his fascination with visible corruption and its concealment. As he wrote of Thomas Griffiths Wainewright, Wilde was himself "the pioneer of Asiatic prose, and delighted in pictorial epithets and pompous exaggerations. To have a style so gorgeous that it conceals the subject is one of the highest achievements" (*CW*, 1002). The drawling, precious prose of the first sentence of *Dorian Gray* is indeed so gorgeous that it conceals the subject: "The studio was filled with the rich odour of roses, and when the light summer wind stirred amidst the trees of the garden, there came through the open door the heavy scent of the lilac, or the more delicate perfume of the pink-flowering thorn." The stronger the perfume, the greater must have been his fear of the stench, the putrescence, of his illness (*CW*, 18).

The urgency of this preoccupation with disease continually breaks through his gorgeous prose. *Dorian Gray* is, among other things, a parable of an artist foreseeing his own physical and mental decay. To follow the development of Wilde's style in relation to his illness is to witness from a new perspective the growth of his philosophical ideas, his humor, and his wit. His wise, acutely psychological insights sound like the thoughts of a man who has determined what he faces and developed a realistic, intellectual defense. His wit was a kind of armor. Besides, a brave front, a fight to the last, a denial of defeat by any means, including laughter, was the very least his mother expected from a son she saw as another Ossian.

The first collected edition of Wilde's poems, which appeared in 1881, included the following sonnet:

> Hélas!
> To drift with every passion till my soul
> Is a stringed lute on which all winds can play,
> Is it for this that I have given away
> Mine ancient wisdom and austere control?
> Methinks my life is a twice-written scroll
> Scrawled over on some boyish holiday
> With idle songs for pipe and virelay,
> Which do but mar the secret of the whole
> Surely there was a time I might have trod
> The sunlit heights, and from life's dissonance
> Struck one clear chord to reach the ears of God:
> Is that time dead? lo! with a little rod
> I did but touch the honey of romance—
> And must I lose a soul's inheritance? (*CW*, 709)

This melancholy lyricism was obviously inspired by the biblical book of Samuel: "Then Saul said to Jonathan, Tell me what thou hast done. And Jonathan told him and said, I did but taste a little honey with the end of the rod that was in my hand, and lo, I must die" (I Sam. 14:43, King James Version). Fearing that his brief, unimportant fling would deprive him of his artistic gifts, Wilde cries out to the gods that he had only touched the "honey of romance" with his "little rod" and so had not really warranted being infected by the dread disease.

Wilde's imagery reveals his longing to escape responsibility—and guilt—for the sexual act that gave him syphilis. He likes to think of his soul as a passive instrument, an aeoleian harp ("a stringed lute on which all winds can play") that drifted until the winds of passion accidentally infected it. Like all obsessive doubters, who prefer that fate decide a situation for them, he proclaims that he has done nothing actively and imagines himself the victim of circumstance. He is angry at fate for punishing him because of a sexual tryst—and not even a homosexual one. His life is indeed a "twice-written scroll," a palimpsest: his art and conduct, no more than a thin veneer, barely cover the indelible traces of the relentless disease. The "idle songs for pipe and virelay" fail to banish his fears. His effort to be happy only depresses him more and mars "the secret of the whole." Because of its honesty and wistful lyricism, this sonnet is almost unique among Wilde's works. The veiled plea for understanding is alien to the witty denials and satiric arabesques of his later work.

The first story that Wilde published after his syphilis recurred was "The Canterville Ghost," which appeared initially in the magazine *Court and Society Review,* on 23 February and 2 March 1887, and was later included in a book of his stories. It is a humorous tale of an American family who buys an old English mansion that is haunted. At first one has the impression that Wilde wanted to poke fun at Americans in a good-natured way and to assuage children's fears of ghosts. The ghost is a bumbling, pathetic old fool who nonetheless elicits one's sympathies when the American children attack him with peashooters and shout "Boo!" The lighthearted banter of the story is followed by a surprisingly maudlin finale: the slapstick ghost turns out to be seriously depressed, almost suicidal. This unexpected twist betrays strong emotions breaking through a defensive posture.

Contemporary critics tended to dismiss "The Canterville Ghost" and similar stories that Wilde wrote during that period. One critic wrote that "they will not add to their author's reputation," adding that "The Canterville Ghost" was "disfigured by some stupid vulgarisms," such as Wilde's quip that "we have really everything in common with America nowadays, except, of course, language." Missing the point, this reviewer added haughtily "and manners." Far more sophisticated reviewers, frustrated by the mixed tone of the stories, felt the same way. Yeats, for instance, wrote that "with its supernatural horse-play," "The Canterville Ghost" was "quite unworthy of more than a passing interest."[33]

Yeats notwithstanding, the story becomes more interesting and its complications and incongruities dissolve if one places it at the proper time in Wilde's life. Written less than a year after his horrifying discovery that he still had syphilis, and rendered more terrible by his having imagined himself cured, the work represents a desperate effort to ridicule his terror of sores, inner rotting, and the loss of his wit and intelligence. By mocking the ghost and his slow deterioration at the hands of the tormenting Americans, Wilde tries to hide his own anxiety. The uneven success of this defense accounts for the uneven tone of the story.

A close look at the story reveals autobiographical elements. The eldest son of the American purchasers of the house was "christened Washington by his parents in a moment of patriotism which he had never ceased to regret" (*CW*, 194). Wilde had his own string of zealously patriotic names that his mother had borrowed from heroes of Celtic mythology. And like Wilde, Washington has a little sister, Virginia; as will be seen, her virginity helps save the ghost from disease and damnation. The pragmatic Washington scours out a blood-stain of the ghost's wife, whom the ghost had murdered, and ridicules the notion that it "cannot be removed"; the supernatural reappearance of the stain suggests that although American optimism improved Wilde's mood, his guilt for "murdering" his wife endured ineradicably.

In 1882 Wilde traveled to America, sponsored by the American representa-tives of Gilbert and Sullivan's operetta *Patience,* which, with foppish Wildean characters, satirized the aesthetic movement. Although he quipped sardon-ically, "I cannot picture America as altogether an Elysium," Wilde was clearly impressed by the strident practicality and "endless frontier" cheer of Ameri-cans.[34] Perhaps he also reflected that the optimism of the doctor who assured him that the syphilis had been cured helped him as little as American opti-mism did in removing the bloodstain. As the son of a prominent physician, Wilde probably knew that mercury, the only relatively effective treatment for syphilis at that time, was at best palliative. If he had believed a doctor who optimistically granted him a clean bill of health, Wilde now blamed himself.

In the story, the ghost's declining spirits and health perhaps indicate the evaporation of a hope that the power of positive thinking might be a cure and illustrate Wilde's contempt for the futility of optimism. On his way to a final, useless attempt to terrorize the Americans, the ghost stops dead in his tracks when he sees

a horrible spectre, motionless as a carven image, and monstrous as a madman's dream! Its head was bald and burnished; its face round, and fat, and white; and hideous laughter seemed to have writhed its features into an eternal grin. From the eyes streamed rays of scarlet light, the mouth was a wide well of fire, and a hideous garment, like to his own, swathed with its silent snows the Titan form. On its breast was a placard with strange writing in antique characters, some scroll of shame it seemed, some record of wild sins, some awful calendar of crime, and, with its right hand, it bore aloft a falchion of gleaming steel. (*CW,* 201)

The Canterville ghost, frightened to death, flees this creature with "wild [Wilde?] sins" on its breast. The adjective *wild* was no accidental choice; in a letter tentatively dated 1889 by Rupert Hart-Davis, Wilde wrote: "Names fascinate me terribly" (*L*, 252). Wilde was to use his own name as an adjective on many occasions.

The ghost has some common symptoms of advanced syphilis, namely, loss of hair ("its head was bald and burnished") and a round, fat white face. These features fit Eugen Bleuler's description of some characteristics of advanced syphilis: "The tone of the mimetic muscles decreases, the naso-labial folds seem wiped out. . . . The finer movements are lost. . . . The *face* assumes a flabby and stupid expression, which often enables one to recognize the paretic immediately."[35] Wilde had a rather fat, flabby face that many people found repulsive; in 1891, Marcel Schwob described him as "a big man, with a large pasty face, red cheeks, an ironic eye, bad and protrusive teeth."[36] Like the horrible specter who frightens the Canterville ghost, Wilde felt in his mouth "a wide well of fire" because of the mercury treatments; such treatments often caused acute stomatitis, an inflammation of the mouth. Lillie Langtry noticed the bad state of his teeth when he was only twenty-two: "His face was large, and so colourless that a few pale freckles of good size were oddly conspicuous. He had a well-shaped mouth, with somewhat coarse lips and greenish-hued teeth."[37] Years later, after Wilde had left prison, André Gide recorded that "his teeth were atrociously decayed."[38] What looked like decay may have been the discoloration and deterioration wrought by mercury treatments.

When the Canterville ghost returns to the scene of his nocturnal horrors, he discovers a pile of old bed curtains, a broomstick, and a "hollow turnip"— the jack-o'-lantern that had been the horrible specter's head. The strange, scary placard with its record of "wild sins" turns out to be a warning, in Gothic letters, that the jack-o'-lantern ghost is:

> Ɏe onlie True and Originale Spook
> Beware of Ɏe Imitationes.
> All others are Counterfeite. (*CW*, 201)

This is Wilde's way of whistling in the dark, asserting that the "ghost" is not real. In other words, the disease is not real but merely a little trouble with his mouth. Years later, in February 1900, he complained of having become "a *neurasthenic*" and mentioned being treated with arsenic and strychnine. Arsenic had been introduced for the treatment of syphilis as early as 1530, when Paracelsus is thought to have used it.[39] Not until 1907 was there a standard arsenic therapy but the drug was occasionally used in Wilde's day.[40]

His perhaps jesting diagnosis of himself as neurasthenic is echoed throughout his work in sadder and sadder laughter. The fake ghost, with "hideous laughter" that "seemed to have writhed its features into an eternal grin" is Wilde himself, who knew that he was always doing the same. Gide recorded that when he met Wilde in January 1895, following a lapse of three years, "Wilde had certainly changed. One felt less softness in his look, something raucous in his laughter and something frenzied in his joy. . . . He went to pleasure as one marches to duty.—'My duty to myself,' he would say, 'is to amuse myself terrifically.'"[41] Wilde seems to allude to the forced quality of his antics in "Lord Arthur Savile's Crime," written at about the same time as "The Canterville Ghost": "Actors are so fortunate. They can choose whether they will appear in tragedy or in comedy, whether they will suffer or make merry, laugh or shed tears. But in real life it is different. Most women and men are forced to perform parts for which they have no qualifications. Our Guildensterns play Hamlet for us, and our Hamlets have to jest like Prince Hal. The world is a stage, but the play is badly cast" (CW, 174). Pathetically, the great wit of the nineteenth century saw himself as a mere clown of forced laughs, as a Hamlet reduced to a jesting Prince Hal.

After his traumatic encounter with the fake spook, the Canterville ghost finds himself too frightened to perform any active haunting, although it remains his "solemn duty to appear in the corridor once a month, and to gibber from the large Oriel window on the first and third Wednesday of every month" (CW, 202). He has no choice but to continue his haunting, despite the commonsense fumigations of the house by the practical Americans. Similarly, Wilde had no choice but to be haunted by the ghostly visitation of his illness in the form of various symptoms. Like the miraculous bloodstain that reappears on the hearth every morning, though it is scrubbed out the night before, Wilde's disease only appeared to have been wiped away.

In suicidal despair, the ghost asks little Virginia, the young daughter in the American family, to help him die. He imagines himself lying dead "in the soft brown earth, with the grasses waving above one's head. . . . To have no yesterday and no to-morrow," an image reminiscent of Wilde's description of his sister, Isola, in "Requiescat":

> she is near
> Under the snow
> Speak gently, she can hear
> The daisies grow. (CW, 724)

The idea of the ghost dying with Virginia's help seems to come from Wilde's lifelong wish to be close to Isola by getting into the grave with her. Like Isola,

Virginia is golden haired, and the ghost reminds her of an old prophecy on the library window:

> 𝔚𝔥𝔢𝔫 a golden girl can win
> Prayer from out the lips of sin,
> 𝔚𝔥𝔢𝔫 the barren almond bears
> And a little child gives away its tears
> Then shall all the house be still
> And peace come to Canterville. (CW, 208)

The ghost enlists Virginia as the golden girl who must weep for his sins, pray for his soul, and so make the barren almond bear in order to release him from his torments. Although she is frightened, she agrees to help him.

In the idea of the renewed fertility of the barren almond and in the scene that follows, there is some suggestion of a sexual encounter between Virginia and the ghost:

He rose from his seat with a faint cry of joy, and taking her hand bent over it with old-fashioned grace and kissed it. His fingers were as cold as ice and his lips burned like fire, but Virginia did not falter, as he led her across the dusky room. On the faded green tapestry were broidered little huntsmen. They blew their tasselled horns with their little hands, waved her to go back. "Go back! little Virginia," they cried, "go back!" but the ghost clutched her hand more tightly, and she shut her eyes against them. Horrible animals with lizard tails, and goggle eyes, blinked at her from the carven chimney piece, and murmured, "Beware! little Virginia, beware! We may never see you again," but the ghost glided on more swiftly. . . . Virginia . . . saw the wall slowly fading away like mist, and a great black cavern in front of her. A bitter cold wind swept around them, and she felt something pulling at her dress" (CW, 208).

The burning of his lips, the horrible lizardlike animals, the fears, the darkness, and the "something pulling at her dress" hint at Wilde's memories, real or imagined, of covertly fondling Isola.

Apart from his wish to be close to his sister, Wilde may have been aware of a bizarre belief, widespread in Victorian England as well as the rest of Europe, that sex with a virgin could cure venereal disease. In "The Folklore of Venereal Disease," J. D. Rolleston, a physician and medical historian, writes that the "cure of a disease by its supposed transfer not only to other persons but also to animals, plants, and even inanimate objects is illustrated in the folklore treatment of several diseases such as whooping cough, epilepsy, warts, boils, pulmonary tuberculosis. . . . In the case of these diseases the transfer is purely imaginary, [but] in the case of venereal disease . . . it may all too frequently actually take place. . . . The person to whom the disease is transferred is preferably a young virgin of either sex. . . . This superstition, which dates back for several centuries, is world wide. . . . The transfer of [syphilis] by sexual intercourse with a virgin of either sex was first mentioned in 1676 by Walter Harris, who stated that in his time it was commonly believed that syphilis could be cured by coitus with a healthy young girl. This superstition is still present especially in country districts."[42] Wilde's mother and father, both of whom were accomplished folklorists, included sections on medical superstitions, charms, and cures in their books on Irish folklore. Although neither mentions this particular belief directly, it seems probable they would have known of it; this was just the sort of eccentric trivia that would have intrigued them.

The implication of this old wives' tale seems to be that by giving someone else a disease, one no longer has it oneself. In *Ancient Legends, Mystic Charms, and Superstitions of Ireland,* Wilde's mother does mention a myth concerning the "transfer of disease" that has just this meaning. For mumps one is advised to "wrap the child in a blanket, take it to the pigsty, rub the child's head to the back of the pig, and the mumps will leave it and pass from the child to the animal." Incidentally, Wilde's mother also included in her book a story about Saint Bridget that seems related to the idea that sex with a virgin cured venereal disease. Depicted as capable of healing lepers by touching them, the saint was "head and chief of all the sacred virgins. . . . She had a virginal chair (*cathedra puellaris*) and was pre-eminent above all the abbesses of Ireland, or of the Scots, for sanctity and power."[43] Oscar was thoroughly acquainted with all his parents' stories and remained quite superstitious into adulthood; moreover, during his marriage he and his wife frequented a fortune teller. He could easily have combined his knowledge of folklore with a fantasy that Isola's embraces would protect him from disease.

To return to the unfortunate Canterville ghost: he does die in the end, with Virginia's help. She is alone with him for hours, and when she returns to her family, she is carrying a little casket of heirloom jewels he had given her. She relates that he is dead but declines to discuss anything that transpired with the ghost behind closed doors. Her being alone with him for hours, his gift of the "family jewels," and her secretiveness are all suggestive of Oscar's longing for sensual closeness with Isola. Wilde's belief in Isola's power to protect him might also be indicated by his always keeping with him the small decorated envelope containing her hair; perhaps he thought of the lock of hair as a talisman that would prevent illness.

Another story, "Lord Arthur Savile's Crime," published in the *Court and Society Review* on 11 and 18 May 1887, also seems at first like a lighthearted and amusing, though shallow, tale. The story concerns a palm reader at a party who tells funny and risqué fortunes until he sees the hand of Lord

Arthur Savile, at which point the palmist grows "curiously pale," shudders, sweats, and stammers, "It is the hand of a charming young man" (*CW*, 172). Lord Arthur, seeing the man's face become "a white mask of horror," insists on knowing the awful thing written in his hand. Finally, after substantial remuneration, the palm reader admits to having observed "murder" written there. Lord Arthur interprets this vision to mean that he is fated to murder someone. Considerately, he decides that he must commit the deed before he marries the girl of his dreams. After two bumbling, inept attempts to do away with relatives, he heaves the palm reader into the Thames one night, feels free at last to marry his beloved Sybil, and lives happily ever after with her.

Like "The Canterville Ghost," this story becomes more interesting and revealing of Wilde's wit and philosophy when one considers his mental torture at the time he wrote it, which was less than one year after the recurrence of his syphilis. His terror of infecting his wife with the disease gives a hidden meaning to Lord Arthur's discovery of "murder" in his palm and also suggests Wilde's own fear of being "murdered" by the disease. As we shall see, Lord Arthur's desire to kill someone before his marriage is related to the hidden identity of the palm reader. Incidentally, Wilde and his wife patronized a palm reader who, like many palm readers of the day, was known as "The Sibyl" of Mortimer Street (*L*, 358).

In this autobiographical story it is not surprising that the description of Lord Arthur's fiancée, Sybil Merton, resembles both Wilde's description of his wife, Constance, when she was still his fiancée and the description of the actress Sybil Vane in *Dorian Gray*, who kills herself when Dorian spurns her. Lord Arthur's Sybil is described as follows: "The small exquisitely-shaped head drooped slightly to one side, as though the thin, reed-like throat could hardly bear the burden of so much beauty; the lips were slightly parted, and seemed made for sweet music; and all the tender purity of girlhood looked out from the dreaming eyes. With her soft, clinging dress . . . she looked like one of those delicate little figures men find in the olive-woods near Tanagra, and there was a touch of Greek grace in her pose and attitude" (*CW*, 177–78). In a letter to Lillie Langtry, Wilde described Constance as "a beautiful girl . . . a grave, slight, violet-eyed little Artemis, with great coils of heavy brown hair which make her flower-like head droop like a blossom, and wonderful ivory hands which draw music from the piano so sweet that the birds stop singing to listen to her" (*L*, 154). Lord Arthur's Sybil also has "violet eyes" (*CW*, 192). Dorian's Sybil, like Lord Arthur's, has "all the delicate grace of [a] Tanagra figurine."

Tanagra figurines were originally made to be put in graves to accompany the dead to the netherworld; these graceful statues therefore probably reminded Wilde of his dead sister. Certainly Sibyl Vane, of *Dorian Gray*, is reminiscent of little Isola: "She was so shy, and so gentle. There was something of a child about her. . . . We stood looking at each other like children" (*CW*, 53). The comparison of Constance to Artemis also suggests that Constance reminded Wilde of his sister. Artemis, the virgin huntress, was also Apollo's twin sister, and Wilde, who was "civilising the provinces by my remarkable lectures" on aesthetics, saw himself as an Apollo, a radiant sungod of prophecy, poetry, and music and, not insignificantly, disease and suffering (*L*, 155). To Bosie, Wilde wrote, "I know Hyacinthus, whom Apollo loved so madly, was you in Greek days" (*L*, 326). The idea of Bosie as a reincarnation of Hyacinthus is intriguing, because Bosie was himself a reincarnation of Isola for Wilde.

On several occasions Wilde compares himself or another writer to Marsyas, the mortal who challenged Apollo to a musical competition and was flayed alive for his pains (*L*, 233). Commenting on *The Ballad of Reading Gaol*, Wilde wrote, "the poem . . . was wrung out of me, a cry of pain, the cry of Marsyas, not the song of Apollo" (*L*, 708). The name Sybil is also identified with Apollo, since Apollo was the god of prophecy. Sibylla, or Sibyl, was the mythical priestess devoted to the service of Apollo, who spoke her oracles in riddles and wrote them down on leaves.[44]

Wilde's description of Lord Arthur's reaction to the vision of murder in his palm is also autobiographical: "With face blanched by terror and eyes wild with grief, Lord Arthur Savile rushed from Bentinck house. . . . The night was bitterly cold . . . but his hands were hot with fever, and his forehead burned like fire. On and on he went, almost with the gait of a drunken man. . . . Once he stopped under a lamp, and looked at his hands. He thought he could detect the stain of blood already on them." Surely this describes Oscar, his eyes wild with grief, suddenly finding out how sick he is: "his hands were hot with fever" and his gait had degenerated so much that he walks "like a drunken man." As if reflecting on the inception of his illness, Lord Arthur "wandered across Oxford street into narrow, shameful alleys. Two women with painted faces mocked him as he went by. From dark courtyards came a sound of oaths and blows, followed by shrill screams." As Lord Arthur wanders through the shameful alleys, he reflects: "It was not the mystery but the comedy of suffering that struck him; its absolute uselessness, its grotesque want of meaning. How incoherent everything seemed! How lacking in all harmony!" (*CW*, 175–76). Perhaps for Wilde the comedy—the laughable, ludicrous part of it all—was that he, a homosexual, had gotten this disease from a woman! The experience was not even worth the disease contracted as its price.

When Wilde was older, he all but admitted this. According to Yeats, after Wilde was released from prison, Ernest Dowson took him aside, implored him to acquire "a more wholesome taste," and intimated that Wilde should visit the local brothel. Wilde obliged, and Dowson, with a cheering crowd, waited outside for him to emerge victoriously. Wilde presently returned and said softly to Dowson, "The first these ten years and it will be the last. It was like cold mutton." Then, loudly, so the crowd could hear him, he added, "But tell it in England, for it will entirely restore my character."[45]

After Lord Arthur returns home from his traumatic evening stroll, he decides immediately to postpone his marriage to Sybil Merton. Looking at her photograph, he is "filled with the terrible pity that is born of love. He felt that to marry her, with the doom of murder hanging over his head, would be a betrayal like that of Judas, a sin worse than any the Borgia had ever dreamed of. What happiness could there be for any of them, when at any moment he might be called upon to carry out the awful prophecy written in his hand?" (*CW*, 178). In this passage Wilde condemns himself as a Judas, a sinner worse than any of the Borgias, for marrying in the full knowledge that he had been infected. The self-accusation of killing his wife could easily have led the homosexual Wilde, frustrated with his sham marriage, to the thought that if he had killed his wife, perhaps he had actually wanted to do so. Because he resented his marriage, he resented his wife, and he felt guilty about this resentment. I believe that unconsciously he equated his desire to escape the marriage with a desire to get his wife out of the way by killing her.

His exasperation with his marriage comes across clearly in *De Profundis* when he admits, "Whether I am married or not is a matter that does not concern me. For years I disregarded the tie. But I really think that it is hard on my wife to be tied to me. I always thought so. And, though it may surprise some of my friends, I am really very fond of my wife and very sorry for her. I sincerely hope that she may have a happy marriage, if she marries again. She could not understand me, and I was bored to death with the married life. But she had some sweet points in her character, and was wonderfully loyal to me" (*L*, 516). This would seem to corroborate his blunter remarks to Frank Harris about his disgust with his wife's body and appearance, especially during her pregnancies:

When I married, my wife was a beautiful girl, white and slim as a lily, with dancing eyes and gay rippling laughter like music. In a year or so the flower-like grace had all vanished; she became heavy, shapeless, deformed. She dragged herself about the house in uncouth misery with drawn blotched face and hideous body, sick at heart because of our love. It was dreadful. I tried to be kind to her; forced myself to touch and kiss her; but she was sick always, and—oh! I cannot recall it, it is all loathesome. . . . I used to wash my mouth and open the window to cleanse my lips in the pure air. Oh, nature is disgusting; it takes beauty and defiles it; it defaces the ivory-white body with the vile cicatrices of maternity; it befouls the altar of the soul.[46]

His revulsion at the thought of being close to her naturally led to his increased hostility and desire to get out of the marriage.

As he brooded about whether he might have wanted to infect his wife, Wilde was driven in his story to play with the idea of putting past events into the future and then attempting to prevent their occurrence. By making Lord Arthur interpret the vision of murder in his palm as a prophecy, Wilde denies his illness as a fait accompli: he has already been murdered by syphilis, as has his wife, he believes. Lord Arthur's assumption that he must actively go out and kill someone seems to echo Wilde's wish that he could prevent his wife's death, and fulfill the inexorable prophecy of the palm reader, by killing someone else instead of her. Such primitive reasoning is evident in his folkloric faith in the curative power of virgins.

Lord Arthur's murder attempts all follow this pattern of denial. Wilde portrays him as an entirely would-be murderer, as if to say that he himself is so unskilled in the arts of murdering, and so foolish and inept, that he could not manage to kill anyone, even if, like Lord Arthur, he planned a murder diligently. To begin with, Lord Arthur finds himself "a good deal puzzled at the technical terms used" to describe various poisons and begins "to regret that he had not paid attention to his classics at Oxford" (CW, 180). The choice of poison, especially a painless one, was not irrelevant to Wilde's own condition, since the mercury treatments he received had painful and unpleasant side effects.

When dynamite also fails, Lord Arthur grows fatalistically melancholy: "He had done his best to commit this murder but on both occasions he had failed, and through no fault of his own. He had tried to do his duty, but it seemed as if Destiny herself had turned traitor. He was oppressed with the sense of the barrenness of good intentions, of the futility of trying to be fine. Perhaps it would be better to break off the marriage altogether. . . . Let Destiny work out his doom. He would not stir to help her" (CW, 189). Wilde is again insisting on his own inability to commit murder. His resolve fails. He has Lord Arthur kill the palm reader who first involved him in this nightmare of prophecy, thus following the practice of the ancient Greeks, who, when they received bad news, killed the messenger who brought it. Wilde, too, equates the message with the messenger, or in this case the diagnosis with the doctor. The palm reader is a doctor in the sense that he offers accurate diagnoses of inner lives. He is even described as resembling "something between a family doctor and a country attorney" (*CW,* 169). Perhaps Wilde also feels he wants to murder the faculty of his own mind that prophesies his fate and forces him to brood over it.

. Lord Arthur's drowning of the palm reader in the Thames could also represent a purification rite or baptism, intended to wash off the stain of the diagnosis and free Lord Arthur to marry. After his traumatic nocturnal wanderings on the evening that he discovers his terrible future as a murderer, Lord Arthur goes home to a bath, which, as Christopher Nassaar has pointed out, symbolizes baptism: "He plunged hastily in, till the cool ripples touched throat and hair, and then dipped his head right under, as though he would have wiped away the stain of some shameful memory. When he stepped out he felt almost at peace. The exquisite physical conditions of the moment had dominated him, as indeed often happens in the case of very finely wrought natures, for the senses, like fire, can purify as well as destroy" (*CW,* 177).[47] This passage contains an obvious fulfillment of the wish, also expressed throughout *Dorian Gray,* that the same senses and sensuality that gave Wilde syphilis could also purify him. Dorian has a similar bath, just after his night walk on the evening he so cruelly discards Sibyl Vane; like Lord Arthur, he feels "refreshed" and almost forgets the "strange tragedy" of his behavior toward her. In the irrationality of desperation, Wilde unconsciously fused the wish to cleanse himself with a spiteful intention to continue his sexual life regardless of the consequences; he now wanted to give other people syphilis, as though he had decided that nothing could help him anymore and he might as well enjoy himself.

The stylistic transformations of Wilde's next literary phase are not immediately understandable in terms of his continuing, intensified desire for purification.[48] Unlike the stories his parents produced, Oscar's fairy tales, novel, and drama *Salome* are characterized by lengthy, excessively detailed, and curiously affected aesthetic descriptions of glittering, ornate decor, which tend to detract from the flow of the narrative. In "The Young King" (1888), the "wild-eyed" young king lusts after beauty. Not content with mentioning that the walls of a palace room are "hung with rich tapestries representing the triumph of Beauty," Wilde goes on to describe "a large press, inlaid with agate and lapus lazuli," and a "curiously wrought cabinet with lacquer panels of powdered and mosaiced gold, on which were placed some delicate goblets of Venetian glass, and a cup of dark-veined onyx" (*CW,* 226).

Elaborate descriptions of precious stones and exotic landscapes drown out the young king's horrified realization that his robe has been produced by brutally exploited slave labor. Yet in his descriptions of workers in a factory one can hear Wilde's rage at the oppression of the masses. When he tells of the terrible lives of galley slaves forced to dive for pearls, he is very much Speranza's son crusading for the underdog. Oscar's elaborate prose is not unlike some of his mother's writing. She was known for her floridly exhibitionistic, sometimes mystical, and passionately overblown essays and poems, yet his identification with her could not account alone for the development of his peculiarly ostentatious style.

Neither are the detailed settings of another of his fairy tales, "The Birthday of the Infanta" (1891), necessary to advance a major theme of the story, the cruelty of the infanta toward the dwarf who loves her: in fact, the details get in the way of the story. When the dwarf goes looking for the infanta in the palace, he sees a curtain and hopes that she will be hiding behind it: "At the end of the hall hung a richly embroidered curtain of black velvet, powdered with suns and stars, the king's favorite devices, and broidered on the colour he loved best," Wilde begins ponderously. Only then does he add: "Perhaps she was hiding behind that?" (*CW*, 242). The more the dwarf searches, the more the interior decoration of the palace clutters up the narrative. When he stumbles into the throne room, hoping to find her there, he seems even more lost among the gorgeous objects; "the hangings . . . of gilt Cordovan leather . . . a heavy gilt chandelier with branches for three hundred wax lights [hanging] down from the black and white ceiling . . . a great canopy of gold cloth, on which the lions and towers of Castile were broidered in seed pearls . . . the kneeling stool of the Infanta, with its cushion of cloth of silver" have little to do with the infanta's disdain or the dwarf's reaction to it (*CW*, 244).

Because Wilde's obsessive thoughts were so powerful, the beauty or aesthetic decoration of his stories became increasingly exaggerated. He was influenced by writers with similarly overblown styles: Edgar Allan Poe and such French authors as Gustave Flaubert, Charles Baudelaire, Stéphane Mallarmé, and especially the decadent Joris-Karl Huysmans. According to Wilde, a book that corrupts Dorian is "a fantastic variation on Huysmans' over-realistic study of the artistic temperament in our inartistic age" (*L*, 313). Wilde's remark in *Dorian Gray* that "it is the spectator, and not life, that art really mirrors" suggests that one appeal of the French decadents for him was that their style helped him in his defense against thoughts of syphilis (*CW*, 17). "Wordsworth went to the lakes, but he was never a lake poet," Wilde remarked. "He found in stones the sermons he had hidden there" (*CW*, 986). Wilde likewise found in these French writers the fantasies about disease and defense against their overt realization that he had hidden in his own work. When these writers hinted at homosexuality or any perverse sexual behavior, they also offered a kind of moral support. The aesthetic qualities of his ornate prose developed into what Freud has called a countercathexis, the diversion of Wilde's preoccupation with his fears into elaborate descriptions of precious stones, fine textiles, aromas, and other aesthetic visions.

Like "The Birthday of the Infanta" and "The Young King," *The Picture of Dorian Gray* contains pages of minute descriptions of aromas, spices, precious stones, tapestries, and objets d'art. Just after commenting on Dorian's sad reflections "of the ruins that Time brought on beautiful and wonderful things," Wilde embarks on a two-page description of each thread or facet of Dorian's treasures: "The most exquisite specimens that he could find of textile and embroidered work, getting the dainty Delhi muslins, finely wrought with gold palmates, and stitched over with iridescent beetles' wings; the Dacca gauzes that from their transparency are known in the East as 'woven air,' 'evening dew;' strange-figured cloths of Java, elaborate yellow Chinese hangings" (*CW*, 109, 110). It is hardly surprising that a contemporary reviewer complained that "the passage quoted earlier from 'The Young King' resembled 'the catalogue of a high art furniture dealer,'" that another critic found the same passage "for all the world like an extract from a catologue of Christies," and that a reviewer of *Dorian Gray* characterized the novel as "the very genius of affectation crystalised in a syrup of words. Reading it, we move in a heavy atmosphere of warm incense and slumbering artificial light."[49]

Wilde's description of the young king as "one who was seeking to find in beauty an anodyne from pain, a sort of restoration from sickness," introduces the salient feature of the fairy tales and *Dorian Gray*: an underlying despair and depression about his sickness always remains behind their decor (*CW*, 225). He sought in his beautiful prose an anodyne from pain and a restoration from syphilis. In writing his fairy tales Wilde endeavored to create for himself a new, aesthetic world that would cloak his obsessive thoughts of his rotting body and soul. Always conscious of his inner ugliness, he became increasingly aware of the ugliness of industrialization and poverty: "Starvation, and not sin, is the parent of modern crime," he wrote in "The Soul of Man under Socialism" (*CW*, 1088). Beset by visions of his future as a putrescent living corpse, he tried to "think lovely thoughts," and the sumptuous detail of his decorative prose coated the dreariness of his bleak visions of illness and degeneration. The uglier his fantasies about syphilis, the more gorgeous his artificial paradises became. The greater his terror, the stronger his need to defend himself against feeling it and the more bountiful his visions of beauty.

A scene in *Dorian Gray* depicts Dorian trying and failing to push disturbing thoughts out of his head with beautiful visions. He has just murdered the painter Basil Hallward but does not "even glance at the murdered man," because he feels "that the whole secret of the thing [is] not to realise the situation." The next morning, however, when he begins to face the necessity of getting rid of the body, he cannot fail to "realise the whole situation," even though he tries desperately not to do so: "He lit a cigarette, and began sketching upon a piece of paper, drawing first flowers, and bits of architecture, and then human faces. Suddenly he realized that every face that he drew seemed to have a fantastic likeness to Basil Hallward. He frowned, and getting up, went over to the bookcase and took out a volume at hazard. He was determined that he would not think about what had happened until it became absolutely necessary that he should do so." At just this point, when Dorian is making his strongest effort to forget the hideous sight of Basil "choking with blood" and dying, Wilde launches into a high-flown description of the book that Dorian has just taken down from the shelf: "It was Gautier's *Emaux et Camées,* Charpentier's Japanese-paper edition, with the Jacquemart etching. The binding was of citron-green leather, with a design of gilt trellis-work and dotted pomegranates" (*CW,* 123). So far Dorian has gotten his mind off the murder. But then, "as he turned over the pages his eye fell on the poem about the hand of Lacenaire, the cold yellow hand 'du supplice encore mal *lavée,*'" that is, a hand "scarcely rid of its torture stain" (*CW,* 126).

Because the beautiful visions alone do not succeed in making Dorian forget, he tries to hide his evil thoughts behind a foreign language. He shudders and goes on to read "those lovely stanzas upon Venice," from which Wilde quotes at length, and reflects,

As one read them, one seemed to be floating down the green waterways of the pink and pearl city, seated in a black gondola with silver prow and trailing curtains. The mere lines looked to him like those straight lines of turquoise-blue that follow one as one pushes out to the Lido. The sudden flashes of colour reminded him of the gleam of the opal-and-iris-throated birds that flutter round the tall, honey-combed Campanile, or stalk, with such stately grace, through the dim, dust-stained arcades. Leaning back with half-closed eyes, he kept saying over and over to himself:—
    "Devant une façade rose,
        Sur le marbre d'un escalier."
The whole of Venice was in those two lines. He remembered the autumn that he had passed there. . . . There was romance in every place. . . . Basil had been with him part of the time, and had gone wild over Tintoret. Poor Basil! What a horrible way for a man to die! (*CW,* 126–27)

The conjuring of colors and elaborate visions leads to an obsessive repetition of lines of French poetry, which Dorian murmurs as though they were a charm to keep away evil thoughts. The charm fails, and he is left with the horrible memory of having murdered his friend.

Inevitably the ideas that were to be repressed break through and show themselves: Wilde's decorative prose also expressed his despair instead of covering it up. His efforts to avoid thoughts of syphilis led him directly back to further ruminations of his condition. This process resembles what Freud termed "the return of the repressed," although Wilde's unwanted thoughts were probably pushed into a corner of his conscious mind rather than relegated to the unconscious. In *Delusions and Dreams in Jensen's* Gradiva, Freud suggests that

it is precisely that which was chosen as the instrument of repression . . . that becomes the vehicle for the return: in and behind the repressing force, what is repressed proves itself victor in the end. This fact, which has been so little noticed and deserves so much consideration, is illustrated . . . in a well-known etching by Felicien Rops; and it is illustrated in the typical case of repression in the life of saints and penitents. An ascetic monk has fled, no doubt, from the temptations of the world, to the image of the crucified Saviour. And now the cross sinks down like a shadow, and in its place, radiant, there rises instead the image of a voluptuous, naked woman, in the same crucified attitude. Other artists with less psychological insight have, in similar representations of temptation, shown sin, insolent and triumphant, in some position alongside of the Saviour on the cross. Only Rops has placed sin in the very place of the Saviour on the cross. He seems to have known that, when what has been repressed returns, it emerges from the repressing force itself.[50]

Wilde had a similar understanding of the way repression works, as a passage in *De Profundis* suggests: "Failure, disgrace, poverty, sorrow, despair, suffering, tears even . . . all these were things of which I was afraid. And as I had determined to know nothing of them, I was forced to taste each one of them in turn, to feed on them, to have for a season, indeed, no other food at all" (*L*, 475). In other words, his deliberate suppression of sorrow led him right back to sorrow.

Wilde goes on to remark that all this was "foreshadowed and prefigured" in his art; he realizes that his repressive effort was doomed to failure. In what follows I trace some of the suppressed themes in Wilde's fairy tales and show how these themes emerge from the suppressing force itself.

"The Happy Prince" opens with another beautiful description: "High above the city, on a tall column, stood the statue of the Happy Prince. He was gilded all over with thick leaves of solid gold, for eyes he had two bright sapphires, and a large ruby glowed in his sword-hilt. . . . He was very much admired indeed" (*CW*, 285). One almost sees Oscar as he liked to see himself. The Happy Prince is, however, very unhappy. One night he relates the following to a little swallow who alights on his shoulder:

When I was alive, and had a human heart . . . I did not know what tears were, for I lived in the Palace of Sans-Souci, where sorrow is not allowed to enter. . . . And now that I am dead they have set me up here so high that my heart is made of lead, yet I cannot choose but weep. . . . Far away . . . far away in a little street there is a poor house. One of the windows is open, and through it I can see a woman sitting at a table. Her face is thin and worn, and she is a seamstress. She is embroidering passion-flowers on a satin gown for the loveliest of the Queen's maids-of-honour. . . . In a bed in a corner of the room her little boy is lying ill. He has a fever, and is asking for oranges. His mother has nothing to give him but river water, so he is crying. Swallow, Swallow, little Swallow, will you not bring him the ruby out of my sword-hilt? (CW, 287)

Wilde reveals his depression—his leaden heart. The ugliness he sees in his own mind becomes the ugliness of the city seen by the Happy Prince. Perhaps he sees himself in the little boy lying ill in a bed in the corner. Feeling like a statue rooted to the ground, Wilde is powerless to change what he sees happening. He would have preferred to hand out the gems and pearls of his wisdom instead of decaying purposelessly.

On this and several other occasions in the story, a little swallow plucks out one of the precious stones encrusting the Happy Prince and brings it to one of the needy people whom the prince wants to help. By the end of the story the Happy Prince has lost all his precious stones and all the gold leaf that had covered him. The mayor and town councillors decide that the statue is too shabby and melt it down. With this sad ending, Wilde formulates among other things the desperate, defensive thought that even though he would die of a degrading scourge and be rejected by all decent men, he would at least succeed in giving away precious wisdom and poetic beauty for the sake of the poor. But unlike the common lot, he could describe his despair. Like Goethe's *Torquato Tasso*, Wilde felt that "when man in his suffering falls silent, a god gave me the gift to say what I feel."

Another story, "The Selfish Giant," hints at Wilde's speculations about his childhood and family life as well as the genesis of his homosexuality. He tells of a selfish giant who refuses to allow the children to play in his garden, where winter comes to stay indefinitely. Because parents are always giants to a young child, the giant could represent Wilde's father: the senior Wilde was also isolated from his children in a selfish way, because he was so often absent from home on professional or philandering excursions.

While winter continues to rage in the selfish giant's garden, a few children sneak in through a hole in the wall and climb up into the trees, which are immediately covered with blossoms and filled with singing birds. In one corner of the garden winter remains, because a tiny boy is unable to climb into a tree; the lowest branch is too high for him. As he stands there weeping, the giant picks him up and places him in the tree, and the tree bursts into blossom. The little boy (Oscar?) flings his arms around the giant's neck and *speculative : reductively allegorical & repetitive.*

It could, but it needn't be

kisses him. After that, the children always come to play in the garden, except for the one little boy who had kissed the giant and whom the giant longs to see again. This could be read as a projection of Wilde's wish as a youngster that his father spend more time with the family.

One day when the giant is very old, he sees that "in the farthest corner of the garden was a tree quite covered with lovely white blossoms. Its branches were golden and silver fruit hung down from them, and underneath it stood the little boy that he had loved. . . . Downstairs ran the giant in great joy. . . . And when he came quite close his face grew red with anger and he said, 'Who hath dared to wound thee?' for on the palms of the child's hands were the prints of two nails, and the prints of two nails were on the little feet. 'Who hath dared to wound thee?' cried the giant; 'tell me that I may take my big sword and slay him.'. . . 'Nay!' answered the child: 'But these are the wounds of Love'" (*CW*, 300–01). The Christ child with the prints of nails on his little feet and hands could represent Oscar, who as a little boy needed his father's love. All his life Wilde identified himself with Christ; in *Salome*, he saw himself as Christ's herald, John the Baptist, and in *De Profundis* he admired Christ as the type of the true artist. The wounds of love in this story might therefore be seen as the masochistic penetration for which the homosexual Wilde longed. The story perhaps reveals Wilde's unconscious belief that he had become homosexual because he had longed for his father's love, but his father had always been a selfish giant, and refused love to the family.

Wilde also reveals in these tales fears about the health of his own young family, particularly his two sons, Cyril and Vyvyan: he seems to have worried about what sort of children he as a syphilitic would produce and how they might blame and judge him for making them ill. In "The Star Child" (1891), he tells how a cruel child remorselessly rejects his parents, a beggar and a leper, but is after many hardships reconciled with them. The star child, a foundling that a poor woodcutter had seen falling down from the sky, becomes, like Dorian Gray, "every year more beautiful to look at, so that all those who dwelt in the village were filled with wonder, for, while they were swarthy and black-haired, he was white and delicate as sawn ivory, and his curls were like the rings of the daffodil. His lips, also, were like the petals of a red flower, and his body like the narcissus of a field where the mower comes not" (*CW*, 276).

This aesthetic description of the star child leads immediately to the assertion "Yet did his beauty work him evil" and to a detailing of the child's pride and cruelty. Like Dorian Gray he is as evil inside as he is attractive to look at: he throws stones at the poor, blind, maimed, and afflicted—all of whom, incidentally, are like his parents in their afflictions—and pierces "with a sharp reed the dim eyes of the mole." One day a poor beggar woman with bleeding feet appears in the village and turns out to be his mother. He mocks her and throws stones at her. As soon as he has sent her away, he discovers that his own skin has become "foul as the toad" and "scaled like an adder" (*CW,* 276, 278); perhaps in the star child Wilde imagined his own children's discovery that the sins of their father were being visited upon them in the form of congenital syphilis. Weeping, the star child repents and goes in search of his parents. After much suffering, he behaves kindly to the leper and is miraculously transformed into his beautiful self; the leper, it develops, is his father, and he, too, with the star child's mother, is transformed. Wilde the leprous father hoped that his sons would forgive him.

CHAPTER 3 WILDE IN HIS LETTERS

T he publication of Oscar Wilde's letters in 1962 forever demolished the image of Wilde as a frivolous, heartless dandy, with little sympathy and much disdain for others. The lesser known dimensions of Wilde—his warmth, generosity, pensive self-criticism, and kindness—emerge from these pages as an extraordinary revelation of his personality.[1] Wilde wrote to all kinds of people—college chums, his parents, editors, male and female lovers, celebrities, shady or down-and-out characters—throughout the diverse situations of his life. These letters show the apparently high-spirited undergraduate who was always descending into chasms of self-doubt, the provoking "professor of Aesthetics" touring America and the English provinces, the self-justifying controversial novelist, the brilliantly successful wit and dramatist, the homosexual besotted by the "gilt-haired boy," and the "soul in pain" eking out an alcoholic, debauched existence.

Rupert Hart-Davis, the editor of Wilde's letters, remarked that they may reveal so much because they were written "to intimate friends without thought of publication" (L, ix). Actually Wilde did intend many of his letters for publication, or at least for posterity. As he remarked in the postscript to one of his undergraduate letters: "I like signing my name as if it was to some document of great importance as 'Send two bags of gold by bearer' or 'Let the Duke be slain tomorrow and the Duchess await me at the hostelry'" (L, 26). Yet he spoke freely in them, as he spoke in person, and inevitably revealed himself. The letters show, more so than his literary productions, that he suffered from a basic conflict that has not been recognized—his desire to be an artist, or at least a thinker, and not the Irish hero and conqueror of the English that his mother wanted him to be. The letters also reveal a deeper unconscious aim that puts the affair with the Marquess of Queensberry in an

entirely new light—namely, Wilde's identification not with his mother's conscious wishes for him to be an Ossianic warrior but with her contradictory
longing to submit to martyrdom on a battlefield.

His quip that he had put his genius into his life rather than into his work as
an artist was not the gleeful admission of a former enfant terrible who was
deliberately giving his profession short shrift in favor of pleasure seeking but
the tortured sigh of a man who felt that he had failed, despite all his efforts, to
fulfill his mother's expectations. He felt a constant tension between his obli-
gation to put all his intellect and artistry into becoming a hero in the political
reality of his time and his own wish to live quietly—neither heroically nor
combatively. Early in 1890 he wrote of *Dorian Gray:* "I have just finished my
first long story, and am tired out. I am afraid it is rather like my own life—all
conversation and no action. I can't describe action: My people sit in chairs
and chatter" (*L,* 255). At the very time when he had achieved one of his
lasting artistic triumphs he was strongly aware that he should rather have put
more energy into performing his heroic role; yet at other times he felt that he
wasted too much on it.

As his letters record, his never-lagging effort at being the hero Speranza
expected sapped the energy he might have used for artistic work. To a college
friend, William Ward, he expressed his longing to withdraw rather than to be
a fighter: "There is a good deal to be said about the necessity of a retreat
especially for literary people. . . . The idea of standing aloof from practical
life is constantly appearing in Greek Philosophy." The same feeling of un-
willingness to involve himself in fighting comes across in a somewhat humorous letter to Mrs. Cunningham Graham, whose lecture on "The Ideals of
Socialism" he declined to attend: "I think your subject is most interesting,
but . . . I want to stand apart, and look on, being neither for God nor for his
enemies. This, I hope, will be allowed" (*ML,* 78, 84).

He expresses this lifelong ambivalence and conflict of conscience mainly
in his letters. Most of his life he felt wearied by the devil-may-care image he
projected to the world, as shown in a letter of late February 1894, written to
an artist who had praised one of his comedies: "Your letter has deeply moved
me. To the world I seem, by intention on my part, a dilettante and dandy
merely—it is not wise to show one's heart to the world—and as seriousness
of manner is the disguise of the fool, folly in its exquisite modes of triviality
and indifference and lack of care is the robe of the wise man. In so vulgar an
age as this we all need masks" (*L,* 352).

In *De Profundis,* his long prison letter to Bosie, he describes Hamlet in a
way that reveals his own tormented feeling of always having to serve two
masters: "[Hamlet] is staggering under the weight of a burden intolerable to

one of his temperament. The dead have come armed out of the grave to impose on him a mission at once too great and too mean for him. He is a dreamer, and he is called upon to act. He has the nature of the poet, and he is asked to grapple with the common complexities of cause and effect, with life in its practical realisation, of which he knows nothing, not with life in its ideal essence, of which he knows much." This perhaps owes something to Samuel Coleridge, who saw in Hamlet's character "the prevalence of the abstracting and generalizing habit over the practical. He does not want courage, skill, will, or opportunity; but every incident sets him thinking; and it is curious, and at the same time, strictly natural, that Hamlet, who all the play seems reason itself, should be impelled, at last, by mere accident to effect his object."[2]

Wilde's next remark about Hamlet describes his own reaction of clowning as a way of coping when called upon to be a real hero: "[Hamlet] has no conception of what to do, and his folly is to feign folly. . . . To Hamlet madness is a mere mask for the hiding of weakness. In the making of mows and jests he sees a chance of delay. He keeps playing with action, as an artist plays with a theory. . . . Instead of trying to be the hero of his own history, he seeks to be the spectator of his own tragedy. He disbelieves in everything, including himself, and yet his doubt helps him not, as it comes not from skepticism, but from a divided will" (L, 504). This most self-perceptive moment of De Profundis was real heroism, because Wilde was here doing battle with his greatest enemy, himself.

In his letters, Wilde's retiring side, which he probably got from his father, emerges strongly. The father was known as a patient researcher on everything from potatoes to Peruvian mummies, from the archaeology of Ireland to the anatomy and physiology of the eye and ear and the treatment of deaf and dumb children. In the Proceedings of the Royal Irish Academy, P. Frogatt designated him "a first-rate scientist trained through personal effort and observation and backed by intuitive genius," who was "no mere 'compiler of abstracts' but a real innovatory 'political arithmetist' with sound though simple methodology . . . [and who possessed] a systematized approach, analytical skill, and deep professional knowledge."[3] His wife confirmed this, by complaining in a letter that her husband's "whole existence is one of unceasing mental activity, and this had made the peculiarities of his nature."[4]

Oscar's temperament was actually closer to his father's than to his mother's. Being a revolutionary or even a self-promoting aesthete suited him less than being an observer. Robert Sherard remembered that "as a schoolboy, so he told me, he had no spirit of adventure, no wish to run away, to join the pirates, to hunt Red Indians, to form secret societies, to go to sea, to be wrecked on desert islands, or to do any of the things which most boys are so very anxious to do. He once told me that he had never climbed a tree. . . . He was all along too bulky to be a boy of action. He 'used to flop about ponderously' is what was said of him."[5] This quiet, contemplative boy often spent his vacations on the continent with his "Darling Mama," as he addresses her at age fourteen in the one letter we have from his adolescence.[6] But he could not be her warrior.

Wilde's early letters, especially those describing an undergraduate trip to Italy and Greece, reveal this natural inclination to be an observer and recorder of details. In a letter to his father, written early in June 1875, Wilde describes in almost filigree detail the chapel of San Lorenzo in Florence and the Biblioteca Laurenziana in its cloisters, where "I was shown wonderfully illuminated missals and unreadable manuscripts and autographs. I remarked the extreme clearness of the initial letters in the Italian missals and bibles, so different from those in the Book of Kells, etc., which might stand for anything. The early illuminations are very beautiful in design and sentiment, but the later are mere mechanical *tours de force* of geometrical scroll work and absurd designs" (*L*, 4). To a tutor at Magdalen he wrote another extremely detailed description, from which emerged scholarly speculations about the cult of the Virgin: "We first came to Genoa, which is a beautiful marble city of palaces over the sea, and then to Ravenna, which is extremely interesting on account of the old Christian churches in it of enormous age and the magnificent mosaics of the *fourth century*. These mosaics were very remarkable as they contained two figures of the Madonna enthroned and receiving adoration; they completely upset the ordinary Protestant idea that the worship of the Virgin did not come in till late in the history of the Church" (*L*, 35).

Wilde often turned his researcher's eye upon himself, particularly on his psychological motivations. In late May 1897, when he had been out of prison only a few weeks, he wrote in a letter: "I think now . . . that I could do *three* articles on prison life. Of course much will be psychological and introspective" (*L*, 581). Of *De Profundis*, he wrote: "It is the most important letter of my life, as it will deal ultimately with my future mental attitude towards life, with the way in which I desire to meet the world again, with the development of my character: with what I have lost, what I have learned, and what I hope to arrive at. At last I see a real goal towards which my soul can go simply, naturally, and rightly. . . . I must finish the letter, that you may understand what I have become, or rather desire to become in nature and aim. My whole life depends upon it" (*L*, 419). Alas, he did not reach his goal.

Even in the early successful days of his American tour of 1881–82, in which his bravura style of aggressive, self-confident bon mots made him a great success in tongue-in-cheek self-promotion, he felt, as letters show, that he was a failure as a serious revolutionary. To John Boyle O'Reilly, an Irish immigrant who had been transported from Ireland to Australia and had escaped to America, Wilde wrote: "I want to see you about my mother's poems. . . . I think my mother's work should make a great success here: it is so unlike the work of her degenerate artistic son" (ML, 47).

Perhaps he was a bit ashamed that his weapon was barbed wit, not bullets. His mother had written about "shining muskets" pointing at Britain and would undoubtedly have loved to have been a gunrunner, if she had had the nerve and the opportunity. Her son contented himself with smuggling subversive ideas into London society. In a letter of October 1890, he obliquely alludes to the erotic idiosyncrasies of Tiberius, the Roman emperor notorious for pedophilia and perversion, and cheerfully dismisses the idea that the latter was guilty of any sexual crime: "I still hope that Tiberius was very wicked, but fear that philology was his only crime" (ML, 91).

The depth of his mother's influence on him is especially pronounced in the letters regarding his employment as editor of a woman's magazine; in that capacity he devoted himself to improving the treatment and status of women. In April 1887 he agreed to take the editorship of a monthly magazine called Lady's World. He wrote that the magazine was "at present . . . too feminine, and not sufficiently womanly. . . . The field of mere millinery and trappings, is to some extent already occupied. . . . We should take a wider range, as well as a high standpoint, and deal not merely with what women wear, but with what they think, and what they feel. The Lady's World should be made the recognised organ for the expression of women's opinions on all subjects of literature, art, and modern life." He went on to say that he was happy to assist in making the magazine "the first woman's paper in England" (L, 195–96). One feels here the happy identification with his mother—not as some heroic figure but as a woman, as his father's wife.

Wilde strove to improve the caliber of Lady's World by assembling many distinguished woman contributors (he even asked Queen Victoria to submit a poem!) and by arguing passionately for the change of the name of the magazine (L, 215).[7] In another letter he states, "I am very anxious that you should make a final appeal to the Directors to alter the name of the magazine I am to edit for them from the Lady's World to the Woman's World." As the rest of the letter shows, Wilde seems to have been drawing the same distinction now drawn by some feminists between lady as a derogatory or frivolous designation for an adult female and woman as a more dignified and respectful honorific.[8]

Wilde went on in the same letter, "The present name of the magazine has a certain taint of vulgarity about it, that will always militate against the success of the new issue, and is also extremely misleading. . . . It will not be applicable to a magazine that aims at being the organ of women of intellect, culture, and position" (L, 203). He added vehemently that this was "undoubtedly" the view of the contributors he intended to use and he mentioned several potential contributors, such as William Thackeray's daughter, who had already complained about the title. The board adopted his position.

The changes he suggested attest to his feminist concerns, which are an expression of his intense identification with his mother as a woman. "I was influenced by my mother. Every man is when he is young," he wrote in *A Woman of No Importance*. A curious epigram in *The Importance of Being Earnest* reveals a moving conflict produced by that influence: "All women," he says, "become like their mothers. That is their tragedy. No man does. That's his" (*CW*, 335). This remark reveals his own tragedy: the difficulty he had in identifying not with his mother as a woman but with her masculine fervor. He joked about this to ward off feelings of despair: "Manliness has become quite effeminate. Only women are manly nowadays," he remarked.[9] The fact was that he could not think of himself as a man. He deeply regretted his lack of willingness to be what his mother wanted him to be. He had a need to identify with his father, too, and probably was equally unable to identify with him completely, since he became a homosexual.

Yet to fulfill Speranza's ideals, Wilde became a warrior fighting British cultural mores, but the figure he presented asked to be derided as well as taken seriously. He transformed himself into a "camp fashion plate," to borrow a phrase from Steven Marcus.[10] During his American tour, Wilde was already establishing himself as a provoking, in fact, militant, critic of British aesthetic tastes, or lack thereof: he dressed and acted as a deliberate caricature of English poets such as Keats and Byron, who were forerunners of Aestheticism. When Wilde stepped off the steamship in New York, a reporter noted that he was wearing a shirt that "might be termed ultra-Byronic, or perhaps décolleté."[11] On the evening of his first lecture in New York, he lingered over Keats, whom he quoted as saying, "I have no reverence . . . for the public, or for anything in existence but the Eternal Being, the memory of great men, and the principle of beauty."[12] Because Wilde could not be an original hero by inclination, he tried to become one through identification with poets who were perceived as heroes, especially in their letters, which reveal their ability to face suffering courageously.[13]

Wilde paid lip service to Speranza's ideals by imitating Keats and Byron; in fact, it seems that he had to settle for imitating them because he could not identify with them. Imitation can be a preliminary stage of identification, but for Wilde imitation had to substitute for identification. When he went to see

Gilbert and Sullivan's *Patience,* which he was officially in New York to promote, he made a quip about the leading character, Bunthorne, that applied to his own divided feelings about his heroic role. "Caricature," Wilde drawled, "is the tribute which mediocrity pays to genius."[14] By this he seems to have wanted to confess that his imitation of Keats and Byron never succeeded in making him feel like the real thing. He could look, but not feel, like these poets. For all the glee he expresses in foppishly aping them, he seems to have considered himself just a mediocre imitation.

In fact, he seems to have felt rather ridiculous: as reporters noted, "Oscar was blushing."[15] In a letter postmarked 29 January 1889, he writes: "Parody, which is the Muse with her tongue in her cheek, has always amused me; but it requires a light touch . . . and, oddly enough, a love of the poet whom it caricatures. One's disciples can parody one—nobody else" (*L,* 239). Had he not loved the British, Wilde could not have caricatured them. In all his comedies, admiration for British mores shines through criticism of British stupidity.

An understanding of the psychological function of this sort of imitation for Wilde will, I believe, add greatly to our comprehension of his peculiar quip about his genius and talent. The letters reveal new reasons for this mysterious aspect of him, because they present all sides of Wilde—not just the satirical dandy of popular misconception.

One would indeed expect to find in the letters the same pattern of carefully crafted, yet curiously ambivalent, emulation that one finds in the rest of his life and work.[16] That Wilde studied the epistolary styles of various writers is suggested in "The Critic as Artist," in which he declares a fascination with the "mere egotism" of "the letters of personalities so different as Cicero and Balzac, Flaubert and Berlioz, Byron and Madame de Sevigné" (*CW,* 1009).[17]

But imitation, because it represents an attempt to identify with another personality, often has as its impetus a need to solve a conflict. Keats and Byron, whose popular images Wilde had already exploited on his American tour, lent themselves exquisitely to Wilde's wish to find models for his letters. Byron's letters, a selection of which first appeared in 1829, and Keats's letters, some of which were first published in 1848, were known to have been most effective in popularizing these poets as heroes and martyrs. Both Keats and Byron were critics of the English and both were kindred spirits in depression and anxiety; their heroic defiance asserted itself as a reaction to feelings of despair and helplessness. By identifying with them, Wilde could try to kill two birds with one stone.

Although Byron was often full of despair, the dash and daring of his life and letters conceal his anguish. Byron's attitude toward his clubfoot—a defor-

mity he overcame by becoming a fine athlete capable of swimming the Hellespont, even remarking that Leander's amatory powers might have been somewhat depleted by such a nightly journey—could only have bolstered Wilde's
attempt to overcome his own incipient deformity as a syphilitic and his
handicap as a homosexual.[18] Byron's apparent triumph over fear and despair
to become a fighter for Greek independence and for an Italian revolutionary
cause probably inspired Wilde even more. And Wilde's knowledge of or
intuition concerning Byron's ambivalent and ambiguous sexuality undoubtedly furthered the identification.

   Longing to feel free of fears about illness, Wilde must have felt encouraged
by Keats's apparent calm in diagnosing himself with tuberculosis. The famous
story of Keats stoically examining drops of blood from his mouth on his
pillow, observing that the color of the blood revealed that it was arterial and
that therefore he must die, would certainly have appealed to a man trying to
find the bravery to face a lingering, ugly death. Keats's acceptance of each new
deadly symptom of tuberculosis with an almost unshakable equanimity, his
attempt never to reveal his despair, and his introduction of the concept of
"negative capability," which he defined as an intention to tolerate "uncertainties, Mysteries, doubts, without any irritable reaching after fact," were heroic
stances to be envied. The criticism of Keats's poetry on political grounds,
because he had sympathized with Leigh Hunt, the English poet and essayist,
and was thus seen as "not only a bad poet, but a bad citizen," only added to
his glory as a martyr.[19]

   In many of their letters—though not their love letters to women—these
poets give the impression that they have transcended, if not resolved, most of
their conflicts and so are free of doubt and at peace with themselves. The
steady self-confidence of Keats and Byron inspired Wilde, who tried to feel
brave and to overcome his doubts and conflicts by affecting an attitude of
utter confidence. As many letters reveal, Wilde was tortured with self-doubt
all his life. In March 1877 he wrote in a letter to William Ward: "I shift with
every breath of thought and am weaker and more self-deceiving than
ever. . . . I get so wretched and low and troubled . . . *with feelings so bitter that
I have lost faith in myself*" (L, 31). Yet Wilde's method, actually his trademark,
was the arrogant certainty with which he affirmed outrageous pronouncements that conflicted with general opinions.

   Thus Wilde developed a similar method of concealing doubts and despair
by a display of certainty. But where Keats and Byron were heroic, Wilde
seems to have felt himself to be a buffoon, to have known that his methods
were the methods of a buffoon. Yet the buffoonery ultimately became heroic,
just as his outrageous statements, which appear to deny all customary truths,

became truths after all. His marvelous humor transcended the tragedy of his situation, as when he claimed that he could not outlive the century, because "if another century began and I was still alive, it would be more than the English could stand!"[20]

An early indication of Wilde's tremendous ambivalence toward his entire public role, and his attempt to resolve it through identification with an ambiguous "heroic" figure, can be found in one of his earliest works, "Ravenna." In this undergraduate poem, which won him the coveted Oxford Newdigate prize, Wilde pays tribute to Byron as a poet, an aristocrat, and an impassioned soldier. Like much of Byron's own poetry "Ravenna" is an imitation of Augustan verse:

> Byron dwelt here in love and revelry
> For two long years—a second Anthony,
> Who of the world another Actium made!
> Yet suffered not his royal soul to fade,
> Or lyre to break, or lance to grow less keen,
> 'Neath any wiles of an Egyptian queen.
> For from the East there came a mighty cry,
> And Greece stood up to fight for Liberty,
> And called him from Ravenna: never knight
> Rode forth more nobly to wild scenes of fight!
> None fell more bravely on ensanguined field,
> Borne like a Spartan back upon his shield!
>
> . . . .
>
> And England, too, shall glory in her son,
> Her warrior-poet, first in song and fight.
> No longer now shall Slander's venomed spite
> Crawl like a snake across his perfect name
> Or mar the lordly scutcheon of his fame. (*CW*, 827–28)

In the last three lines Wilde also imagines himself as a great name, but a great name injured by "Slander's venomed spite." Wilde would have identified far more easily with the side of Byron that resembled himself. Like the Wildes, Byron was a bit of an arriviste: having spent his formative years living in impoverished surroundings in Aberdeen, Scotland, he become an English lord only when he suddenly got his inheritance at age ten. Thus, like Wilde, he was an outsider among the aristocratic English. Like Wilde's Irish lilt, Byron's trace of a Scottish accent branded him as a foreigner among the English. Both men adopted English accents at university. Byron, like Wilde, affected youth, and said his poems were "the effusions of a boy"—a phrase Wilde borrowed, particularly when he sent a poem to Gladstone.[21]

Oscar Wilde at about age two, dressed in children's finery of the period.

Envelope decorated by Oscar Wilde, in which he kept a lock of hair belonging to his sister, Isola.

Caricature of Wilde in his aesthetic phase at Oxford. (Courtesy Clark Library)

Oscar Wilde (standing) as first-year student at Oxford in 1875. Wilde's brother, Willie, is seated on the right; on the left is his friend J. E. C. Bodley. (Courtesy Clark Library)

Wilde (seated) with two Oxford friends in 1876. Reginald Harding (left) was known as "Kitten," and William Ward (center), as "Bouncer." (Courtesy Clark Library)

Oscar Wilde as a young man.
(Courtesy Clark Library)

Broadside-style ballad
that appeared in
London after Wilde's
arrest. (Courtesy
Clark Library)

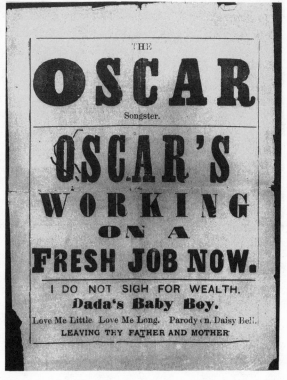

THE
OSCAR
Songster.
OSCAR'S
WORKING
ON A
FRESH JOB NOW.
I DO NOT SIGH FOR WEALTH.
Dada's Baby Boy.
Love Me Little. Love Me Long. Parody on Daisy Bell.
LEAVING THY FATHER AND MOTHER

OH! OSCAR WILDE,

WE NEVER THOUGHT

That You Was Built That Way.

Now wonders they will never cease, and
    as each day we read,
The papers, why we oft say, well, "I am
    surprised" indeed,
For people who we think are 18 carat
    turn out brass,
And what we thought a Lion's roar's the
    braying of ass,
We read of pious preachers who turn out
    to be sad rakes,
But Oscar Wilde, he fairly earns the
    baker and the cakes,
He's got into a mess, and he will take
    some getting out,
You've climbed Jane's ladder, Oscar but
    you've got stuck up the spout.

Chorus.

Oh! Oscar, you're a Daisy, you're a Sun-
    flower and a Rose,
You're a thick old "Dandylion," from
    your pimple to your toes,
You're the sweetest lump of "Boy's Love"
    that's been picked for many a day,
Oh! Oscar Wilde, we never thought, that
    you was built that way.

You've been "An Ideal Husband," in your
    tin pot way no doubt,
Though "A Woman of no Importance,"
    was your wife, when you were out,
At least that's what the papers say, of
    course they can't be wrong;
They seemed to say that Oscar's fun was
    very, very, strong,
He would'nt treat a "Lady" no not even
    Totty Fay,
But with the pretty boys, he liked to

pass his time away,
Champagne, and Chicken suppers, and
    he'd also give them pelf,
He was fond of manly beauty, he's so
    beautiful himself.

The Marquis of Queensberry, it would
    seem got Oscar "Wild(e)"
He must have been a silly little silly, to
    get riled,
You know there is a saying Oscar, "hard
    words break no bones,"
And folks who live in houses made of
    glass, should not throw stones.
The Marquis got the best of it, and
    knocked poor Oscar out,
They did'nt use no 4 oz gloves, 'twas "raw
    uns" there's no doubt,
He got one in the windbag, and he cussed
    the "Queensberry Rules"
For Oscar, and his second, Taylor looked
    a pair of fools.

At Hollaway our only "Oscar," does his
    fate bewail,
And says he'd rather be at the "Savoy"
    than be in jail,
The Idol of Society, the Poet and the Pet
Can't get a Hock and Seltzer, or yet
    smoke a cigarette,
The "Golden Haired Divineties," seen in
    the Strand each night,
Are quiet excited at the news, and says
    it serves 'em right,
For blacklegging in any trade, is very
    mean and wrong,
And the papers say, that Lord knows who,
    they'll have before so long.

Broadside-style ballad that appeared in London after Wilde's arrest. (Courtesy Clark Library)

OSCAR'S
WORKING ON A FRESH JOB NOW.

The Oscar trial is ended, and his dream of love is
  o'er,
And now in jail, he does bewail,
His funny little capers. he won't cut for two
  years more,
He'll have to start upon a job, he's never done
  before,
His very tender feelings will be mangled now and
  torn,
When he has to rise each morn, and grind the
  golden corn,
And instead of ham and chicken, and such dainty
  bits of scran,
For dry toke and pint of skilly, he'll be putting out
  his can:

Chorus.—

Oh! Oscar Wilde your tricks, has got you in a fix,
You've lost your precious liberty, and got to live
  on skilly go-lee,
Instead of going to plays, you'll have to go to
  prayers,
Then "All in a row" off you'll go, climbing the
  golden stairs.

Well, Oscar cannot grumble, that he's not been
  tried enough,
For twice should be, a fill say we,
The lawyers on each side no doubt, have done
  their best to bluff,
The juries but the second one, for Oscar cut up
  rough,
The evidence no doubt, was pretty hot
Of letters, such a lot, and mostly tommy rot;

For when men write of rose leaf lips, and say
  they're kissing mad,
About another man, why! you can bet they've got
  it bad.

There's no doubt some of the witnesses, were quite
  as bad as he,
And did as fall, to claim black-mail;
With Wilde, and Taylor, safely lodged in jail they
  ought to be,
And to carry on the same old game, should not
  be free,
The case has caused a lot of blood and hair to fly,
For the Marquis had a try, and blacked Lord
  Thingumys eye,
Although a lot of people seem to say, they must be
  fools,
To start in Piccadilly, fighting under Queensberry
  rules.

For two long weary years, from business Oscar has
  retired,
To sleep alone, and break some stone,
The public of his plays and poetry, seem to soon
  have tired,
Although his company by them, till lately was de-
  sired,
When he his sentence got 'tis said that Oscar
  seemed quite dazed,
In fact was quite amazed, and seemed to be going
  crazed,
And no doubt for the next two years, he will need
  all his pluck,
When instead of dainty bits, he has to tackle
  Indian buck.

Photo of Wilde's wife, Constance, published in *To-Day* in 1894.

Caricature of Oscar Wilde by E. B. Duval, 1882. (Courtesy Clark Library)

Caricature of Oscar
Wilde, 1882. (Courtesy
Clark Library)

Political painting by George Cruikshank, 1883. Wilde is standing on the roof at top
right-hand corner. (Courtesy Clark Library)

Lina Munte as Salome, in the first French production of the play, which opened in
1896. (Courtesy Clark Library)

O. V. Gzovskaia as Salome, in a Russian production of the early 1920s. From *Firebird,* a Russian review of art and literature. (Courtesy Clark Library)

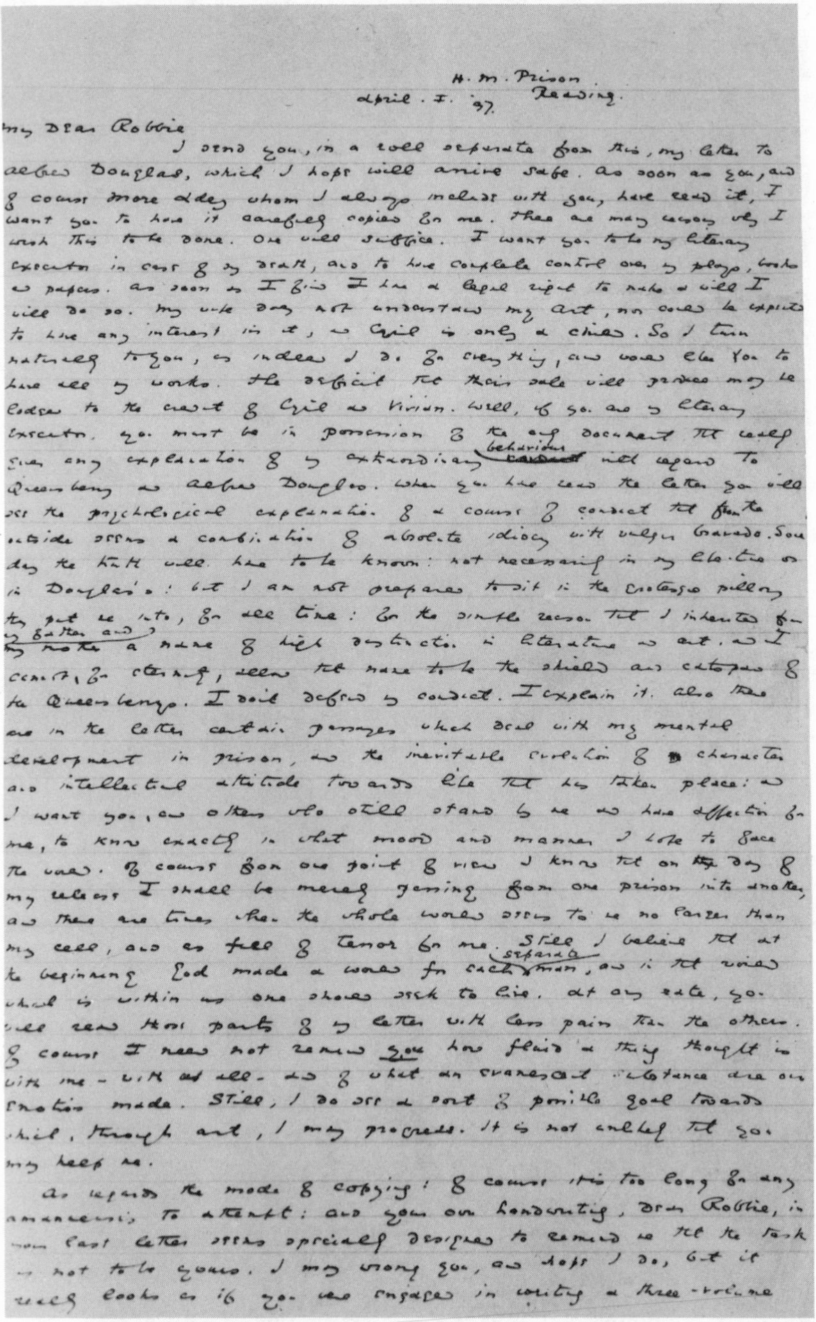

H. M. Prison
Reading.
April. I. 97.

My Dear Robbie

I send you, in a roll separate from this, my letter to Alfred Douglas, which I hope will arrive safe. As soon as you, and of course More Adey whom I always include with you, have read it, I want you to have it carefully copied for me. There are many reasons why I wish this to be done. One will suffice. I want you to be my literary executor in case of my death, and to have complete control over my plays, books and papers. As soon as I find I have a legal right to make a will I will do so. My wife does not understand my art, nor could be expected to have any interest in it, and Cyril is only a child. So I turn naturally to you, as indeed I do for everything, and would like you to have all my works. The deficit that their sale will produce may be lodged to the credit of Cyril and Vivian. Well, if you are my literary executor, you must be in possession of the only document that really gives any explanation of my extraordinary behaviour with regard to Queensberry and Alfred Douglas. When you have read the letter you will see the psychological explanation of a course of conduct that from the outside seems a combination of absolute idiocy with vulgar bravado. Some day the truth will have to be known: not necessarily in my lifetime or in Douglas's: but I am not prepared to sit in the grotesque pillory they put me into, for all time: for the simple reason that I inherited from my father and mother a name of high distinction in literature and art, and I cannot, for eternity, allow that name to be the shield and catspaw of the Queensberrys. I don't defend my conduct. I explain it. Also there are in the letter certain passages which deal with my mental development in prison, and the inevitable evolution of character and intellectual attitude towards life that has taken place: and I want you, and others who still stand by me and have affection for me, to know exactly in what mood and manner I hope to face the world. Of course from one point of view I know that on the day of my release I shall be merely passing from one prison into another, and there are times when the whole world seems to me no larger than my cell, and as full of terror for me. Still I believe that at the beginning God made a world for each separate man, and in that world which is within us one should seek to live. At any rate, you will read those parts of my letter with less pain than the others. Of course I need not remind *you* how fluid a thing thought is with me – with us all – and of what an evanescent substance are our emotions made. Still, I do see a sort of possible goal towards which, through art, I may progress. It is not unlikely that you may help me.

As regards the mode of copying: of course it is too long for any amanuensis to attempt: and your own handwriting, dear Robbie, in your last letter seems specially designed to remind me that the task is not to be yours. I may wrong you, and hope I do, but it really looks as if you were engaged in writing a three-volume

Letter from Wilde to Robert Ross, written on 1 April 1897 from Reading Gaol. In it he wrote: "I know that on the day of my release I shall be merely passing from one prison into another."

Byron was also full of private torments. In fact, somewhere in her collection of critical essays, entitled *Men, Women, and Books,* Wilde's mother praised Byron's "literature of despair" and called him the "poet of doubt."[22] Like Wilde, Byron had a warlike mother, but political convictions did not inspire Mrs. Byron's random rages, one of which involved her throwing a poker and tongs at her son.[23] As G. Wilson Knight pointed out in "Christ and Wilde," "the nature of [Wilde's] relation to his mother . . . recalls Byron's [too close relation to his mother]. . . . Like Byron, Wilde was a lover of children . . . and both exerted a strong fascination over women. Both often appeared effeminate, and yet both were capable, when challenged, of disconcerting feats of male strength. Wilde's love of flowers and interest in both male and female dress . . . were allied with a robust physique, physical courage, and a devastating wit to give him a position of artistic and social dominance that proved intoxicating both to others and to himself. From youth onwards he maintained, like Byron, a boyish immaturity, often difficult to distinguish from the integration of a seer."[24]

Perhaps the only way that Wilde could try to identify himself with the heroic side of Byron was to recognize himself sympathetically in the troubled Byron, the privately tormented soul: the Byron of the ambivalent sexuality, who became a hero because he felt weak and degraded by his mother's taunts about his clubfoot and who, like Wilde, turned for consolation to his sister's caresses. In *De Profundis,* Wilde sums himself up in relation to Byron: "I was a man who stood in symbolic relations to the art and culture of my age. . . . Byron was a symbolic figure, but his relations were to the passion of the age and its weariness of passion. Mine were to something more noble, more permanent, of more vital issue, of wider scope" (*CW,* 466). One can find buried in his essays and dramas acute psychological observations, along with philosophical reactions to the scientific discoveries of the day. But for his age he was a symbol of the nonheroic side of Byron—the "passion" and "weariness of passion." As he said to David Hunter-Blair, one of his Oxford friends: "Somehow or other I'll be famous, and if not famous, I'll be notorious."[25]

Incidentally Wilde saw Keats in the same slandered light. As an undergraduate, Wilde tried to enlist the aid of Keats's biographer, Richard Monckton Milnes, in removing a medallion profile above Keats's grave, which Wilde found hideous and referred to as "this ugly libel of Keats" (*L,* 42).

Wilde's identification with Keats was complicated. He affected to deplore the popularization of Keats's love letters to Fanny Brawne, which had provoked the deprecation of Keats as a notorious sensualist. Matthew Arnold's conferral of disapproval—he disdained their "unpleasing" sexuality— probably helped to promote Keats as much as his defense of Keats as a man of

"flint and iron" who invested "intellectual and spiritual passion" in his poetry.[26] The day before the letters to Fanny Brawne were auctioned off at
Sotheby's, Wilde wrote a sonnet, "On the Sale by Auction of Keats's Love
Letters" (L, 182). Comparing the sale of the letters to the gambling by Roman
soldiers for Christ's clothes, the sonnet protests too much the invasion of a
poet's privacy:

> These are the letters that Endymion wrote
>   To one he loved in secret and apart:
>   And now the brawlers of the auction-mart
> Bargain and bid for each poor blotted note,
> Ay! for each separate pulse of passion quote
>   The merchant's price. I think, they love not art
>   Who break the crystal of a poet's heart
> That small and sickly eyes may glare or gloat.
>
> Is it not said that many years ago
>   ·   In a far Eastern town some soldiers ran
>   With torches through the midnight, and began
> To wrangle for mean raiment, and to throw
>   Dice for the garments of a wretched man,
>   Not knowing the God's wonder, or His woe? (CW, 815)

But Wilde went to the sale and actually purchased several of the letters. He
apparently had very mixed feelings about their sale and popularity.[27] In De
Profundis he referred to this sonnet when he raged against Bosie's intention to
publish letters that Wilde had sent him from Holloway Prison: "The letters
that should have been to you things sacred and secret beyond anything in the
whole world! These actually were the letters you proposed to publish for the
jaded decadent to wonder at. . . . Had there been nothing in your own heart to
cry out against so vulgar a sacrilege you might at least have remembered the
sonnet he wrote who saw with such scorn the letters of John Keats sold by
public auction in London, and have understood at last the real meaning of my
lines [here he quotes the last three lines of the octave]" (L, 455).

If Wilde had really wanted his letters to remain secret he would never have
sent them to Bosie; he was in prison because Bosie had left some of Wilde's
letters in the pocket of an old suit and a blackmailer had gotten hold of them.
Keats's masochistic attitude resembles Wilde's. Wilde wrote to Bosie from
prison: "I am going to see if I cannot make the bitter waters sweet by the
intensity of the love I bear you. . . . I am determined not to revolt but to
accept every outrage through devotion to love, to let my body be dishonoured. . . . You have been the supreme, the perfect love of my life; there can

be no other" (*L*, 397–98). Keats wrote to Fanny Brawne: "I have no limit now to my love. . . . I have been astonished that men could die martyrs for religion—I have shuddered at it. I shudder no more—I could be martyred for my religion—Love is my religion—I could die for that. I could die for you. My Creed is Love and you are its only tenet. You have ravished me away by a Power I cannot resist."[28]

To identify with Byron was for Wilde to attempt to reconcile Speranza's democratic revolutionary idealism with her ambitions toward some sort of aristocracy. She had expressed, in one of her sporadic flights from socialist ardor to social climbing, great regard for Thomas Carlyle's more reactionary views: "I quite agree with him. No democracy. Why should a rude, un-cultured mob dare to utter its voice? Let the best reign, Intellect and Ability—you and I if they choose and an admirable world we would make of it—but not the machine masses."[29] If Wilde heard such about-faces often in his youth, he must have been full of conflict indeed. In fact, the sentiments preceding her admiring remark about Carlyle completely contradict it: "Writing for money is a very dull thing compared to writing for a Revolu-tion," Speranza complains; "I am longing to light up another [revolution.] Will you help me?"[30]

Like Byron, Keats appealed to Wilde partly on snobbish grounds, not just as a poet-patriot but as a member of the English race. To the Reverend Matthew Russell, S.J., the Irish editor of the *Dublin University Magazine,* Wilde wrote in a letter: "I am so sorry you object to the words '*our* English land' [in Wilde's sonnet]. It is a noble privilege to count oneself of the same race as Keats or Shakespeare. However, I have changed it. I would not shock the feelings of your readers for anything" (*L*, 40). Needless to say, Wilde, an Irishman, was not of the same race as Keats or Shakespeare. He backed down and changed his poem in the knowledge that he would never be accepted by the English.

The letters about Keats reveal much more than Wilde's snobbery; they are full of self-revelations of his homosexual and masochistic fantasies. In a letter to Monckton Milnes, Wilde called Keats "a Martyr, and worthy to lie in the City of Martyrs [that is, Rome, where Keats is buried]. I thought of him as a Priest of Beauty slain before his time, a lovely Sebastian killed by the arrows of a lying and unjust tongue" (*L*, 41). He considered Keats's grave "the holiest place in Rome." Wilde's sonnet "The Grave of Keats" underscores this preoc-cupation with Keats as a martyr by describing him as "The youngest of the martyrs," who is "Rid of the world's injustice, and his pain" (*CW*, 776).

His choice of the adjective *lovely* to describe the image of Saint Sebastian shot full of arrows seems bizarre, unless we assume that Wilde is really expressing a different, unconscious meaning, namely, a sexual fantasy of being helplessly bound and enjoying penetration by another male. Indeed, portraits of Sebastian (like Bernini's beatific and obviously orgasmic sculpture of Saint Theresa) often portray a figure who appears to be experiencing unalloyed bliss, despite, or because of, all the "arrows" sticking into him.

After his release from prison, Wilde took the name of Sebastian Melmoth. In this name change we see an identification with Sebastian, and hence with Keats, as a martyr. There is a curious reference in one of Wilde's letters that indicates the name probably also stood for Wilde's desire to die like a hero. On 29 May 1897, Wilde wrote: "*Melmoth* is the name of that curious novel of my grand-uncle [*Melmoth the Wanderer,* by Charles Maturin]. . . . The book is now an extinct volcano, but I come from it like Empedocles, I hope, if the Gods prove kind to one who denied them" (*ML,* 148). Empedocles—who appears as a romantic hero in Matthew Arnold's poem "Empedocles on Etna"—was a philosopher who plunged into the volcanic crater on Mount Etna in an attempt to prove his divinity. Strangely enough, both Keats and Wilde's mother had used the same volcano imagery to invoke their heroic ambitions. In defending his poetry, Keats had said: "I would jump down Aetna for any great public good—but I hate a mawkish popularity."[31] Speranza had proclaimed that she was "first cousin to Aetna and half-sister to Vesuvius."[32] Her son, who in her wake felt like an "extinct volcano," still hoped to shoot off a few sparks for any worthy political cause.

Wilde, however, could never have become an active fighter like Byron and could never have showed in boyhood any of the "fine fierceness" and "rapt ardour" that he admired in Keats (*ML,* 90). The best he could do was to become an intellectual soldier, a quality expressed in his aggressive wit. He always saw himself as a hero manqué, and his final artistic effort, *The Ballad of Reading Gaol,* concerns a soldier who is executed. Because Wilde was unable to fight with pistols and swords, he allied himself with those who did. His friend Robert Sherard was always getting into brawls and wrote several books belligerently castigating anyone who had attacked Wilde. Wilde once advised him not to fight more than six duels a week (*L,* 391). In a letter to Reggie Turner, Max Beerbohm recounted, "I must tell you a sweet tale of Oscar told me by Will [Rothenstein, a portrait painter]. Will and Oscar were conducted by Sherard to a kind of thieves' cellar in Paris, where they mixed freely with the company—mostly cut-throats. Sherard, as is his wont, got drunk and frightful and rising from his chair assumed an attitude of defence, saying in a loud voice that anyone who attacked Mr Oscar Wilde would have to reckon with *him* first. 'Hush, Robert, Hush!' said Oscar, laying a white hand of plump restraint upon Sherard's shoulder, 'hush, you are defending me at the risk of my life!' Isn't it lovely?"[33] Bosie's bellicosity is legendary as well: apart from constantly picking fights with Wilde and throwing tantrums everywhere he went, he also shot off a pistol in the Berkeley Hotel (*L*, 446). After Wilde's death he was always taking people to court, or being taken to court himself, for libel. He did in fact serve six months in Wormwood Scrubs Prison in 1923 for libeling Winston Churchill. Not surprisingly, he was the son of the man who invented the Queensberry rules for boxing.[34] Pugilism ran in his family.

The Picture of Dorian Gray was one of Wilde's first major intellectual acts of aggression. It was a book designed to provoke the English, and he fought for its rights in his letters. When critics denounced it as immoral, he attacked what he saw as their anti-intellectualism. In a letter he deplored "this puritanism [of the moralistic critics] . . . that is always marring the artistic instinct of the English." The first of his letters to the editor of the *St. James Gazette,* a paper that had published an extremely negative review of the novel, might certainly be read as a record of the arrogant and utterly self-assured side of Wilde in performance, successfully living up to Speranza's heroic ideal: "Sir, I have read your criticism of my story . . . and I need hardly say that I do not propose to discuss its merits or demerits, its personalities or its lack of personality. . . . I am quite incapable of understanding how any work of art can be criticised from a moral standpoint. The sphere of art and the sphere of ethics are absolutely distinct and separate." He went on to "object . . . most strongly" to the newspaper's placarding the town with posters that read: "Mr. Oscar Wilde's Advertisement; A Bad Case" (*L*, 261).

His objections were of course calculated to ignite the ire of the editor: "Whether the expression 'A Bad Case' refers to my book or to the present position of the Government, I cannot tell." He added spitefully that it was "silly and unnecessary" of the editor to use the word "advertisement." Then he piled on the contempt:

I think I may say without vanity—though I do not wish to appear to run vanity down—that of all men in England I am the one who requires least advertisement. I am tired to death of being advertised. I feel no thrill when I see my name in a paper. . . . I wrote this book entirely for my own pleasure, and it gave me very great pleasure to write it. Whether it becomes popular or not is a matter of absolute indifference to me. I am afraid, sir, that the real advertisement is your cleverly written article [that is, the review that had blasted the book]. The English public . . . take no interest in a work of art until it is told that the work in question is immoral. (*L*, 257)

Another letter that Wilde wrote in defense of *Dorian Gray* owes something to Keats's defense of his poem *Endymion,* which also got bad reviews. Keats wrote: "I have not the slightest feel of humility towards the public. . . . I would be subdued before friends, and thank them for subduing me; but among the multitudes of men I have no feel of stooping; I hate the thought of humility to them. . . . I never wrote one single line of poetry with the least shadow of public thought."[35] Wilde develops to an extreme caricature Keats's view of this sense of independence from public opinion and insists that "the pleasure that one has in creating a work of art is a purely personal pleasure, and it is for the sake of this pleasure that one creates. The artist works with his eye on the object. Nothing else interests him. What people are likely to say does not even occur to him. . . . I write because it gives me the greatest possible aesthetic pleasure to write. If my work pleases the few, I am grati- fied. . . . As for the mob, I have no desire to be a popular novelist" (L, 266).

If emulation of Keats and Byron as heroic martyrs was part of Wilde's conflicted wish to create himself as an Ossianic warrior-bard, the results were, as one might expect, that he became a kind of hero *malgré lui*. His life, like his poems, seems a "serious parody" of their lives, to borrow a phrase from Edward Shanks, who remarked: "Wilde's downfall and his wretched death in Paris make but a sordid caricature of Byron's mysterious exile from England and his heroic death in Greece."[36] Matthew Arnold had summarized Byron's career in terms that also might have described Wilde. Arnold wrote: "We talk of Byron's *personality*. . . . The power of Byron's personality lies in . . . '*the excellence of sincerity and strength*' [Swinburne]. . . . Byron found our nation . . . fixed in a system of established facts and dominant ideas which revolted him. The mental bondage of the most powerful part of our nation, of its strong middle class, to a narrow and false system of this kind is what we call British Philistinism. . . . The great middle class, on whose impregnable Philistinism he shattered himself to pieces—how little have . . . these felt Byron's vital influence!"[37]

Reacting to this description, and seeing himself portrayed in the person of Byron, Wilde characterized Byron's achievements with great ambivalence. In "The Soul of Man under Socialism," he classes him among "a few men who have been able to realise their personalities completely." But he adds: "Most personalities have been obliged to be rebels. Half their strength has been wasted in friction. Byron's personality, for instance, was terribly wasted in battle with the stupidity, and hypocrisy, and philistinism of the English: Such battles do not always intensify strength: they often exaggerate weakness. Byron was never able to give us what he might have given us" (CW, 1084).

Wilde saw his own life being "wasted in battle with the stupidity, and hypocrisy, and philistinism of the English" and his own inability to realize his personality—to give us "what he might have given us" artistically. As a letter about *Dorian Gray* shows, he found no solution: "Lord Henry Wotton seeks to be merely the spectator of life. He finds that those who reject the battle are more deeply wounded than those who take part in it" (*L*, 259). Yet actually joining a battle only deepened Wilde's conflict: he was too much in a battle with himself to take sides.

In his most basic conflict, which underlay all others, Wilde tried to reconcile a private longing for homosexual submission with the guilt he felt for not even wanting to be a hero. In some of the letters written after he emerged from prison, he felt oppressed and shameful because of his "life of senseless pleasure and hard materialism and a mode of existence unworthy of my mother's son" (*L*, 587). In a letter of approximately 3 June 1897 he wrote to an old friend that he was "not ashamed of having been in prison" but was "thoroughly ashamed of having led a life unworthy of an artist. . . . I do not interest myself in that British view of morals that sets Messalina [the debauched wife of Emperor Claudius] above Sporus [the castrated, degraded pathic of Emperor Nero]: both pleasures are matters of temperament, and like all sensual pleasures . . . slay the soul. . . . My reckless pursuit of mundane pleasure . . . my whole attitude towards life, all these things were wrong for an artist" (*L*, 594–95).[38]

His languishing desire for penetration can be inferred from more than his identification with Saint Sebastian or his wish to be dominated by Bosie. In three letters—the one written about 3 June 1897, one postmarked 9 June 1897, and one dated 12 July 1897—Wilde reiterates his rejection of the British view that Messalina is better than Sporus but adds that "both are equally vile," a remark that reminds one how torn he felt, no matter what role he chose (*L*, 594, 621, 604).

The culmination of his conflicts was undoubtedly the perilous legal game Wilde played with the Marquess of Queensberry. It was a duel that he wanted to fight before all England and indeed all the world. In *De Profundis*, he characterized the trial as "a tragi-comedy on a high stage in History, with the whole world as the audience, and myself as the prize for the victor in the contemptible contest" (*L*, 504). Wilde's final provocation of the marquess' hatred and destructiveness did not come about by chance, through carelessness, or even through omnipotent fantasies of being able to defeat his opponent in court. Wilde reached the pinnacle of a lifelong effort when he wrestled before the public with this aristocrat, whose credentials he admired because he had adopted his mother's snobbery. He never expected any other outcome than Queensberry's victory. As he wrote in *De Profundis,* "Those of my friends who really desired my welfare implored me . . . not to face an impossible trial" (*L*, 430). Virtually everyone had warned Wilde about the inevitable outcome of the trials, and Frank Harris had even procured a yacht for a quick, adventurous getaway.[39]

Wilde made sure to get himself "raped" as a man and as an artist by this powerful Englishman; he wanted to play Sporus to Queensberry's Nero.[40] Although he said at least twice in *De Profundis* that he had not wanted to be the "catspaw" between Bosie and his father, he also alluded obliquely with another feline image to his fantasy of being overpowered and destroyed: "In the most wonderful of all his plays, Æschylus tells us of the great Lord who brings up in his house the lion-cub. . . . And the thing grows up and shows the nature of its race . . . and destroys the lord and his house and all that he possesses. I feel that I was such a one as he" (*L, 445, 462, 461*). "How I used to toy with that tiger, life," he was to remark after his release from prison. He returns again and again in *De Profundis* to this image of the powerful feline; in one place he refers to his homosexual encounters with male prostitutes as "feasting with panthers" (*L, 492*).

In the same long letter he mentions a threatening letter Queensberry had written to Bosie, which was full of "obscene threats and coarse violences" (*L, 445*). He goes on to reveal that for Queensberry the trials had been great sport: "As for the cost of the trial, you may be interested to know that your father openly said in the Orleans club that if it had cost him £20,000 he would have considered the money thoroughly well spent, he had extracted such enjoyment, and delight, and triumph out of it all. The fact that he was able not merely to put me in prison for two years, but to take me out for an afternoon and make me a public bankrupt was an extra refinement of pleasure . . . the crowning point of my humiliation, and of his complete and perfect victory." (Queensberry, incidentally, had a paranoid streak that barely covered his own deeply repressed homosexuality; late in life, and after Wilde's imprisonment, he complained of being hounded by "the Oscar Wilders.")[41]

In his courtroom drama Wilde made sure to include a poetic and stirring defense of homosexuality. In his performance before the court he was an Irish hero and a martyr for his mother's sake: symbolically he was penetrated by his father in that self-destructive moment. The Marquess of Queensberry had been made to play the role of the unconscious father, and Wilde played both sides of his mother's role as he saw it. With her masculine fervor she had provoked scenes in courtrooms, sparring with his father's mistress at one trial and loudly claiming victory for a seditious article in another. He also played her unconscious feminine role: Speranza had struggled all her life with a conflict between her desire to be a warrior and her masochistic enjoyment of self-abasement. In October 1849, while a young woman, she wrote in a letter: "I am indignant to be obliged to follow Zenobia like the Elijah chariot wheels of my conqueror but after all, like a true woman, I love to be a slave when I find a real King."[42] About one year later she wrote: "I am trying to subdue the melancholy in me by exercise. I ride twice a week and canter furiously—do you know this *ruling* is a grand thing—even a horse and yet in love I like to feel myself a slave—the difficulty is to find anyone capable of ruling me. I love them when I feel their power."[43]

It seems that Bosie was a means to this ultimate goal—a mere detour, a stand-in, and not the real object of Wilde's love at all. Wilde himself was often mystified by his love of Bosie and somehow perceived that he was attracted to Bosie's destructiveness. In a letter of 23 September 1897 he wrote enigmatically: "He ruined my life and so for that very reason I seem forced to love him more: and I think that now [that he is finally here visiting] I shall do lovely work" (*L*, 648).

Wilde sensed that the scene he succeeded in creating with the marquess was a re-creation of an earlier scene or fantasy. In a letter of early 1886, he says: "Our most fiery moments of ecstasy are merely shadows of what somewhere else we have felt, or of what we long someday to feel. . . . I know there is no such thing as a new experience at all" (*L*, 185). One might even say that the purpose of Wilde's art was to rehearse the supreme act of identification with his mother for the purpose of becoming the love object of his father, being castrated ("beheaded" like Jokanaan in *Salome*), and finally being annihilated. The purpose of his life was to stage this unconscious fantasy in reality. Essentially his courtroom drama put the finishing touches on his life, which he spoke of as a work of art: having played out his deepest fantasy in the arena of a London court, he seems to have felt that the life into which he had put his genius was finished, so that he had less and less interest in producing art. As he wrote to Frank Harris on 13 June 1897, "I no longer make *roulades* of phrases about the deep things I feel. When I write directly to you I speak directly. Violin-variations don't interest me" (*L*, 609). Wilde was tired. To Robert Ross he wrote: "Bosie has also written to me to say he is on the eve of a duel! . . . I have written to him to beg him *never* to fight duels, as once one does it one has to go on. And though it is not dangerous, like our English cricket or football is, still it is a tedious game to be always playing" (*L*, 592).

In spite of his fatigue, he wanted to wage war against prison abuse and tried to do so by enlisting the aid of reformers who were in sympathy with his mother's political goals. He asked some of them to write letters to the papers about prison reform. To Michael Davitt, an Irish writer and politician who "had been frequently imprisoned for Fenian, land league, and similar activities," Wilde wrote: "I have been sent a cutting from a Liverpool paper which states that you intend to ask a question about the treatment of A.2.II [an insane prisoner named Prince] in Reading Prison. . . . I sincerely hope that you are *in some way* stirring in this matter. No one knows better than yourself how terrible life in an English prison is" (*L,* 586). By May 1898 he felt that he had been somewhat successful in his efforts at reform: "I think that, aided by some splendid personalities like Davitt and John Burns, I have been able to deal a heavy and fatal blow at the monstrous prison-system of English justice. There is to be no more starvation, or sleeplessness, nor endless silence, nor eternal solitude, nor brutal floggings. The system is exposed, and, so, doomed" (*L,* 851).

Wilde wrote several long essaylike letters on prison reform to the editor of the *Daily Chronicle,* who published them. Written in remarkably straightforward language addressed to a broad audience, the letters reveal the mind of a precise, compassionate observer of human suffering; they show an entirely different side of the man whose trademark was cynicism and who by this time was regarded by the public as a fiend, a reckless destroyer of the lives of young boys. In one of them he outlines, with great simplicity, the abuses of prison:

> The necessary reforms are very simple. They concern the needs of the body and the needs of the mind of each unfortunate prisoner.
> With regard to the first, there are three permanent punishments authorised by law in English prisons:
>   1. Hunger
>   2. Insomnia
>   3. Disease
> The food supplied to prisoners is entirely inadequate. (*L,* 722)

Discussing cruelty to children in prisons, Wilde describes a small boy he had seen "in the dimly lit cell right opposite my own. . . . The child's face was like a white wedge of sheer terror. There was in his eyes the terror of a hunted animal. The next morning I heard him at breakfast-time crying, and calling to be let out. His cry was for his parents. From time to time I could hear the deep voice of the warder on duty telling him to keep quiet."

Wilde observes that the child "was not even convicted of whatever little offence he had been charged with. He was simply on remand. That I knew by his wearing his own clothes, which seemed neat enough. He was, however, wearing prison socks and shoes. This showed that he was a very poor boy, whose own shoes, if he had any, were in a bad state."

Wilde goes to great lengths to explain the psychological effects of prison on children: "People today do not understand what cruelty is. They regard it as a sort of terrible mediaeval passion, and connect it with the race of men like Eccelino da Romano, and others, to whom the deliberate infliction of pain gave a real madness of pleasure. But men of the stamp of Eccelino are merely abnormal types of perverted individualism. Ordinary cruelty is simply stupidity. It is the entire want of imagination." Wilde condemns the "want of imagination" that fails to understand "the peculiar psychology of a child's nature. A child can understand a punishment inflicted by an individual, such as a parent or guardian, and bear it with a certain amount of acquiescence. What it cannot understand is a punishment inflicted by society. It cannot realise what society is." He goes on to explain that because of this "the terror of a child in prison is quite limitless."

After making recommendations for the treatment of children in prison, including the sort of food they should be allowed to have and their education, Wilde goes on to protest the flogging of the half-witted inmate named Prince, who, Wilde writes, was "becoming insane, and being treated as if he were shamming." In vivid, poetic language he evokes with sympathy the man's condition: "There, in the beautiful sunlight, walked this poor creature . . . grinning like an ape, and making with his hands the most fantastic gestures, as though he was playing in the air on some invisible stringed instrument, or arranging and dealing counters in some curious game. All the while these hysterical tears, without which none of us ever saw him, were making soiled runnels in his white swollen face."

With pitiless detail he makes us almost eyewitnesses to the man's flogging: "On Saturday week last I was in my cell at about one o'clock occupied in cleaning and polishing the tins I had been using for dinner. Suddenly I was startled by the prison silence being broken by the most horrible and revolting shrieks, or rather howls, for at first I thought some animal like a bull or cow was being unskillfully slaughtered outside the prison walls. . . . He had had twenty-four lashes in the cookhouse on Saturday afternoon" (L, 573). Wilde wrote several letters in hopes of preventing Prince from being beaten again. His pleas were ignored, and a week later, on 6 June 1897, he reported to Robert Ross: "It makes me sick to think that [he] has been flogged again. It fills me with despair" (L, 599).

Apart from such attempts at reform, Wilde made one final literary effort, *The Ballad of Reading Gaol*. This tale of a soldier hanged for murdering his wife might be seen as Wilde's final reflection on his own role as an unwilling soldier in his mother's lifelong war. He was torn by conflict throughout the writing and felt that he was never able to make it a great poem. In a letter he wrote: "The poem suffers under the difficulties of a divided aim in style. Some is realistic, some romantic: some poetry, some propaganda. I feel it keenly, but as a whole I think the production interesting: that it is interesting from more points of view than one is artistically to be regretted" (*L*, 654). In another letter he wrote, "I am occupied in finishing a poem, terribly realistic for me, and drawn from actual experience, a sort of denial of my own philosophy of art in many ways. I hope it is good, but every night I hear cocks crowing in Berneval, so I am afraid I may have denied myself, and would weep bitterly, if I had not wept away all my tears" (*L*, 751). Wilde was living in Berneval, France, at the time. His remark about the cocks crowing indicates that he saw himself as both Judas and Christ. Knowing that he would never regain his heroic laurels in the form of admiration of his artistry by the English, he doubted the worth of his art. He wondered "whether it is worthwhile fighting on against the hideous forces of the world. Personally I don't think it is, but Vanity, that great impulse, still drives me to think of a possible future of self-assertion" (*L*, 676). In the heydays of his successful comedies, his art helped him feel as though he had become a hero as a successful playwright who lorded it over the English. In a world that ostracized him, he was no longer able to achieve this artistic heroism.

But if the greatness of a human being can be measured by attempts to rise above conflicts, then Wilde did achieve a certain heroism. With resolution and humor he tried to accept what had happened to him and to accept himself at his best and worst. He knew that he had set himself an impossible task, as a letter to Robert Ross reveals: "This is my first day alone, and of course a very unhappy one. I begin to realise my terrible position of isolation, and I have been rebellious and bitter of heart all day. Is it not sad? I thought I was accepting everything so well. . . . I found a little chapter, full of the most fantastic saints . . . with smiles carved to a *rictus*, almost, like primitive things. . . . I laughed with amusement when I saw them" (*L*, 576).

He was laughing at himself and at his ability to force a grin to cover his despair. In a letter of early June 1897 he longs for his own chalet, where he could be "not king over others—I am tired of that—but a king without subjects, *un roi dans le desert,* lord over my own soul only, over my own soul at last" (*L*, 597). When he was just beginning work on *The Ballad of Reading Gaol* he wrote, rather desperately, "For myself, of course, the aim of life is to realise one's *own* personality—one's *own* nature, and now, as before, it is through Art that I realise what is in me" (*L*, 751). He was pleading with himself to be himself, but he could not choose who to be. As he wrote in December 1897, "I was a problem for which there was no solution" (*L*, 685). At times like this, he reminds us of the Herod in one of Johann Nestroy's parodies, who wishes to know who is stronger: I, or I.

In his despairing effort to accept everything, he accepted too much: "I am leading a very good life, and it does not agree with me," he wrote at one point (*ML*, 176). But as long as he could still smile and play, he got some enjoyment from his ruined life. In a letter crammed with exclamation points and child- ish glee he describes a fete with strawberries, cakes, apricots, and grenadine syrup that he held for the little children of Berneval in celebration of Queen Victoria's jubilee. Although he reverted almost immediately to his old life with a vengeance and sprinkled his letters with anecdotes about teenage boys whose homosexual favors he had enjoyed, his perseverance in the face of the universal rejection he had so dreaded was extraordinary. As he wrote, "To have survived at all—to have come out sane in mind and sound of body—is a thing so marvellous to me, that it seems to me sometimes, not that the age of miracles is over, but that it is only just beginning" (*L*, 607).

CHAPTER 4 THE DIALECTICS OF *THE IMPORTANCE OF BEING EARNEST*

In a letter of August 1897, written just a few months after his release from prison, Wilde wrote, "Nemesis has caught me in her net: to struggle is foolish. Why is it that one runs to one's ruin? Why has destruction such a fascination? Why, when one stands on a pinnacle, must one throw one-self down? No one knows, but things are so" (L, 629). A cruel dialectic had always driven him to fill, in an endless round, two opposite roles. To be hero and victor or martyr and victim for the Irish revolution: these were the imperatives he felt his mother had thrust upon him. Speranza could never decide which role she preferred for herself and so foisted the dilemma onto her son.[1]

Wilde sought endlessly the impossible resolution of this problem. The increase of success in one role intensified his need to succeed in the other. A letter of July 1894, written when *The Importance of Being Earnest* was incubating in his mind, complains: "I . . . went and sat with my mother. Death and Love seem to walk on either hand as I go through life: they are the only things I think of, their wings shadow me" (L, 358). During Oscar's trials, she threatened to disown him if he left London, although all his friends had urged him to flee: "If you stay, even if you go to prison, you will always be my son, but if you go, I will never speak to you again."[2] It was difficult to sustain simultaneously the glory of victory and the pain of defeat, except perhaps during the stirring moments in his trial when he gave the impassioned speech on the "Love that dare not speak its name." He made a hostile British courtroom audience applaud his daring performance and sympathize momentarily with the plight of the homosexual in society. He had bought this success with his final self-destruction. *Ananke,* or inexorable necessity, drove him from one side of his conflict to the other in a perpetual whirlwind of infernal choices and made Oscar Wilde the jester into a tragic figure.

It is one of the curious facts of Wilde's life that he owed his enormous success as a literary figure to his homosexual enslavement by Lord Alfred Douglas. The relationship began with the conquest of Bosie: "I . . . saw quite clearly . . . my position in the world of Art, the interest my personality had always excited, my money, the luxury in which I lived, the thousand and one things that went to make up a life so charmingly, so wonderfully improbable as mine was, each and all of them, elements that fascinated you and made you cling to me," Wilde wrote in *De Profundis* (*L*, 445).

Bosie's autobiography makes it clear that Wilde was right. Bosie had fallen in love with the public Oscar Wilde, the Lord Henry Wotton in *The Picture of* ✓ *Dorian Gray,* the Lord Darlington in *Lady Windermere's Fan,* the Lord Illingworth in *A Woman of No Importance,* and the Lord Goring in *An Ideal Husband:* "I was a boy and he was a blasé and very intellectual and brilliant man who had immense experience."[3] Frank Harris claims that at the first meeting with Wilde, Bosie "admired him, hung upon his lips with his soul in his eye" and that "Oscar was . . . enormously affected by . . . Lord Alfred Douglas' name and position. . . . No doubt Oscar talked his best [at their first meeting] because he was talking to Lord Alfred Douglas."[4] Bosie tried to amend this portrayal of himself, writing that "what really happened, of course, at that interview was just the ordinary exchange of courtesies." But he could not help confessing that "I was very much impressed, much more than I have admitted."[5]

Winning this young aristocrat was a social triumph that made Wilde feel he had finally become a peer. Bosie, despite his insignificance, was the son of the Marquess of Queensberry, a Scottish noble with an inherited title and an influential, though notorious, representative of British aristocracy. This success drove Wilde inexorably to failure. In spite of, or rather because of, his triumph, he was immediately the victim of emotional turmoil, for he felt tortured by Bosie. In a letter of March 1893 he begs him not to "make scenes with me. They kill me. . . . I cannot see you, so Greek and gracious, distorted with passion" (*L*, 336). In November of the same year he wrote, as he did more than once, to Bosie's mother, to complain that Bosie was "sleepless, nervous and rather hysterical . . . aimless, unhappy, and absurd" (*L*, 346). Even in a letter Wilde wrote to Bosie in the highest spirits, to crow about how well the writing of *Earnest* was going, he sighed at the end: "When we are out of tune, all colour goes from things for me, but we are never really out of tune" (*L*, 363). Swooning in Bosie's arms, yielding to his every whim, Wilde felt guilt about enjoying domination rather than being dominating.

Until 1891, the year he met Bosie, Wilde as a writer had expressed mainly the private, retiring side of his personality—the philosophical, introspective,

humanistic Oscar Wilde rather than the Mephistophelian dandy he presented to the public. Before 1892, the wit that charmed and conquered the
English, the wit that reverberates throughout his comedies, was manifested
mostly in his public behavior and his personal letters, not so much in his art.
Wilde's need to impress Bosie, and to generate the considerable capital
needed to maintain him in style, changed all that. Nothing sold better than
Wilde's wit. His best known, most public voice, the voice that lit up drawing
rooms and made Bosie fall in love with him, the repartee, quick and deadly as
pistol shots, now became the voice of his art.

Without such a pressing need for cash, Wilde might have continued to
spend his wit freely at social occasions without exploiting its commercial
possibilities. He might have remained a witty gentleman. Given the added
expenses of life with Bosie, however, he began to turn his wit into financial
gain. But his bondage to Bosie was creative not only financially but also
artistically. His extreme ambivalence toward the British aristocracy, expressed through his aggression as well as his libidinal longing, became sublimated as the basic theme of his comedies. The relationship to Bosie stimulated his wish for acceptance as a peer—not just as an equal but as an official
member of the peerage. That yearning provoked his ever-ready criticism of
this social class. In all his comedies, he laughs at his attempts to ingratiate
himself with nobility and his equally strong wish to kick them where it hurt
most.

The docile submissiveness to Bosie mobilized Wilde toward a fighting Irish
provocation of the "screaming scarlet Marquis," as he called Bosie's father.
Wilde, ready and needing to fight, found Bosie's father a worthy enemy. An
aggressive pugilist fond of impromptu public sparring, the Marquess of
Queensberry provoked Wilde adroitly, making scenes at the Café Royal,
throwing a tantrum at Wilde's home, and plotting to disrupt the opening
night of The Importance of Being Earnest by throwing a grotesque bouquet of
phallic vegetables at Wilde.

Meanwhile, Wilde's status, through his association with Bosie, had risen so
much in his own mind that he began to see Bosie's status as sufficient support
for asserting his homosexuality even more openly. An inflated sense of self-
importance was leading to scenes like one remembered by Backhouse, who
recounts how he, Wilde, and Verlaine all got drunk on champagne and
adjourned to the Moulin Rouge, "where it happened that the heir to the
Throne of England, Albert Edward Prince of Wales, was conferring the honour of his presence. . . . After the performance, we all formed a sort of line of
honour for the passing of the great man. Oscar told us, purring with high
satisfaction: 'You'll see that His Royal Highness will stop and speak to me,' but

he was too optimistic, for, though Albert Edward evidently recognised Wilde, he absolutely ignored him and passed out to his waiting brougham without a bow."[6]

Wilde's inflated self-confidence was bruised by this encounter. As he was happily writing to Bosie that "my play is really very funny: I am quite delighted with it," he had become angry enough to defend his honor as a homosexual against his attacker: "Your father is on the rampage again—been to Café Royal to enquire for us, with threats etc. I think now it would have been better for me to have had him bound over to keep the peace, but what a scandal! Still, it is intolerable to be dogged by a maniac" (L, 362, 360).

Throughout this period—the early and mid-1890s—Wilde and Bosie were flagrant in their public display of affection toward each other as well as toward young grooms, newspaper boys, and male prostitutes. At the height of his career as a writer, Wilde felt he had the authority to take the stage as an obvious homosexual, convinced that his protests would be dignified by his status as an intellectual in the artistic and social empyrean. It is difficult to say how much of all this was the result of conscious deliberation or of unconscious impetuosity.

With the brilliant success of his last play, The Importance of Being Earnest, which Max Beerbohm and others hailed as a masterpiece, Wilde conquered the English. He was an Irish hero. The reviewer for the New York Times gushed that "Oscar Wilde may be said to have at last, and by a single stroke, put his enemies under his feet."[7] Nearly all the critics now outdid themselves trying to place the thickest crown of laurels on the head of a playwright whose earlier comedic efforts, though adored by the British public, had drawn mixed reviews from the British press. With Earnest Wilde won the almost unanimous praise of the British press and the heart of the public. Only another Irishman, George Bernard Shaw, denigrated the play—and one cannot help thinking that his reaction came out of sheer envy.[8] Recalling those days of heady success, Wilde's old friend Ada Leverson wrote: "It is really difficult to convey now in words the strange popularity, the craze there was at this moment for the subject of my essay; 'To meet Mr. Oscar Wilde' was put on the most exclusive of invitation cards."[9]

Wilde's conquest of the British was now beyond challenge. He possessed the body as well as the soul of the eminent Lord Queensberry's son. And he had made thousands of pounds with his comedies, which were playing to packed houses: A Woman of No Importance alone brought its author one hundred pounds a week.[10] When, if not now, would it be time for him to face the battle? The cause for which he began to mobilize himself was ambiguous: was it Irish patriotism or the civil rights of the homosexual? They merged in his mind. In a letter written after his prison term he remarked: "A patriot put in prison for loving his country loves his country, and a poet put in prison for loving boys loves boys" (L, 705).

The four comedies, although they are not part of an integrated whole, seem to culminate in The Importance of Being Earnest. They can be understood as the visible part of his increasingly oppressive conflict. In his first three comedies, he attempts to conquer by deliberately tempering his rage against the British, making the aristocracy on stage arrogant, empty, supercilious, and exploitative, yet charming, splendidly behaved, brilliantly witty, and at least occasionally moral. His emotional involvement is evident only upon close inspection. It sneaks into the text, producing the tragic choices and heroic renunciations of characters in these comedies. It is important to note, however, that what he invented for his characters was eventually played out in his own life. He was drawing up the blueprints for his own catastrophe when he wrote his funniest plays.

Mrs. Erlynne of Lady Windermere's Fan, for example, does not reveal that she is the mother of Lady Windermere, whom she abandoned as an infant. The daughter has fantasies about her long-lost mother's purity, fantasies that would be demolished if she found out that Mrs. Erlynne, a woman with a considerable past, is her mother. Mrs. Erlynne accepts the martyrdom that society has inflicted on her for her sexual sin, as Wilde was to do later. She is a fallen woman, treated as an outcast. Her daughter will never know she exists: this was exactly Wilde's punishment after his prison term. His sons were not allowed to see him or even to know where he lived, and like Mrs. Erlynne, he tried to console himself with "not repentance, but pleasure" (CW, 425).

There is Mrs. Arbuthnot of A Woman of No Importance. Just like Wilde following his imprisonment, she becomes a recluse from society and goes about under an assumed name in the hope that no one will discover her son's illegitimacy and shame the two of them. In De Profundis, Wilde alludes to his own social and moral isolation by quoting one of her lines in the play: "Where I walk there are thorns" (CW, 467). There seems to be at least an unconscious connection between the play and the eventual fate of its author. He sums up his situation with another of Mrs. Arbuthnot's lines: "[for me] the world is shrivelled to a handsbreadth" (L, 470).

In his first three comedies, Wilde's conflict can be discovered even in the literary form of his work, in the uneasy, surprisingly inappropriate mixture of farce and morality play, as when Hester, a prim young woman, dampens a marvelous stream of wit with puritan moralizing about English society, which she sees as "shallow, selfish, foolish . . . all wrong, all wrong" (CW, 449). The curious descents in Wilde's first three comedies, from sharp wit to strident moralizing, evaporate in the paradoxes of *The Importance of Being Earnest*. The first three comedies show an embittered Wilde, the homosexual outcast who thunders against his society like his alter ego, Jokanaan. Not a trace of this humorless disapproval remains in *The Importance of Being Earnest*. No dour Jokanaan formulates confrontations. Instead, paradoxes take over, guilefully embracing rather than confronting opposing views. Upper-class British gentlemen accept and reject matrimony: they plan to marry but would not dream of allowing such a trifle as matrimony to interfere with extramarital amusements. "Why is it that at a bachelor's establishment the servants invariably drink the champagne? I merely ask for information," inquires Algernon. Lane, the butler, replies: "I have often observed that in married households the champagne is rarely of a first-rate brand." That paves the way for Algernon's and Wilde's chief point: "Good heavens! is marriage so demoralizing as that?" (*CW,* 321).

Only while he was writing his last play did Wilde relinquish the idea that he might find a compromise that would allow him to go on living without provoking a catastrophe. Like the protagonist of a Greek drama, he accepts the inevitability of a tragic end, the insolubility of his conflict. The uninterrupted laughter throughout *Earnest* and the avoidance of descents into shrill morality that had marred his earlier plays are the result of his acceptance. "The increasing seriousness of things . . . that's the great opportunity of jokes," wrote Henry James, whom Wilde considered to have little sense of humor.[11] "Life is far too important a thing ever to talk seriously about it," Wilde remarked at the time when he was plotting his downfall (*CW,* 390). The entire *Importance of Being Earnest* declares that the whole of life is a joke. For the public, the title was a joke; for Wilde it was a warning and a prediction. It was indeed important to remind himself how earnest his situation was. He remarked in conversation: "Humanity takes itself too seriously. It is the world's original sin. If the cavemen had known how to laugh, history would have been different."[12] In *A Woman of No Importance,* he writes: "The world has always laughed at its own tragedies, that being the only way in which it has been able to bear them. . . . Consequently, whatever the world has treated seriously belongs to the comedy side of things" (*CW,* 462).

In *The Importance of Being Earnest,* laughter does much more than entertain the English. It was a curtain behind which he was preparing his end. Wilde laughs because he is free now to understand the inevitability of his fate. He relaxes, like the suicide who has made the fatal decision. Knowing well that his love of demolishing British mores reflects his ineligibility for a listing in Debrett's *Peerage,* he lets the formidable Lady Bracknell, the gorgon of British society, remark: "Never speak disrespectfully of society. . . . Only people who can't get into it do that" (*CW*, 374). He has the freedom to reveal this now that his brilliant play writing has insured his increased standing in British society.

A letter written in August 1894, while he was working on *The Importance of Being Earnest*, reveals his readiness to abandon all attempts to control his fate: "My play . . . lies in Sibylline leaves about the room, and Arthur [the butler] has twice made a chaos of it by 'tidying up.' The result, however, was rather dramatic. I am inclined to think that Chaos is a stronger evidence for an Intelligent Creator than Kosmos is: the view might be expanded" (*L*, 362). He feared, yet at the same time welcomed, the chaos that would come. The integration of his personality was weakening. His syphilis had also had sufficient time to ferment. By asserting that chaos was evidence of an intelligent creator, he tried to see his disintegration as a great creative culmination. Detecting similar thoughts almost a half-century later in Thomas Mann's *Dr. Faustus*, one may be inclined to think that Wilde intuitively saw connections between syphilitic deterioration, perhaps in gradual loss of inhibition and the surprising increase of creative output.

It is difficult to consider Wilde's provocation of Queensberry as simply a sudden outburst of rage. Consciously it was a defense against Queensberry's attempt to expose Wilde as a homosexual.[13] Unconsciously it was more complicated. While Queensberry went around trying to pick fights with Wilde, Wilde could, by suing him, call London's attention to the problem of being a homosexual, thus unconsciously calling attention to his own homosexuality. To call attention to one's sexuality is the expression of a sexual wish, a sexual dare. Queensberry's behavior sent such a message. Judging by his obsessive interest in Wilde and his paranoid thoughts of being "hounded by the Oscar Wilders," he allowed Wilde glimpses of unconscious sexual excitement. One day he told his son that he was not surprised at Bosie's fondness for Wilde, calling Wilde "a wonderful man." But that same afternoon Queensberry sent a letter filled with disgust and threats to cut off funds if Bosie continued to see him.[14] Wilde took up the glove. The urge to sue the marquess became irresistible: "The only way to get rid of a temptation is to yield to it." Consciously Wilde felt, as he complained to Bosie, that he had been forced to "wrestle with Caliban." After joking himself through life and through three comedies that gave him the status he had desired, and finding himself at the crest of a victorious career as an English writer, Wilde felt driven to force the world he had conquered to see and accept that the brilliant playwright was a homosexual. It had now become important to be truly earnest. Everything had to be risked. A homosexual Irishman challenged the English world.

Provoking Queensberry also meant unconsciously squaring things with his own father. Convoluted as his relationship with his father was, it is not difficult to see that the challenge of Queensberry was the endgame of Wilde's Oedipal conflict. An impressionable and sensitive ten-year-old when his father's insane lover, Mary Travers, sued his mother for libel after she complained to Mary's father, Oscar probably felt dishonored by his father's public philandering. The crude jingles sung about his parents after the infamous trial that impoverished his father and shamed his mother would not have reassured him about his legitimacy or anything else. About eleven years later, at the time of his father's death, when Oscar was a university student, he spoke with great admiration of his mother's tolerance in allowing one of his father's lovers to sit by his deathbed, heavily veiled in black. His plays are filled with characters who, like Jack Worthing in *Earnest,* are either illegitimate or misinformed about who their parents are.

Oscar, probably also envious of his father's exploits, grew up to emulate him by becoming a highly public philanderer himself. The episode with Queensberry has a double function: it can be seen as an attempt to fight his father and to submit to him sexually. Though young Oscar resented his father's philandering, he must have resented even more being passed over for the women in his father's affections. With a grand gesture he embarked upon becoming the ultimate Oedipal victor and victim: to kill and to submit to his father at once was a dialectical triumph.[15]

Writing under pressure to make money, he took the ready-made plot of his double life as a homosexual and spoofed it in the double lives of Jack and Algernon. The first three plays had raised him to the intellectual heights of his generation, but the fourth, he felt, should take him to the summit and be the comedy of all comedies. What was to be the narrative? Something totally unimportant so that spur-of-the-moment solutions to any private conflicts that arose as he was writing the play could be easily inserted at any point. It must unmask the empty formalities of the English mores of his day, naturally. He summoned all his talents. Marriage and hidden lives had been a focus of his interest for some time. Marriage was not just his personal problem but a great problem of English high society at that time. Jack's supposed illegitimacy crept into his thinking as a derivative of most painful self-doubts. The conflicting unconscious visions of his future would show up—his being revealed as an aristocrat and his going to prison as a social outcast. The bitter recognition that life was earnest had to be laughed at as if it were a stupid joke.

He had lived for this end. The more successful he became, the more he knew that the time had come accidentally; he had gotten into position to fight the last battle by suing Lord Queensberry for libel. He knew that the public humiliation would come, having been sufficiently warned. At the same time he had a curious sense that the result of his action would at least offer relief from his life of constant doubt. It would take all choice out of his hands. And there was another secret element in this last dramatic arrangement. His humiliation, if it came, and it would come, was what his mother had wanted. Thereby it could be both a gift for her and a punishment: "Each man kills the thing he loves" (*CW*, 844).

This last comedy, the final flourish in his lifelong struggle to assume the roles thrust upon him by his mother, is thus a drama of identity and at the same time of the death of his identities. The main characters, Jack and Algy, are so interchangeable in dress and spirit, as are the women, Gwendolen and Cecily, that Wilde seems to want to impress on his audience that they have no identities of their own. They are carbon copies. The scene in which the women ask the men questions in unison, and the men reply in unison, brings home this denial of difference. At the same time, there is an artificial splitting of characters into several different identities: Jack and Algy both adopt the name of Ernest in order to assume another role. Identity is unstable: easily assumed, carelessly discarded.

The marriage theme that dominates the play may have arisen, at least in part, from Wilde's recognition that by going around openly as a homosexual, he had brought his marriage almost to the point of collapse. In his last comedy his characters do what he liked to pretend he never did in real life: they disguise themselves when they want to do something they consider wicked or socially unacceptable. Jack explains the reason for his two identities as Jack and Ernest by saying that he has to adopt a "very high moral tone on all subjects" in his role as guardian to young Cecily but that "as a high moral tone can hardly be said to conduce very much to either one's health or one's happiness if carried to excess, in order to get up to town I have always pretended to have a younger brother of the name of Ernest, who . . . gets into the most dreadful scrapes" (*CW*, 326). English gentlemen hid their forbidden activities behind other names or identities; Irish heroes and martyrs would not.

In a letter of February 1892, written shortly after Wilde completed the first of his famous series of social satires, *Lady Windermere's Fan,* he insisted that comedy was a serious business: "To those of us who do not look on a play as a mere question of pantomime and clowning, psychological interest is everything" (*L,* 313). Although Wilde's comedies look quite flippant and seem free of any serious message, they were always serious expressions of trenchant social criticism. Wilde's wit opens a door into a world of social and psychological truth that the hilarious surface of his comedies does not lead one to suspect. The main ingredients of his wit are easily identified: he overturns trite truisms and stands social mores on their head: "I hope you have not been leading a double life, pretending to be wicked and really being good all the time. That would be hypocrisy" (CW, 343). Every quip in the play—and there is quip after quip after quip—follows this principle. The question is, why, when his method of producing mental pyrotechnics seems so monotonously unchanging, does every flash still surprise and even delight us? Why don't we get tired of the formula? Why don't we get bored?

The title almost promises a colossal bore: *The Importance of Being Earnest* sounds like a moralistic tract, not a comedy. But we soon detect that the title was meant in earnest. In an interview, Wilde enlarged upon the philosophy of the play: "We should treat all the trivial things of life very seriously, and all the serious things of life with sincere and studied triviality."[16] What is serious in Wilde's trivial wit are well-placed arrows aimed at British pretension: "I was obliged to call on dear Lady Harbury. I hadn't been there since her poor husband's death. I never saw a woman so altered; she looks quite twenty years younger," Lady Bracknell announces (CW, 328). She exposes the hypocrisy of unfelt or unneeded social proprieties: she is ever so compassionate; then, with a lightning turn of phrase, she annihilates. The greatest heresy in England is to proclaim that one is different, to refuse to blend in with time-honored customs of how things are done or are not done. But Wilde, in all of his witty japes, is announcing that he is not just different but illicitly different, and hinting that he is going to live openly as a homosexual. The style of the quips reveals his conflict between wanting to show, ostentatiously and fearlessly, that he is different and being afraid to do so. He compromises by revealing that he is different but leaves the nature of his difference obscure.

The merciless repetition of this formula—never outwardly rejecting social convention but killing it by turning it upside down—becomes in his hands a serious technique for dramatizing the essential relativity of truth. In *An Ideal Husband* Wilde defined falsehoods as "the truths of other people." Wilde did not even wish to disguise his formula; he advertised his literary method for jokes. *The Importance of Being Earnest* is his manifesto. One feels that by his wit he frees himself and tries to free his audience, at least momentarily, from all inhibitions.

Wilde achieved his aim of disguising the trivial as serious and vice versa through the use of paradox, a style produced by the dialectical tension between his opposing life goals. Paradox balances and complements one truth with its opposite, so that "truth" is a continually evolving synthesis of thesis and antithesis. "The very essence of romance is uncertainty. If I ever get married I'll certainly try to forget the fact," remarks a young dandy in the opening scene of *The Importance of Being Earnest*. Paradoxically, the very thing that dulls a romance is absolute certainty, the evaporation of mystery. Uncertainty creates doubt and anxiety, but Wilde, in an existentialist mood, attempting to fulfill opposing wishes, saw the same silly propensity in all mankind, who, as Montaigne pointed out, is "as fit to be laughed at as able to laugh."[17] The "very essence of romance," which is hoping, wishing, and dreaming of fulfillment, dies as soon as one is certain of a partner's love and fidelity. Wilde observed, as did Freud and number of romantic poets, that romantic love thrives on expectation and frustration, never on fulfillment.

He perfects the form of the paradox in *The Importance of Being Earnest*. Its seemingly silly, nonsensical inversions of commonplace truisms are direct hits on British civilization, especially one of its cornerstones, the institution of marriage: "Divorces are made in heaven," remarks Algernon, an aristocrat of this civilization. This looks like trivial fluff, but it was a criticism pointed at the heart of the attitude of the Anglican church toward marriage: "What . . . God hath joined together let not man put asunder."[18] He must have known that he spoke for his generation. Marriage has always had a bad press, but Wilde gave divorce a heavenly seal of approval. A remark he made in "The Truth of Masks" sums up the dialectic of *The Importance of Being Earnest*: "In art, there is no such thing as universal truth. A Truth in art is that whose contradictory is also true" (*CW*, 1078).

Even Wilde's characters are paradoxes. Lady Bracknell, dowager of an important family, is a formidable symbol of power and privilege, adamantly opposed to marriages of unequal rank. But she is herself an arriviste who married for money: "I do not approve of mercenary marriages. When I married Lord Bracknell I had no fortune of any kind. But I never dreamed for a moment of allowing that to stand in my way" (*CW*, 374). She is what she isn't, and yet she is. Algy, her nephew, is "an extremely . . . an ostentatiously eligible young man. He has nothing, but he looks everything" (*CW*, 375). Algy's friend Jack, a foundling of indeterminate social origin, is a highborn scion of the aristocracy. Lady Bracknell's daughter, Gwendolen, engaged to Jack and apparently in love, assures him, "I never change, except in my affections" (*CW*, 382). The picture of respectable femininity and conventional opinion, Gwendolen is enviably uninhibited about announcing that what she finds most attractive in a man is weakness: "Outside the family circle, papa, I am glad to say, is entirely unknown. I think that is quite as it should be. The home seems to me to be the proper sphere for the man. And certainly once a man begins to neglect his domestic duties he becomes painfully effeminate, does he not? And that makes men so very attractive" (*CW*, 362).

All this sounds like the material of which thousands of farces are made, and yet one senses that these remarks hide a truth. They seem asocial, even antisocial, but they are neither. They merely show two sides of social convention in an unending dialectical struggle. Without serious content, Wilde's wit could not have survived a century of great social conflict so triumphantly. In Gwendolen Fairfax's dialogue, Wilde shows that he knows the trick of justifying feminism by praising male chauvinism, while at the same time making feminism laughable.[19] He dramatizes a remark he made in *A Woman of No Importance:* "Women love us for our defects. If we have enough of them, they will forgive us everything, even our own gigantic intellects" (*CW*, 463).

From the opening line of *The Importance of Being Earnest*, Wilde does not know which is more amusing—the approval or the denial of class distinctions. Act 1 begins with Algernon, a young dandy, playing the piano. He asks his butler, "Did you hear what I was playing, Lane?" Ideally the English butler personifies paradox: he is the perfect servant in the person of the perfect gentleman. Lane's reply demonstrates this: "I didn't think it polite to listen, sir." Why is this response surprising? One notices the condescending criticism behind the seeming expression of utmost respect. But no sooner has Wilde hit at the aristocrat than he helps him back to his feet with a remark that accepts the presumption of the aristocrat over the artist: Algy gets back at Lane by announcing, "I don't play accurately—anyone can play accurately— but I play with wonderful expression. As far as the piano is concerned, sentiment is my forte. I keep science for Life" (*CW*, 321). Behind Wilde's barbed remark one can feel his bitter knowledge that brilliance and wit do not make an aristocrat and that being an aristocrat does not make one an artist.

Algy then alludes to that afternoon's tea: "Speaking of the science of Life, have you got the cucumber sandwiches cut for Lady Bracknell?" Algernon insists on gobbling every last one and prevents his guest, Ernest, from even touching them. Cucumber sandwiches, the *dernier mot* in English delicacy, epitomize decorous taste and mindless restraint. Never intended to satisfy the appetite, they symbolize a courteous and reserved negative hospitality. They are meant to be sampled ceremoniously. It was quite like Wilde to seize upon these refined refreshments to show the greed and rapacity behind the polite English restraint—the opposite of all that the English tea ceremony is supposed to represent. In this scene and throughout the play, the British tea, the emblem of civilized decorum, becomes the occasion for revealing the self-aggrandizing aggressiveness behind the refinement of the manners.[20]

Algy turns the conversation to marriage, the chief theme of the play. Neither he nor his butler has anything good to say on the subject. When Ernest arrives, he is happy to learn that the woman he loves, Gwendolen, has also been invited to tea. Algy is not encouraging about the success of the romance. Dialectically demolishing the traditional notions of love and romance, he puts the thesis ("The way you flirt with Gwendolen is perfectly disgraceful") right next to the antithesis ("It is almost as bad as the way Gwendolen flirts with you"). Ernest insists that he is in love with her and has come to town "expressly to propose" to her. Algy's synthesis of his previous thesis and antithesis is another unexpected twist: "Girls never marry the men they flirt with. Girls don't think it right," he tells Ernest with a provocative negativism; he then adds that in any case he will not allow him to marry Gwendolen, who is his cousin, until Ernest clears up an unexplained problem, "the whole question of Cecily" (CW, 323).

What Algy is actually provoking is one of those frequent self-revelations of Wilde's that make little sense in the context of the play—and are interesting to the biographer precisely because of that. It turns out that Ernest has left his cigarette case, with the incriminating inscription "From little Cecily with her fondest love to her dear Uncle Jack," lying around Algy's house. Here Wilde seems to bring into the play an opportunity for Algy to engage in a little extortion. Wilde and Bosie had both been the prey of homosexual blackmailers. Wilde got to know Bosie when he rescued him from an entanglement with a blackmailer, and extortion was such a regularly anticipated event of their lives together that Wilde wrote to Bosie in a letter: "I would sooner [be blackmailed by every renter in London] than see you bitter, unjust, hating" (L, 336).[21] The fact is that Algy could have fought off objections to Ernest's marriage plans much more simply and convincingly.[22] The cigarette case was a representation of many such cases, along with other gifts, that Wilde had distributed among the male prostitutes he frequented and that later became incriminating evidence, evidence he must have feared unconsciously while he was writing The Importance of Being Earnest.

The cigarette case introduces another central theme of the play and of Wilde's life: the hidden identity. We meet here another derivative of Wilde's unconscious problems caused by homosexuality and the life he led. It develops that Ernest is an assumed name taken by Jack whenever he is "in town" to enjoy the profligate life of a dandy; when he returns to the country he again becomes Jack and takes on the role of a rather stern and tedious uncle toward his ward, Cecily. He tells Cecily that he has a wicked younger brother named Ernest, who is always getting into trouble, running up debts, and making it necessary for him to go to town and bail him out. Having discovered all this,

Algy reveals that he, too, has the same sort of double life: he has an imaginary invalid friend whom he calls Bunbury; whenever he wants to get out of an undesired social engagement he invokes Bunbury's ill health and says he must visit him. The fact that Algy has the same problem shows that Algernon and Ernest are just different editions of the same individual.

There is a bizarre moment in the play when all the protagonists decide to speak in unison because they are trying to avoid an argument. "Could we not both speak at the same time?" one young lady asks the other, and speaking together they say: "Your Christian names are an insuperable barrier! That is all!" The young men reply in unison: "Our Christian names? Is that all? But we are going to be christened this afternoon" (CW, 371). Being in unison with the world, converting to what is expected: how pleasant it would have been for Wilde—a dream in which conflict was avoided. But Wilde could not do this, nor did he want to—and less so than ever now, at the point of his greatest success. Only from the point of view of the play does speaking in unison eliminate the conflict that was threatening on the horizon.

When Algernon's guests, Gwendolen and her imposing dowager mother, Lady Bracknell, arrive for tea, he distracts Lady Bracknell so that Jack can propose to Gwendolen. In this marriage proposal scene, and in Algernon's proposal to Cecily in act 3, Wilde seems to be making fun of the idea that men choose. Women have decided everything in advance. The hilarious conversation between Jack and Gwendolen that follows, presented as a series of proposals and counterproposals, seems to be designed to reveal the ineffectiveness of argumentation and analysis in deciding one's fate. No matter how clear the thesis, no matter how strong the antithesis, no matter how ingenious the synthesis, fate rolls on inexorably. Jack asks Gwendolen if he may propose, and she replies that it "would be an admirable opportunity" and that she is "fully determined to accept." He cries, "Gwendolen!" and she asks what he has got to say to her. "You know what I have got to say!" he replies. "Yes, but you don't say it," responds Gwendolen (CW, 331). He knows his fate—that he must propose to Gwendolen. Wilde recognizes that purpose and action are the human links in the causal chain of nature. In conversation Wilde remarked, "When a man acts he is a puppet. When he describes [his actions] he is a poet" (CW, 1024).

The marriage proposal joke gets repeated when Algernon asks for Cecily's hand and discovers that his engagement has already been arranged by her. She says, "You silly boy! Of course. Why, we have been engaged for the last three months. . . . Yes; it will be exactly three months on Thursday." Algernon replies, "I didn't know," and Cecily remarks that "very few people nowadays ever realise the position in which they are placed" (CW, 359). The amusing double paradox of the tender little Cecily as an aggressive manipulator, and the conquering male, Algy, as the victim of his heart, deny free will while making a joke of ananke. Understanding that he was driven to behave in the way he did, that he was powerless to stop himself from carrying out his fate, Wilde smiled at his dilemma. In *De Profundis* he wrote: "The important thing . . . is to absorb into my nature all that has been done to me, to make it part of me, to accept it without complaint, fear, or reluctance. . . . Whatever is realised is right" (*L,* 469).

While Jack is still on his knees to Gwendolen, Lady Bracknell interrupts the marriage proposal and orders Gwendolen downstairs to the carriage while she interrogates Jack about his age, wealth, and family background. It is not surprising to find beneath the most hilarious scene of the play the deepest, most painfully unsettled question of Wilde's life. His mother, born Jane Elgee on Lower Leeson Street, a very modest area of Dublin, had tried to claim that her name was a corruption of Alighieri and that she was actually descended from Dante. When Frank Harris asked Wilde what the O'Flahertie in his name stood for, he got a pompous reply: "The O'Flaherties were kings in Ireland, and I have a right to the name; I am descended from them." Seeing that he had offended Wilde by laughing, Harris, imagining "the greatest of the O'Flaherties, with bushy head and dirty rags, warming enormous hairy legs before a smoking peat fire," explained that he found it humorous "that Oscar Wilde should want to be an O'Flahertie."[23] Wilde laughed too, but the question must have persisted: Was he, Oscar Fingal O'Flahertie Wills Wilde, a descendant of Irish kings? Was he really his father's son? Or his mother's bastard? She herself may well have been illegitimate, as Brian de Breffny, an Irish genealogist, has recently argued.[24] Inquiring into Jack's background, Lady Bracknell asks him if both his parents are living. "I have lost both my parents," he replies. "Both?" exclaims Lady Bracknell, "To lose one parent may be regarded as a misfortune. . . . To lose both seems like carelessness." This is a curious answer. Does she not believe him? Does she feel that he is unwilling to disclose his lineage? Ernest goes on to explain that he was a foundling discovered in a handbag in the cloakroom at Victoria Station and remarks that his parents "seem to have lost me. . . . I don't actually know who I am by birth" (*CW,* 333).

In spite of all Wilde's achievements, Bosie could always make him feel his illegitimacy. Wilde, from a family with only an acquired title, never got over the sense of being an arriviste. In July 1897, he wrote a letter that protests Bosie's snobbish attitude toward Wilde's friend Robert Ross, who, like Wilde, was a commoner. The letter shows all too clearly how socially inferior Wilde felt, because it so strongly protests Bosie's breezy sense of social superiority, an attitude that Wilde, for all his arrogance, apparently envied deeply: "What [Bosie] must be made to feel is that his vulgar and ridiculous assumption of social superiority must be retracted and apologized for. I have written to tell him that *quand on est gentilhomme on est gentilhomme,* and that for him to try and pose as your social superior because he is the third son of a Scotch marquis and you the third son of a commoner is offensively stupid. Questions of title are matters of heraldry—no more. I wish you would be strong on this point; the thing should be thrashed out of him" (*L*, 624).

In the play, Lady Bracknell goes on to compare Ernest's story about his origins to the "worst excesses of the French revolution." Apparently she is unable even to conceive of a commoner as a suitor for her daughter and suggests a way out of the dilemma. He *must* have been an aristocrat lost by his parents, perhaps in the French Revolution. In the motif of the handbag, Wilde seems to have been inspired by the Moses legend: the foundling of uncertain origin, often illegitimate, is actually a prince, a leader, and a hero. A dominant theme in all cultures, and a primary fantasy of humanity, is to rise from lowly or ordinary origins to great heights. The depth of this obsession with his social standing is clear in the scene that follows Lady Bracknell's inquisitorial conversation with Jack: she forbids him to see or to think of marrying her daughter unless he can "acquire some relations as soon as possible, and . . . produce one parent, of either sex, before the season is quite over" (*CW*, 334). The lady is willing to give him a second chance: he should hurry up and fulfill the required social formalities by inventing some parents for himself.

In act 2, an old governess, Miss Prism, who has been with Jack's family for years, is in love with the rector of the local church. The flirtation between the elderly Miss Prism and the rector seems introduced as mere filler; both seem stock characters, and she appears to be a woman of no importance. But as her name indicates, she comes to refract important issues. It turns out that she is the deus ex machina who will reveal the true identity of the foundling: Miss Prism is the woman who accidentally misplaced Jack in the handbag and left him at Victoria Station, and she knows that he is actually Ernest Moncrieff, an English lord. This episode of the hero returning home and being recognized by his old nurse may be a parody of a well-known scene in the *Odyssey*.[25]

She flirts with the rector, Canon Chasuble—an exemplary case of clothes making the man—though there is not much character beneath his canonic vestments. Apart from being made into a Homeric nurse and the artificial deliverer of Jack from his identity problem, Miss Prism, with her sidekick, Canon Chasuble, is used only to restress Wilde's basic theme of the play:

women make men marry. A misanthrope Miss Prism can accept; "a wom-anthrope never!" she scolds (CW, 345).

By the end of act 3, the young men are engaged to the young women. The girls discover, however, that the men are not named Ernest. They insist that they would not want to marry anybody who is not named Ernest. One wonders why. Of course Wilde wanted to stress that at this point in his career it was important to be earnest. But he wanted to laugh at the idea that he had to choose one identity or role in order to do so, to show how unimportant it really was whether he, the double of Jack, was earnest or not. He wanted to negate the importance of social status, yet he could not accept for his charac-ter Ernest, who is a representation of himself, the status of a relatively low-born Irishman.

Smarting under the idea that he was not an aristocrat, Wilde sustained the fantasy that he was of noble birth yet could not help laughing at the whole idea of class differences. In Jack he re-created himself as an antihero. He is a social misfit in the eyes of the British aristocracy, having been found in a handbag at Victoria Station. But he is unable and unwilling to carry this idea to the bitter end. Victoria Station is not allowed to introduce the finishing touch to the comedy.

In the final scene, the antihero finds out that he is Ernest Moncrieff, a highborn aristocrat. When he learns that he was really given the name Ernest at birth, the name he has been adopting whenever it suited his convenience, he remarks: "it is a terrible thing for a man to find out suddenly that all his life he has been speaking nothing but the truth" (CW, 383). True to his old habits, Wilde plagiarizes Molière's bourgeois gentilhomme, who remarks that it is amazing to discover that all one's life one has been speaking prose. Wilde had hoped all along that by hiding himself, whether behind other people's ideas or behind his paradoxes, he might avoid telling the truth, as much as he would have liked to trumpet it in all directions. He was now headed for the grand culmination of his life, his last paradox. He was a homosexual, he was known to many as a homosexual, he wanted to be known openly as a homosexual, yet he sued for libel the very man who told the truth about him, that he was indeed "posing as a sodomite."

André Gide, who by chance met Wilde in Algiers in January 1895, while The Importance of Being Earnest was in rehearsal, saw that Wilde was "fren-zied in his joy," driven irresistibly toward disaster. "A fatality was leading him on; he could not and would not elude it. He seemed to put all his concern, his virtue, into overexaggerating his destiny and losing patience with himself." He remembers Wilde saying, "Not happiness! Above all, not happiness. Pleasure! We must always want the most tragic." When Gide listened to

Wilde's tale of being insulted and pursued by Bosie's father, he became alarmed and asked, "But if you go back there, what will happen? Do you know what you are risking?" Wilde became vague. Gide concluded that "the dramatic turn which surprised and astounded London, abruptly transforming Wilde from accuser to accused, did not, strictly speaking, cause him any surprise."[26]

A scene that Wilde wrote for the original four-act version of *The Importance of Being Earnest* seems to confirm that while writing the play, he was under the influence of a premonition. He inserts, without visible motivation, an extensive scene: Algernon is arrested for not paying his debts to the Savoy Hotel. As he is about to be taken away to Holloway Prison—incidentally, the prison in which a short time later Wilde was first to be detained—he says airily: "Well, I really am not going to be imprisoned in the suburbs for having dined in the West End." The solicitor counters: "The bill is for suppers, not for dinners." Algernon brushes away the rebuff with another refusal to be detained in the suburbs. The solicitor acknowledges that "the surroundings I admit are middle class; but the gaol itself is fashionable and well-aired; and there are ample opportunities of taking exercise at certain stated hours of the day." Algernon, horrified, cries: "No gentleman ever takes exercise" (*CW*, 351). One shudders to observe Wilde watching, with eyes wide open yet not seeing, what his unconscious was preparing.

Wilde's ultimate solution was indeed paradoxical: his courtroom made him a helpless and passive victim, but it became the background for his most active defiance of society; when the case was already a lost cause, his famous speech on the "Love that dare not speak its name" drew cheers. Toward Bosie, who had all the time pushed him into action, he behaved submissively. But in *De Profundis,* he remembers: "This urging me, forcing me to appeal to Society for help [in initiating the libel suit against Queensberry], is one of the things that makes me despise you so much, that makes me despise myself so much for having yielded to you" (*L*, 492–93). The court scenes were the closest he came to filling both roles of hero and martyr at once.

Paradoxically, by sending his body to prison, he was actually freeing his mind: the burden of trying to defy the dialectic of his fate, of deciding when to assume which role, would be lifted. But as he had quipped so knowingly: "There is only one thing worse than not getting what one wants: getting what one wants." Once incarcerated, what Wilde ate, what he wore, how his hair was cut, when he could speak—these were all decided for him. He was never confronted with the anxious ambivalence from which he crafted his paradoxes. The arrogant certainty, emphatic negativism, and manifest inconsistency woven into his stylistic signature, the paradox, had all been reactions to normal everyday doubts and decision making. He had gotten the aesthetic thrill of creating paradoxes out of the angst of making up his mind. Even after he was finally given permission to write in prison, he did not produce anything creative beyond *De Profundis,* his lengthy love letter to Bosie, containing a curious mixture of love and hate.

His mind never regained its famous effervescence, its elastic response to stress. There were to be no more virtuoso displays of witty paradox, no more comedies like *The Importance of Being Earnest.* He had played out his roles: as a hero and as a martyr he was a has-been, an out-of-work actor. In 1900, shortly before he died, he ran into Anna, comtesse de Brémont, an old friend of his mother's, in Paris. He spoke of his life in the past tense: "I have lived. . . . I have lived all there was to live."[27]

Never able to live both roles at once, always doubting from the confines of one role whether he ought to be playing the other, he remained in the grip of his uncertainties until he died. In *The Picture of Dorian Gray,* he had remarked: "The things one feels absolutely certain about are never true" (*CW,* 161). Nowhere is this expression of tormenting doubt clearer than in the pose of warlike certainty in his pronouncements about homosexuality: "Yes: I have no doubt we [homosexuals] shall win, but the road is long, and red with monstrous martyrdoms" (*L,* 721).

Gradually, over the course of his career, he tried to arrive at the philosophic view that uncertainty, like his sexuality, was to be displayed and celebrated, not hidden and feared. "Who wants to be consistent?" he wrote in 1889. "The dullard and the doctrinaire, the tedious people who carry out their principles to the bitter end of action, to the *reductio ad absurdum* of practice. Not I" (*CW,* 971).

Final certainty and acceptance of his fate helped him occasionally to transform his barbed witticisms into humor comparable to that of the prisoner Freud mentions in his article "On Humour": the man being led out to be hanged on a Monday sees the gallows and remarks ironically, "Well, that's a nice beginning of the week." This humor, though now a little the worse for wear, still had some grandeur. It was a magnificent death rattle, which, as Freud put it, "insists that it cannot be affected by the traumas of the external world; it shows, in fact, that such traumas are not more than occasions for it to gain pleasure."[28]

In *The Importance of Being Earnest* and in some of his darkest hours during and after prison, Wilde was quite capable of pulling himself up from the lowest depths by such humor. *The Importance of Being Earnest* was the culmination of Wilde's effort to accept the fact that uncertainty is an inescapable ingredient of life. By laughing, he freed himself for the moment from this anguish. When Jack protests, "You always want to argue about things," Algy answers, "That is exactly what things were originally made for!" (*CW*, 335). Wilde even tries to praise the healthy result of uncertainty, doubt, and imperfection: when Jack tells Gwendolen that she is "quite perfect," she replies, "Oh! I hope I am not that. It would leave no room for developments, and I intend to develop in many directions" (*CW*, 378).

A torn and tortured soul, Wilde could philosophically take comfort in thinking and in observing himself. He was aware of his lifelong attempt to defend himself against the dread of doubting with a show of certainty. He placed the crown of thorns on his head not to convince but to be convinced. He recognized in his martyrdom as a homosexual a need to convince himself of his allegiance to his sexual identity: "Martyrdom was to me merely a tragic form of skepticism, an attempt to realise by fire what one had failed to do by faith." Always the dandy, Oscar Wilde on the witness stand, sporting a flower in his buttonhole, playfully parrying questions, and pontificating about the nobility of the "Love that dare not speak its name," was never less sure of himself. His worst hours as a famous writer denigrated and defrocked in the dock at the Old Bailey were his finest hours as a man, but from there he descended quickly, steeply, to a total dissolution of his creative powers and an ignoble, sordid death in a seedy Paris hotel.

CHAPTER 5 *DE PROFUNDIS*: DYING BEYOND HIS MEANS

Between January and March 1897, approximately four months before his release from Reading Gaol, Wilde wrote a lengthy letter to Bosie Douglas, a letter seething with love and hate. Now known as *De Profundis,* a title chosen by his friend Robert Ross, the letter was accurately named: it emerged from Wilde's lowest depths, after he had served nearly twenty months of his two years of hard labor, many of them in solitary confinement.[1]

Wilde's opening complaint of the "long and fruitless" time he endured in prison while waiting for some word from Bosie leads one to expect a sad letter of unrequited love, the expression of a wounded and rejected soul. But *De Profundis* is more than such a letter. In fact, it is much more than a letter. The form was an expedient that Wilde seized upon to circumvent prison rules, which dictated that he could write only letters. Sitting in prison, the time of his release drawing nearer, Wilde had to consider his reentry into society. He would want to return as an established man of letters whose prison experiences had led him into new artistic ventures. This fallen angel of comedy and conversation, this novelist, dramatist, essayist, critic, and poet, would naturally attempt to create a new literary work. But his options were limited. Each sheet of writing, considered a letter by officials, had to be handed over to the guard at night and was subject to censorship. Isolated from the intellectual and artistic world that had been his life's blood, from the adoration and conversation of friends who had stimulated his thought, he did the best he could, confined as he was to a stark cell with a glaring jet gaslight that hurt his eyes. He may have been able to see and revise the manuscript on the sly with the help of a kindly warden, but he never had the freedom of mind and ease of composition that he had possessed before prison.

His first choice of a title, "Epistola: In Carcare et Vinculus" (Letter: In Prison and in Chains), shows that he did not intend to write an ordinary letter, that in fact he thought of the work as literary art, belles lettres. He wanted to write a formal epistle in the style of the old Roman writers— Horace, Cicero, or Ovid—or to give himself the authority and status of the Gospel writers. The term *epistola* calls to mind Ovid's *Tristia* and *Epistolae ex Ponto,* letters the great Roman poet wrote from exile. Wilde's epistola thus became an apocalyptic vision of his past and future life, of his anticipated and longed-for redemption of the writer Oscar Wilde. *De Profundis* includes confession, moments of self-analysis, howls of self-pity. It is both a history and a justification of Wilde's life, an *Apologia pro Vita Sua*—in the style of Cardinal Newman—an explanation of that life. Reading it, one is moved by the sufferings of a brilliant, isolated mind trying to prove that the self-inflicted catastrophes of his life have had meaning and purpose, that in the end they will reveal order and coherence in the rise and fall of Oscar Wilde.

De Profundis may appear at first to contain more chaos than rhyme or reason. Buffeted between highly personal complaints, vicious attempts to wound Bosie, and an intense, kindly longing to embrace him, Wilde seems engulfed by inner conflicts. The contents of this work relate to Bosie insofar as a lover is the most imaginable recipient of a letter full of the deepest intimacies as well as the highest and most philosophical thoughts about life. But it is easy to discern the exposition of many philosophical thoughts and problems that cannot be directed at Bosie's interests or understanding: Wilde knew well that Bosie was not up to his own intellectual level—indeed, he chose Bosie in part for that deficiency.

Strewn through *De Profundis* are philosophical ideas about art and literary creation. Wilde begins with the nihilism of Goethe's Mephistopheles and progresses almost immediately, in typical Wildean fashion, to the bright light of Christ as an optimistic philosopher. Wilde writes, "In a manner not yet understood of the world [Christ] regarded sin and suffering as being in themselves beautiful, holy things, and modes of perfection." This was of course a deliberate blasphemy, the opposite of Christian doctrine, and so Wilde adds: "It *sounds* a very dangerous idea. It is so. All great ideas *are* dangerous" (*L,* 486). He had experienced how dangerous his sins were for his genius.

In *De Profundis,* Wilde is attempting to reconcile his destructive and his creative urges, to prove that the destructive urge produces creativity and is necessary to it. In *Faust,* Mephistopheles—like Wilde, "the spirit that eternally denies"—remarks:

I am a portion of that part which once was everything
a part of darkness which gave birth to Light.[2]

Wilde, living Mephistopheles' philosophy that "everything that is worthy of
creation is worthy of being destroyed," always felt that annihilation inspired
him. The darkness of sin and despair, the depths of a depression that seemed
to be leading only to death, the decay and destruction of Dorian Gray, might
all become the womb of poetry and philosophy. The idea that destruction is
pregnant with creative possibilities unifies the many different themes of *De
Profundis*. Bringing together his hatred of Bosie and his love of Bosie, Wilde
hopes to recover enough creative energy to resurrect himself as a great writer
and personality.

From the moment of Wilde's sentencing on 25 May 1895, when he literally
shook with horror, the dynamic wit, for whom defiance had been a way of
life, made no attempt to defy anyone. He was dazed for months afterward. His
warder remembered that each morning after Wilde cleaned his cell and
arranged his eating tins in their required order, "he would step back, and
view them with an air of childlike complacency."[3] Weakened by diarrhea,
weight loss, waning and painful eyesight and pain in the eyes, and a recurrent
ear infection, forbidden to speak to other prisoners, he feared he was going
insane. In a petition to the Home Secretary of 2 July 1896, Wilde pleaded,
"For more than thirteen dreadful months now, the petitioner has been subject
to the fearful system of solitary cellular confinement: without human intercourse of any kind; without writing materials whose use might help to
distract the mind: without suitable or sufficient books, so essential to any
literary man, so vital for the preservation of mental balance: condemned to
absolute silence. . . . The despair and misery of this lonely and wretched life
[has] been intensified beyond words by the death of his mother, Lady Wilde,
to whom he was deeply attached, as well as by the contemplation of the ruin
he has brought on his young wife and his two children. . . . He is deprived of
everything that could soothe, distract, or heal a wounded and shaken mind"
(*L*, 402–03). He had fallen into a deep depression, from which he was never
to recover. Several visitors, including Frank Harris and Robert Ross, recorded
their alarm upon seeing that he had difficulty in speaking—he actually
preferred not to do so—and wanted to hear them talk instead. "Very unlike
Oscar," Ross said.[4]

Out of this reversal of personality, and during the last part of his imprisonment, came the *Epistola,* a letter nearly devoid of his famous wit but still
characteristically Wilde: the minute he puts pen to paper his innate dis-
putatiousness quickly regenerates. Trying to emphasize a thesis, he imme-

diately becomes antithetical. Efforts to analyze and blame himself invariably yield to strenuous blasts of self-exoneration and self-glorification. "I will begin by telling you that I blame myself terribly," writes Wilde in the fourth paragraph of De Profundis, reiterating this self-blame for several more lines. But the paragraph ends with a condemnation of Bosie: "I am not speaking in terms of rhetorical exaggeration but in terms of absolute truth to actual fact when I remind you that during the whole time we were together I never wrote one single line" (L, 425–26). This bombast is incidentally a Wildean lie, a beautifully big lie. Bosie, the source and substance of his four great comedies, was always in the background and often by his side as he wrote.

These two voices in De Profundis, the voice of self-blame and the voice of self-glorification, create a dramatic dialogue between the tragedian Wilde and the Wilde who steps back to observe, with ironic remove and occasional flashes of humor, his continually unfolding tragedy. One minute Wilde is tearing his hair and beating his breast over his sins or Bosie's; the next he has a smirk on his face. Sorrowing that "loathing, bitterness and contempt should for ever take that place in my heart once held by love is very sad to me," pained because Bosie had wanted to publish Wilde's love letters without permission, Wilde begs Bosie to write to him personally instead. Plunging from pathos to bathos in the same sentence, Wilde reminds Bosie that Bosie's love letters will be ignored by the world: "though the world will know nothing of whatever words of grief or passion, of remorse or indifference you may choose to send as your answer or your appeal" (L, 242). Wilde could not resist heckling Bosie and harping on his infantile need for attention. But it was Wilde who was so preoccupied with what the world would think of him and of his writing. With high seriousness, Wilde begins a sentence: "If you find in [my letter] something of which you feel that you are unjustly accused"; with sneering wit he completes it: "Remember that one should be thankful that there is any fault of which one can be unjustly accused." Always chasing a tragic tone with a humorous remark, Wilde keeps his reader off-balance. The constant flux makes reading De Profundis a disorienting experience.

Wilde's propensity for setting in motion a perpetual dialectic is a significant stylistic link between De Profundis and Wilde's comedies, as well as between the last epoch of glorious creativity just before his trials and his artistic sterility after prison. De Profundis is certainly anything but witty, although there are in it traces of Wilde's wit, which did not leave him till his last breath. But De Profundis shares with Wilde's comedies certain essentials of structure. "Divorces are made in heaven" (from The Importance of Being Earnest [CW, 323]) expresses Wilde's thinking in the same way as a remark in

De Profundis: "The sentimentalist is always a cynic at heart" (L, 501). Both depend on ellipsis. The essential critical thought is hidden. Economy of logic was always Wilde's genius.

Indeed, De Profundis is in its way a kind of play, a tragicomedy. On the surface it is a letter of complaint and constant rebuke, but it is also a conversation between Wilde and himself, in which Bosie is introduced merely to represent Wilde's ambivalence. In De Profundis, Wilde managed, in spite of prison rules, to produce an act of a play in the form of a letter. It may seem surprising to consider this dark and searing document a play. But one recalls George Bernard Shaw's opinion of De Profundis, that "no other Irishman had yet produced as masterful a comedy."[5] Shaw, once again showing a touch of envy, caught the likeness between Wilde's thinking in De Profundis and that in Earnest—the likeness of their unconscious content.

At the point when Wilde felt the need to restore himself as a writer—he would, in only a short time, have to face a vengeful public that would no longer accept and admire him as the brilliant playwright he had been—he would try to resume this position by again proving his prowess as a dramatist. In a sense he must have felt the need to pick up where he had left off when he was put into prison. Before writing any of his successful comedies, he proclaimed in "The Critic as Artist" a formula for dialogue that he followed in each subsequent dramatic work, including now De Profundis: to "invent an imaginary antagonist, and convert him when [one] chooses by some absurd sophistical argument" (CW, 1046). He was particularly drawn to the form of dialogue in which one character contradicts another, and often himself. Although a great deal of interesting thought is expended in the arguments, no real conclusion is formulated. Each attempt to draw the argument to a conclusion immediately creates opposition.[6]

Dialectical reasoning is not just a basic source of Wilde's wit but the underlying structure of all his work. As a dialogue, De Profundis is Wilde's last drama. It is a drama depicting the struggle of one man against his society and against the deadening conformity imposed by prison rules and regulations. And in Wildean fashion it is a drama in which the hero speaks out of both sides of his mouth. As soon as he has settled the mask of the accuser over his face, he changes into the persona of an accused little boy defending himself. The question Wilde once asked about Max Beerbohm, "Does he ever take off his face and show you his mask?" sounds like an epigraph for De Profundis. De Profundis is the final crest in a wave that begins with "The Decay of Lying" and "The Critic as Artist." These early dialogues are, like the comedies and like all of Wilde's best work, self-dramatizations.

From the beginning of De Profundis, Wilde writes with Bosie's responses in mind, addresses him as if he were hearing his replies: "I have no doubt that in this letter in which I have to write of your life and of mine, of the past and of the future, of sweet things changed to bitterness and of the bitter things that may be turned to joy, there will be much that will wound your vanity to the quick. [Bosie parries.] If it prove so, [Bosie nods bitterly] read the letter over and over again till it kills your vanity. [Bosie gestures that he is unjustly, unfairly accused.]" (L, 424–25). Throughout the letter, Wilde challenges Bosie and defends himself against Bosie's imagined retorts. "There is, I know, one answer to all that I have said to you, and that is that you loved me: that all through those two and a half years during which the Fates were weaving into one scarlet pattern the threads of our divided lives you really loved me. [Bosie looks quizzical.] Yes: I know you did" (L, 444). The reader is continually treated to scenes that depict Bosie's typical responses: "Those incessant scenes that seemed to be almost physically necessary to you, and in which your mind and body grew distorted and you became a thing as terrible to look at as to listen to" (L, 429).

Dialogue, especially in the form known as apostrophe, in which the writer turns away from the audience to address an imaginary figure, is a natural form for one who makes an art of antinomy. Wilde seems to recognize this in "The Critic as Artist" by having one character accuse the other of being an antinomian—presumably not in the technical religious sense, but in the sense of being a believer in opposition and contradiction—and getting the reply that antinomianism is essential and far more important than any moral sense of right and wrong. In De Profundis also Wilde declares: "I am a born antinomian" (L, 468).

Negativism, in the sense of having an automatic negative reaction to any statement made by anyone, even or especially himself, was such a fundamental aspect of Wilde's intellectuality and art that one is impelled to seek a reason for it. He says no to any statement and then says no to his own no: "Whenever people agree with me, I always feel I must be wrong" (CW, 416). As an Irishman and especially as the son of a volcanically patriotic mother, he was indoctrinated from birth to be negative to anything British. But many Irish poets have been in the same position and have not had Wilde's form of wit, so that this negative attitude toward the English cannot be assigned exclusively to national politics. There are people—as every psychoanalyst knows—whose development remains in a sense fixated in this phase. Wilde is a good example of this personality type and of the creativity one can develop in spite of it, or perhaps even because of it. Wilde defends himself against his difficulty in accepting difference by affecting to celebrate difference rather than to fear it. His defense against recognizing and accepting his own difference reveals itself in his frequently noted copying of other writers' styles. At the same time he controls his fear of difference by underscoring his difference constantly, as if being different is the guiding star of his life. Differentness was the lifelong task to which Wilde devoted his life as a work of art, as well as a significant source for his choice of dialogue and drama as the forms of his art.

The manuscript of *De Profundis,* written on prison paper ruled in blue, covers twenty folio sheets, each of four pages. Each page was carefully numbered by prison authorities. The official rules allowed Wilde to work on only one page at a time and prohibited his having the entire document in front of him. Given Wilde's extremely constrained working conditions, his poor health, isolation, and despair, it is not surprising that his treatise appears rambling, undisciplined, or carelessly constructed at first glance. Many critics have complained of a lack of form in the letter.[7] But Rupert Hart-Davis, the editor of Wilde's letters, feels that Wilde must have been allowed to look over more than one sheet at a time: Hart-Davis points out that several sheets appear to be fair copies and that Wilde in his cover letter quotes at length "from memory" so much of the manuscript that he must have had it in front of him. Following Hart-Davis, Ellmann writes that because of the compassion of Major J. O. Nelson, a newly appointed warden, Wilde was able to revise the letter "throughout" and that "some pages appear to have been totally rewritten and substituted for an earlier version."[8] Given Ellmann's findings, Wilde seems to have had ample opportunity to revise the letter.[9]

In fact, the letter is far from formless. As the last of Wilde's "dialogues," it expresses an underlying consistency of purpose: to free himself from the emotional paralysis that had gripped him in prison. He needed Bosie now to re-create the Oscar Wilde whose comedies had taken London by storm. As always, when Wilde retreated into himself, he needed company. His wit and philosophy were alienated and antisocial, but the more deeply he burrowed into himself to be alone, the more he appreciated Bosie's presence. Wilde's comedies arose in the wake of Bosie's temper tantrums. Bosie's endless explosions, endless chattering, and endless demands had, paradoxically, inspired the best of Wilde's art.[10]

De Profundis has been thought of as a dialogue before. Robert Sherard reportedly remarked that "the peevish recriminations . . . resemble a work by Socrates and his good lady [Xantippe]." Every line of the letter shows the push and pull, the question and response of dialogue. As if foreseeing the literary criticisms about a lack of form, he insists (to Bosie): "I cannot reconstruct [this] letter or re-write it. You must take it as it stands, blotted in many places with tears, in some with the signs of passion or pain, and make it out as best you can." Bosie, who stands here for all literary critics to come, is being reminded: "As for corrections and errata, I made them in order that my words should be an absolute expression of my thoughts, and err neither through surplusage nor through being inadequate. . . . As it stands . . . my letter has its definite meaning behind every phrase. . . . Wherever there is erasion or substitution, however slight, however elaborate, it is because I am seeking to render my real impression, to find for my mood its exact equivalent" (L, 502– 03). Although Wilde is deeply critical of himself in the last remark, he also seems to want to repeat what he had reportedly said about one of his earlier works: "Who am I to tamper with a masterpiece?"

The first sentence of De Profundis reveals the internal division that is the driving force behind the work: "After long and fruitless waiting I have deter- mined to write to you myself, as much for your sake as for mine" (L, 424). Throughout his epistola, he discloses self-accusations that are too painful to be acknowledged through diatribes against Bosie. This is a basic ploy in the often-unintentional self-analysis of the creative writer—and a method Wilde recognized in "The Critic as Artist" when he wrote: "Man is least himself when he talks in his own person. Give him a mask, and he will tell you the truth" (CW, 1045). A writer can often express and analyze his or her feelings more easily by assigning them to an invented character.

By setting up Bosie as the antagonist in his dialogue, Wilde was casting him as representative of his own unconscious resistances. Warning Bosie that the letter will contain "much that will wound your vanity," Wilde reminds him- self that his own vanity, which has been demolished by prison, must not stand in the way of self-criticism as he emerges from the underworld. Forced to have his hair cut, to step into a dirty bath that other prisoners have bathed in, to wear the hideous striped prisoner's uniform, to be degraded by physical illness along with all the weight of his troubles, Wilde submitted silently. On the other hand, in a letter of 6 May 1897, just twelve days before his release, he again clutched at vanity: at the end of a long list enumerating clothing and accessories that he deems necessary, including two dozen white hand- kerchiefs, a dozen with colored borders, and plain mother-of pearl studs, he flourishes: "Also, some nice French soap, Houbigant's, if you can get it . . . either 'Peau d'Espagne' or 'Sac de Laitue' . . . also a case of scent; Canterbury Wood Violet. . . . There is a wonderful thing [for graying hair] called Koko Marikopas . . . a wonderful hair-tonic; the name alone seems worth the money, so please get a large bottle. I want, for psychological reasons, to feel entirely physically cleansed of the stain and soil of prison life, so these things are all—trivial as they might sound—really of great importance" (L, 535). The restoration of his vanity, of Oscar Wilde, the toast of London, had been one of the purposes of *De Profundis*—but so too had the restoration of his entire sense of himself, his basic self-esteem.

There is an overt impulse toward self-analysis in the letter, which shows in his description of his art as "the great primal note by which I revealed, first myself to myself, and then myself to the world" (*L*, 447). In a letter to Robert Ross, Wilde claims that *De Profundis* is "the psychological explanation of a course of conduct that from the outside seems a combination of absolute idiocy and vulgar bravado." But in the next sentence he again argues with himself: "I don't defend my conduct. I explain it" (*L*, 512). Actually, he explains and accuses himself by explaining and accusing Bosie. The more bitter the accusation of Bosie, the more it reveals Wilde's own feelings of guilt—as other letters show.

Early in *De Profundis* Wilde cries out: "You surely must see now that your incapacity of being alone: your nature so exigent in its persistent claim on the attention and time of others: your lack of any power of sustained intellectual concentration . . . were as destructive to your own progress in culture as they were to my work as an artist?" In truth, however, it was Wilde who was unable to be alone. Enforced solitude—especially the social ostracism he faced after prison and the poverty that in the best of circumstances would prevent him from rejoining high society—was torture. On his first day alone after prison, after the old friends who had met him at the boat and helped him get to France had departed, he wrote: "I begin to realise my terrible position of isolation." When in early September 1897 he finally returned to Bosie against the advice of his friends and against all common sense—since the terms of his wife's will forbade it and since she and her advisers had indicated that they would cut off all funds if he did so—he wrote: "My going back to Bosie was psychologically inevitable. . . . I cannot live without the atmosphere of Love; I must love and be loved, whatever price I pay for it." A year before he died, his letters were full of pathetic pleas for visits. To Robert Ross he wrote: "Is there *any* chance of your coming? . . . I am ill and lonely" (*L*, 576, 644, 793).

Wilde's jibe that Bosie lacked "any power of sustained intellectual concentration" was, sadly, another comment on his own inability to write anything, apart from *The Ballad of Reading Gaol* and some letters, after he left prison. In February 1898 he moved to Paris on the theory that he would be able to write there: "It is my only chance of working. I miss an intellectual atmosphere. . . . I have no brains now, or energy" (*L*, 700). Indeed, all he could write were letters, letters increasingly querulous in their demands for money. With the loss of his sense of himself and of identity, he lost his ability to create.

Wilde's self-loathing was a poignant source of his rage against Bosie for not loving him. He is obsessed in *De Profundis* with some lines in a letter that Bosie wrote to him: "When you are not on your pedestal you are not interesting. The next time you are ill I will go away at once" (L, 439). Wilde relates how these lines came back to him again and again, how he brooded over them—no doubt because he felt stung by their truth. Being ignored was even worse than being spat upon. He had lost his pedestal; he had lost his professional career as a conversationalist. It distressed him that he had been loved by Bosie only for his glamour and glitter and money, not for himself.

The strong ambivalence that deepened his depression, even as it fired his creativity, is explicit in a letter of March 1896 to Robert Ross. His wish to "feel more pleasure" immediately produces the reflection that he feels "dead to all emotions except those of anguish and despair." The thought of the "horror of death" inspires "the still greater horror of living." This greater horror, far from being a melodramatic expression or an idle phrase, involved the real dread of having to go out into the world again, which he tried to master by writing *De Profundis*. The real world opening up before him threatened to plunge him into depths far more profound than the experience of prison had. The more he longed to resurrect himself as a writer, the more keenly he felt the loss of that identity; in the same letter he complains: "I fear you will find it difficult to read this, but as I am not allowed writing materials, I seem to have forgotten how to write: you must excuse me" (L, 399). He was really trembling with the fear of having lost his creativity—of knowing that indeed he had lost his ability to create.

As I have mentioned, officially he was allowed to write only letters, and until about July 1896, very few letters. Under the regime of a particularly callous prison warden, Henry Isaacson, who wanted to "knock the nonsense" out of Wilde and punished him by taking his books away, he had been allowed pen and paper only to write to solicitors, the Home Office, or a few friends. His letters were sometimes censored: on at least one occasion a prison official cut out with scissors a reference to Bosie. J. O. Nelson, the warden who replaced Isaacson, was much kinder and gave Wilde all the paper he wanted.[11] It remains unclear whether Nelson ever had the authority to relax the rules that much. Perhaps to play it safe, Wilde and Nelson decided together that whatever he would write would be called a letter. Ellmann suggests that Wilde "devised a stratagem in which Major Nelson was to indulge him. He would write a letter to Alfred Douglas, as he was allowed to do by rule, but such a letter would also offer an autobiographical account of his last five years."[12]

There were, after Nelson's arrival on the scene, few external obstacles in the way of Wilde's wish to restore himself as a writer. Broken in body and spirit, he was unable at first to seize the opportunity. Only a few months before his release, when the anxiety about his future forced him to prepare for the outside world, did he take advantage of his new writing privileges.

The closer the date of his release, the more terrifying became the thought of living as a "pariah dog," an ex-criminal, a pauper, and a despised exile from the art and society that gave his life meaning.[13] He writes in De Profundis, "I, and such as I am, have hardly any right to air and sun. Our presence taints the pleasure of others. We are unwelcome when we reappear. . . . Our very children are taken away. Those lovely links with humanity are broken. We are doomed to be solitary" (L, 465). The greatest curse for this man who thrived on conversation was to be alone, rejected, despised. He foresaw that his isolation in society would seem even greater than his isolation in prison. Prison had been terrible, but now he sensed that the worst torments would come after his release, in moving from "a sort of eternity of fame to a sort of eternity of infamy" (L, 470). Absolute triumph would be followed by utter ignominy.

A number of Victorian autobiographers before him had experienced profound despair. Loss of faith in religion or philosophy had threatened to crush Thomas Carlyle and John Henry Cardinal Newman. John Stuart Mill was thrust into a crisis by his conflict over love and hatred for his despotic father.[14] Out of the fragments of an inner battle they tried to resurrect themselves. Although Wilde had never lost faith in himself—only in his public—the search of these men for meaning when all seemed meaningless appealed to him.[15] In the autobiographies of Carlyle, Newman, and Mill, one can discern a step-by-step progression from confused and tormenting self-doubt to self-assurance and hope—a gradual conversion, a death of the old self and a spiritual rebirth of a new personality.[16] Carlyle spoke of moving from a despairing phase he labeled the "everlasting no" through a "center of indifference" to an end phase: the "everlasting yea."[17] Newman, modeling his autobiography on Saint Augustine's Confessions, typically writes: "From the end of 1841, I was on my death-bed, as regards my membership with the Anglican church."[18] This spiritual death was the prerequisite for his spiritual rebirth, his conversion to Catholicism.

The self-salvation model of crisis autobiography had ostensibly inspired Wilde in the writing of De Profundis. Indeed, Richard Ellmann suggests that De Profundis is meant to "follow, like a parable, his progress from pleasure to pain and then, in the last months, to a change of heart and mastery of pain. Remorse, purgation, and hope would all play their parts. . . . [He] might write something comparable to Pilgrim's Progress."[19] All these stages of spiritual salvation should certainly have played a part. But because remorse was conspicuously absent, purgation could hardly follow. In the three-step process of inner turmoil, spiritual death, and spiritual rebirth, Wilde had gotten as far as spiritual death. Conversing with Vincent O'Sullivan, an Irish-American poet and novelist, after prison, Wilde compared himself to Lucien de Rubempré and Julien Sorel and said, "Lucien hanged himself, Julien was executed, and I died in prison."[20] By that time, Wilde had realized that *De Profundis* had failed miserably to effect his resurrection.

During Wilde's first three months in prison, when little reading material was available to him, he read *Pilgrim's Progress* and the Bible.[21] In July 1895, he managed through the intervention of a member of the Home Office to get books that greatly influenced the writing of *De Profundis*. Among them were the *Confessions* and *De civitate Dei* of Saint Augustine and Cardinal Newman's *The Grammar of Assent, Apologia pro Vita Sua, Two Essays on Miracles,* and *The Idea of a University* (*L,* 399n). Wilde devoured these works and in July 1896 bitterly complained in a petition to the Home Secretary that although he had been "by special permission . . . allowed two books a week to read" the prison library was "extremely small and poor" and that "the books kindly added at the prisoner's request he had read and re-read till they have become almost meaningless to him: he is practically left without anything to read" (*L,* 403). He got more books as a result of this petition, among them Carlyle's *Sartor Resartus* and Newman's *Critical and Historical Essays.*

Newman's autobiography, *Apologia pro Vita Sua,* was part of the intellectual and emotional background of *De Profundis* (*L,* 405). When Wilde had been struggling with religion as an undergraduate, he had found comfort in reading Newman's *Apologia.* In a letter of March 1877, Wilde writes to a friend at Oxford: "I have dreams of a visit to Newman, of the holy sacrament in a new Church, and of a quiet and peace afterwards in my soul" (*L,* 31).[22] In another letter of the same period, Wilde speaks of a young undergraduate who, influenced by Newman, is considering abandoning Anglicanism for Catholicism. Wilde alludes to this potential conversion as the seduction of the young man by a prostitute; he was of course using an epithet often employed in those days by Protestants denigrating the Catholic church.[23] Newman's decision to live as a celibate, made as early as age fifteen, suggests an aversion to heterosexuality, if not suppressed homosexuality. Like Wilde he had been accused of seducing young men, true, not into sexual acts but into the Roman Catholic church. Wilde was aware of the accusations made against Newman and of the sexual innuendos that could be drawn from them.

Newman's descriptions of being "profoundly troubled" and of feeling that "confidence in me was lost—but I had already lost full confidence in myself" struck a familiar chord.[24] The peaceful state of mind that Newman claims to have experienced after his conversion appealed to Wilde; he must have envied Newman's claim of having "no anxiety of heart whatever." Wilde, too, would have liked to have been able to say, as Newman did, that "I have been in perfect peace and contentment; I have never had one doubt."[25] The only state of perfect peace Wilde could imagine was death: "While I was in Wandsworth Prison I longed to die. It was my one desire," he wrote (*L*, 471).

What enabled Newman and many of the autobiographers of spiritual crisis to find form and purpose in their lives was the ancient Christian system of biblical typology.[26] This system made it possible to avoid responsibility and feelings of guilt, because all experiences are seen as part of a divine, a providential scheme that will have a positive outcome. Events and persons in the Old Testament are interpreted as necessary precursors of events and persons in the New Testament. Typology reassures that no event is random, that whatever happens in whatever way had to happen that way in order for the divine plan to be completed.

In prison, Wilde's reading was restricted to religious pamphlets and to the Bible for so many months that biblical stories and their symbolism were uppermost in his mind by the time he got around to writing *De Profundis*. Avrom Fleishman characterizes the work as "an exercise in biblical rewriting and in a typological redaction of personal experience," in which "the language of typology appears throughout."[27]

The possibility of finding through typology meaningfulness and optimism in what was a crushing fall from the glittering heights fit Wilde like a glove, particularly in that interpretation of meaning could be used to seek the truth or, perchance, to hide it. The idea that no event is random freed him from having to take responsibility for his actions. Northrop Frye comments, "What typology really is as a mode of thought, what it both assumes and leads to, is a theory of history, or more accurately of historic process: an assumption that there is some meaning and point to history."[28] The point that Wilde wanted to illuminate in *De Profundis* was that the suffering of pain, and even death, be it physical or spiritual, leads to redemption—in his case, redemption as a writer with, he hoped, enhanced creative powers. Like Newman, Wilde would use typology for self-justification.[29] Wilde would be intrigued by this theory, particularly because in contrast to psychology, which only explains, it provides an optimistic vision of future redemption.[30]

In his sorrow and despair, describing himself as "a disgraced and ruined man," Wilde spoke in the spirit of Psalm 130, which intones: "Out of the depths [de profundis] have I cried unto thee, O Lord." The psalm, with its mixture of mournful appeal for pardon and concessions of guilt combined with the speaker's confidence that he will be forgiven, is the canvas upon which *De Profundis* was painted. In *De Profundis* Wilde is casting himself in the role of David, who is thought to be the author of the Psalms. Avrom Fleishman remarks that Wilde wanted to "confess the depths of his own sins—sexual and familial in David's case, as in [his own]." And confession is traditionally the first step toward redemption. David is a type of Christ, so apparently Wilde was trying to see a type of Christ in himself.[31]

Yet even as Wilde seeks to justify himself with typology, he is overcome with the realization that it is nonsense. In 1890, seven years before Wilde wrote *De Profundis,* he had already commented in "The Critic as Artist" that "the mode of thought that Cardinal Newman represented—if that can be called a mode of thought which seeks to solve intellectual problems by a denial of the supremacy of the intellect—may not, I think, survive" (*CW,* 1010). In *De Profundis,* Wilde uses typological exegesis but at the same time denies the validity of this system of interpretation. Mentioning "the cry of Isaiah," which in typological thinking was connected with the coming of Christ, he says that it "had really no more to do with [Christ's] coming than the song of the nightingale has to do with the rising of the moon" (*L,* 482).

In the same typical Wildean way, he flirts with the idea of conversion only to ridicule it. He sees himself as one searching for a *vita nuova,* like Newman, like Augustine, like Dante (*L,* 467).[32] As a first step in refashioning his personality he had compared himself to Dante. But then he admits that the new life is just going to be the old one: "This new life, as through my love of Dante I like to call it, is of course no new life at all, but simply the continuance, by means of development and evolution, of my former life" (*L,* 475).

There is a significant difference between Wilde and other autobiographers in this genre. They wanted to change themselves, whereas he had a fantasy that somehow the world would change so that he would not have to. Initially he blames himself: "Nobody, great or small, can be ruined except by his own hand. . . . Terrible as what you [Bosie] did to me was, what I did to myself was far more terrible still" (*L,* 465–66). This fleeting impulse to understand what he did to himself altered even as he was writing. Wilde thunders at Bosie: "You see that I have to write your life to you, and you have to realise it" (*L,* 448). He wanted Bosie to live up to the figure Wilde makes of him for his own purposes. Addressing Bosie as the embodiment of his own self-negation, he fashions his advice to him along the Christian autobiographer's lines. To provoke in Bosie the spiritual crisis and renewal that ought to be part of his own development as a Christian autobiographer, Wilde writes: "If there be in [my letter] one single passage that brings tears to your eyes, weep as we weep in prison where the day no less than the night is set apart for tears. It is the only thing that can save you" (*L,* 424–25). But we must not forget that when Wilde blames the character Bosie in *De Profundis,* Bosie represents the culpable part of Wilde.

Self-blame, though nearly always disguised as a thundering indictment of Bosie, inevitably plunges Wilde into despair—probably because Wilde knows that he has only himself to blame. In the beginning of one letter he announces: "You must read this letter right through, though each word may become to you as the fire or knife of the surgeon, that makes the delicate flesh burn or bleed" (*L,* 425). He wishes on Bosie the punishment that he himself fears from the world and actually accepts, at least tentatively, as deserved. His threats to end the friendship loom over the entire letter, but hurtling from one extreme to the other, he insists on knowing why Bosie has not been writing to him ("Your silence has been horrible") and at the end he extends his affection, with hopes for a reunion "in some quiet foreign town." His human need for love breaks through.

Gazing at his image, he sees Bosie's faults, which are actually his own faults projected onto Bosie. He can tolerate self-accusation only by accusing Bosie. Blaming his young lover, he begs for his affection. He seeks the healing touch of love that all depressed people seek. The great cynic in the end needs to love and be loved: "Ah! Had you been in prison—I will not say through any fault of mine, for that would be a thought too terrible for me to bear—but through fault of your own, error of your own, faith in some unworthy friend, slip in sensual mire, trust misapplied, or love ill-bestowed, or none, or all of these— do you think that I would have allowed you to eat your heart away in darkness in solitude, without trying in some way, however slight, to help you to bear the bitter burden of your disgrace?" Airing his own faults under the guise of airing Bosie's, Wilde cannot be faulted: "Do you think that I would not have let you know that if you suffered, I was suffering too: that if you wept, there were tears in my eyes also: and that if you lay in the house of bondage and were despised of men, I out of my very griefs had built a house in which to dwell until your coming" (*L,* 463). Wilde was in reality too self-critical not to blame himself. His description of the loving benevolence that he would have bestowed on Bosie had Bosie been imprisoned spreads a narcissistic balm on the gaping wound of Wilde's self-accusations. Unable to see himself realistically enough to acknowledge that these are self-accusations, he has no real hope of self-resurrection through self-transformation. The old narcissistic Wilde will never die, so the new self-analytic Wilde is aborted.

To justify his terrible experiences as a necessary phase in his development as a writer, Wilde dwells on his memory of a horrifying afternoon five months into his prison term, when he was transferred from Wandsworth Prison to

Reading Gaol, an experience that darkened any hopes he may have had for being allowed to live peacefully after his release:

From two o'clock till half-past two on that day I had to stand on the centre platform of Clapham Junction in convict dress and handcuffed, for all the world to look at. . . . Of all possible objects I was the most grotesque. When people saw me they laughed. Each train as it came up swelled the audience. Nothing could exceed their amusement. That was of course before they knew who I was. As soon as they had been informed, they laughed still more. For half an hour I stood there in the gray November rain surrounded by a jeering mob. [One of the hecklers spat in his face.]³³ For a year after that was done to me I wept every day at the same hour and for the same space of time. (L, 491)

This degrading experience allowed him to exalt himself as an important martyr, one who "stood in symbolic relations to the art and culture of my age" (L, 466). He interprets his weeping in front of the mob as a good and necessary part of his development, for "a day in prison on which one does not weep is a day on which one's heart is hard, not a day on which one's heart is happy." His sorrows have, he claims, deepened his understanding of himself and of other people, so that he can now sympathize with sorrow.

Avrom Fleishman has suggested that "it is but a short step from Clapham Junction to Golgotha."³⁴ Wilde's vision of himself at Clapham Junction as Christ being abused on the road to Golgotha would allow him to find a reason for his humiliation in his ultimate resurrection. Christ was ordained to suffer and be crucified so that he could return to life with increased power and authority; Wilde longed to see the same reward in his own sufferings. As his prose poem "The Master" (written at least ten months before he was imprisoned) reveals, he was disappointed at not yet having made it as far as Golgotha. As I mentioned earlier, Wilde's works of art were blueprints— unconscious plans for his life: "Every single work of art is the fulfillment of a prophecy," he wrote in De Profundis (L, 481).

In "The Master," published in July 1894, Wilde's unconscious wish to be crucified and his feeling that he is being slighted when no one bothers to nail him to the cross, are quite transparent. In the story, Joseph of Arimethea, on his way home from the Crucifixion, meets a disheveled and lachrymose young man who is masquerading as Christ, having "wounded his body with thorns, and [set] on his hair . . . ashes as a crown." When Joseph offers him condolence for Christ's death, the young man cries: "It is not for Him that I am weeping, but for myself. I too have changed water into wine, and I have healed the leper and given sight to the blind. I have walked upon the waters, and from the dwellers in the tombs I have cast out devils. . . . All things that this man has done I have done also. And yet they have not crucified me" (*CW*, 865).

When Jesus Christ yielded up the ghost, no less than an earthquake and mass terror made up for his degradation: "And behold, the veil of the temple was rent in twain from the top to the bottom; and the earth did quake, and the rocks rent; and the graves were opened; and many bodies of the saints which slept arose, and came out of the graves after his resurrection" (Matt. 27:51– 53, King James Version). Admiring these special effects, Wilde must have felt like the damp firecracker in his charming story "The Remarkable Rocket"; in it, the explosive dries off just enough to be successfully ignited but fails to explode and, as he is fizzling out, gasps: "I knew I should create a great sensation" (*CW*, 310).

It made sense for Wilde to try to rebuild his image by continuing to compare himself to Christ: he felt crucified as a homosexual. ("A pillory is a terrific reality.") Slowly but surely, because he "could not bear [his sufferings] to be without meaning," he tried to find some purpose in them. Of himself and Bosie he wrote, "Nature was in this matter a stepmother to both of us" (*L*, 491, 467, 413). He wanted to put the blame for his sufferings on anyone else—if not Bosie, then Mother Nature—anyone but himself. He had tried to be a savior, but he was now a savior in considerable need of being saved himself.[35]

Comparing his sufferings to those of Christ, Wilde sounds much like other Christian autobiographers, although he is not one. He discovers late in life that "the secret of life is suffering." Christian typology comes in handy at this point. One cannot help remembering that Oxford was the site of his probable exposure to syphilis and of his first opportunities to participate in homosexual activity: "When I was at Oxford [I remember] saying to one of my friends . . . that I wanted to eat of the fruit of all the trees in the garden of the world." Following typological thinking, in *De Profundis* he has to be the fallen Adam who mystically foreshadows Christ, who thereby becomes the new Adam, fallen but redeemed, and through the same spiritual metamorphosis the redeemer. Wilde now condemns his own desire to experience only pleasure. In dithyrambic prose he unfolds the creative power of suffering: "Failure, disgrace, poverty, sorrow, despair, suffering, tears even, the broken words that come from the lips of pain. . . . The other half of the garden had its secrets for me also." He sees in the pain of Christ a prerequisite for producing great art: "I now see that sorrow, being the supreme emotion of which man is capable, is at once the type and test of all great art" (*L*, 473–75).

Sorrow becomes for Wilde the new path to creative possibilities. As in the Christian types of suffering of Old Testament figures, his sufferings will be justified by the great art that he hopes his sorrow will lead him to produce. He even clings to typological language to convince himself that all his pain, self-inflicted as it was, was a secretly planned part of his artistic development: "Of course all this is foreshadowed and prefigured in my art. Some of it is in 'The Happy Prince:' some of it in 'The Young King,' notably in the passage where the Bishop says to the kneeling boy: 'Is not He who made misery wiser than thou art?'" At this point he needed the fantasy that there was a divine plan behind his utter failure to give him the strength for what remained of his future.[36]

He seized upon the story of Christ, who had been brought back to life. The situation being what it was, it would have made little sense for Wilde to resurrect Oscar Wilde the dandy and wit. The idea of becoming a Christ figure had, however, been brewing for some time. In *Salome* Wilde had already found a vehicle for projecting his wish to be, if not Christ himself, then at least his prophet, Jokanaan. The character of Jokanaan, who is critical of the aristocracy and disdainful of the blandishments of women, is a projection of Wilde. In the person of Salome, Wilde created a superb representation of sexual perversity—oral greed and anal sadism culminating in necrophilia. She is, as discussed earlier, a revenant of his sister, Isola, but he projects upon her some of his own most morbid desires. He was once even photographed in costume as Salome.[37] Probably having foreseen himself in a dungeon like Jokanaan, Wilde seems in *De Profundis* to gather strength from the anger of the holy man against his society. He reveals that he unconsciously identifies his aggressive homosexuality with his defiant wit: "What the paradox was to me in the sphere of thought, perversity became to me in the sphere of passion" (*L*, 466). Much more than a casual quip, this remark deserves analysis. It is part sad confession, part inaccurate attempt to reconstruct his life before prison: he seems to mean that he dried up as an artist and philosopher when he exchanged the labor of intellectual acrobatics for perversity—that satiation of an appetite that left no him no energy or inclination for the unique expression of his genius through paradox. In fact, he did not exchange sublimated artistic labor for sexual indulgence. He was always engaged in both activities, but toward the latter part of his artistic career he became more and more sexually self-indulgent, more promiscuous, less careful, less devoted to art, and more devoted to boys.

His famous paradoxes were, among other things, his way of proclaiming his idiomatic, deviant, subjective truth of the moment—truths uttered, like Jokanaan's truths, to shock the aristocracy into reforming itself. His perversity, his homosexuality, was his reality, the basis of his subjective truth: he was a homosexual—a homosexual prophet. Like Jokanaan's violent cries into a

moral wilderness, Wilde's paradoxes were intellectual denunciations, a form
of sadomasochism. He proclaimed his truths in such a way that he confused,
rather than enlightened, his listeners and was punished—decapitated—for
his aggression: his image was beheaded.

Wilde's affinity to other crisis autobiographers does not go beyond a vague
yearning to resurrect himself and a perverse desire to do so by being different
from them. Ultimately he asserts not that he is like Christ but rather that
Christ is like the artist, which means of course that Christ resembles Wilde:
"I see a far more intimate and immediate connection between the true life of
Christ and the true life of the artist. . . . Christ [is] the true precursor of the
romantic movement. . . . Christ's place is indeed with the poets" (L, 476–
77). Instead of Wilde trying to be a type of Christ, Christ becomes a type of
Wilde, a romantic poet, as Wilde liked to see himself. He endures all his
terrible sufferings not so much to be like Christ but because in the topsy-
turvy Wildean version of typology, Christ's sufferings make him a type of
good artist, and Wilde's suffering is the ordained way of becoming a good
artist like Christ. In fact, ten pages near the end of De Profundis are devoted to
the praise of Christ, who comes to bear a remarkable similarity to Oscar
Wilde.

Wilde imagines Christ as a poet and hero rising, as he himself rose, from
nonaristocratic beginnings to a kind of self-made nobility: "There is still
something to me almost incredible in the idea of a young Galilean peasant
imagining that he could bear on his own shoulders the burden of the entire
world: all that had been already done and suffered, and all that was yet to be
done and suffered: the sins of Nero, of Ceasar Borgia . . . oppressed nationalities, factory children, thieves, people in prisons, outcasts" (L, 477). This
Christ is an Atlas, with superhuman, heroic strength, shouldering all that
Wilde's mother wanted her Ossianic Oscar to bear: the burdens of oppressed
nationalities and oppressed minorities. Returning obsessively to the theme of
the heroic self-made Christ, Wilde writes: "Out of the carpenter's shop at
Nazareth had come a personality infinitely greater than any made by myth or
legend" (L, 481). Out of a middle-class Dublin surgeon's home had come
Oscar Wilde, a personality ordained to follow the grandiose imaginings of his
mother. Wilde's mention of Christ in the carpenter's shop was probably
prompted by a thought of Sir John Everett Millais's painting Christ in the
House of His Parents, in which the young Christ shows his cut hand to his
mother while sheep—Christ's future flock—nose in at the window. The irrev-
erence of Millais's painting is the background for Wilde's image of himself
as Christ—and indeed, as Wilde confesses toward the end of De Profundis:
"Religion does not help me" (L, 468).

Wilde has a way of picking out similarities between himself and Christ: "One always thinks of him as a young bridegroom with his companions." This was, alas, exactly the kind of young bridegroom Wilde had been, always leaving his wife for his male companions. "I see no difficulty at all in believing that such was the charm of his personality that his mere presence could bring peace to souls in anguish" (L, 478). This is patting himself on the back for a quality he actually possessed. When he goes on to claim that "to live for others as a definite self-conscious aim was not [Christ's] creed," he is trying again to reconcile his need to live for himself with his mother's need that he live for Ireland: "While Christ did not say to men, 'Live for others,' he pointed out that there was no difference at all between the lives of others and one's own life" (L, 479–80).

The point of all this was to write a crisis autobiography modeled after what he thought Newman's *Apologia* was like—to show that he had undergone a transformation or entered a new and better state of being, that he had become a serious and sorrowing artist and had been reborn as a result of his immense, enduring emotional turmoil. To the last moment Wilde intended to appear at least as if he were going write a crisis autobiography in the Christian style but then do the opposite. Triumphantly Wilde sounds his final note: "We are no longer in Art concerned with the type. It is with the exception we have to do" (L, 489). He dispenses with the Christian type that has been all along inform-ing his autobiographical explorations and announces that he will consider only the exception—that is, himself. "For [Christ] there were no laws: there were exceptions only" (L, 488).

These sudden reversals are typical. An early reviewer of his poetry said, "Mr. Wilde imitates Keats, but in Keats there is nothing in the least like these passages; they can indeed be paralleled in Whitman, but Whitman's offences rest on a somewhat different ground. . . . Mr. Wilde may talk of Greece; but there is nothing Greek about his poems; his nudities do not suggest the sacred whiteness of an antique statue, but rather the forcible unveiling of some insulted innocence."[38] Another critic wrote, "His method is this: he takes some well-established truth, something in which the wisdom of centu-ries and the wit of the greatest men have concurred, and asserts the contrary."[39]

The question is why he did so. Wilde himself offers no direct answers. The inner process that produced his wit also produced *De Profundis*. He never directly discusses the sources of his strange need to display clever and precise imitations of other writers while flaunting his contempt for imitation. His simultaneous fascination and disgust with imitation is felt in all his work. Implying that Christ is actually like himself, rather than the other way around, is an attempt to reconcile his need to imitate him with his denial of all imitation. In the desperate struggle not to imitate, he has to imitate Christ because he sees him as a complete original, but he defends himself even against that imitation: "Above all, Christ is the most supreme of Individualists. Most people are other people. Their thoughts are someone else's opinions, their life a mimicry, their passions a quotation" (*L,* 479).

In one of Wilde's prose poems he recounts sardonically a conference between a group of iron filings who are debating whether or not they should go and visit the magnet and who, predictably, find themselves on their way before they even realize it. The same feeling, perhaps, went into his observation that "autobiography is irresistible" (*CW,* 1010). He yields to the urge, in all his works, to reveal that he needs to imitate and to deny that he imitates. Banking on this urge, he contents himself with the notion that he "never reads Flaubert's *Tentation de St Antoine*" without signing his name at the end: "All the best Hundred Books bear my signature in this manner."[40]

When Max Beerbohm reviewed *De Profundis,* he observed that

some of the critics, wishing to reconcile recent enthusiasm with past obloquy, have been suggesting that *De Profundis* is quite unlike any previous work of Oscar Wilde— a quite sudden and unrelated phenomenon. Oscar Wilde, according to them, was gloriously transformed by incarceration. Their theory comprises two fallacies. The first fallacy is that Oscar Wilde had been mainly remarkable for his wit. In point of fact, wit was the least important of his gifts. Primarily he was a poet, with a life-long passion for beauty; and a philosopher with a lifelong passion for thought. His wit, and his humour (which was of an even finer quality than his wit), sprang from a very solid basis of seriousness, as all good wit or humour must.[41]

The seriousness was his profound interest in understanding human nature, especially his own. He was really a sad observer, a poet concealing the warmth of his personality—his "beautiful, kindly humor," as Frank Harris wrote.[42] At the same time he was trying to externalize in the form of wit the self-destructive elements that had been raging inside. The main aspect of his personality was not witty and charming but tragic. In one sense comparing himself to Christ was the last jest of a man whose great talent was spent in turning the struggle for internal stability into a joke. One can discern the difficulty of understanding and evaluating Wilde in the inability of those who denigrated him as a weeping Pierrot to see the tragic face behind the mask. They took the buffoon's face for the reality rather than perceiving the clown whose heart was broken (*L,* 490).

In a letter to Frank Harris of 18 February 1899, Wilde remarked that he had written to his publisher, Leonard Smithers, regarding a new printing of

The Importance of Being Earnest: "It is so trivial, so irresponsible a comedy: and while the public liked to hear of my pain—curiosity and the autobiographical form being elements of interest [in *The Ballad of Reading Gaol*] I am not sure that they will welcome me again in airy mood and spirit, mocking at morals, and defiance of social rules. There is, or at least in their eyes there should be, such a gap between the two Oscars" (*L,* 780). Thus it is difficult to say whether the new Wilde was genuine or just a new pose—he was both.

Wilde left prison on 19 May 1897. With Reading Gaol behind him, he could see himself as a saint, or at least as someone who was sincerely striving for sainthood. Wilde's self-analyses always end in an attempt to make himself out as a saint rather than a sinner. In a postcard of mid-June 1897 he recounted that he had just been to the local church at Berneval-sur-Mer to see a first communion: "very sweet, and flowerlike with children. The curé's hopes are at their highest. *Sed non sum dignus,"* he complains (*L,* 606). Simply trying to accomplish peace with himself, he avoids both conflict and change. He could become a saint only in fantasy, and he was ready to fulfill at least one part of this fantasy—that no saint exists who is without sin: "The only difference between a saint and a sinner is that every saint has a past and every sinner has a future," he proclaims serenely.

Like a saint, he had been dying for the sins of others, the nameless homosexuals of his age. He deemed this sacrifice Christ-like. In the old days he had always forgiven Bosie yet failed to change him. Explaining to himself his lack of success, he says: "Only one whose life is without stain can forgive sin." Now Christ-like he has hope that his new status of near holiness will alter Bosie's character. Hoping for greater power to transform both of their characters, he tries to impress Bosie with the idea that his sufferings have ennobled him: "My forgiveness should mean a great deal to you now" (*L,* 465).

By the end of *De Profundis* much of his bitterness has evaporated, and his love for Bosie breaks through; he signs himself "Your affectionate friend." The appeal to Bosie, the need to revisit mentally all the scenes of their scandal, show that the wish to change or understand himself yields to the longing to return to his old life. He told Robert Ross that the *Ballad of Reading Gaol* was not really about his prison life but about his life at Naples with Bosie, which he deemed the source of "all the best stanzas" (*L,* 731n). And indeed, no sooner was he out of prison than he went right back to being "hand in glove with all the little boys on the boulevard," as Bosie said. In two letters of late December 1898, Wilde wrote: "I am leading a very good life, and it does not agree with me. There is a sad lack of fauns in the pinewoods at

Napoule. . . . I have two special friends, one called Raphael, the other Fortune—both quite perfect, except," he adds, like the old Wilde, "that they can read and write" (*ML*, 176–77). In a letter of September 1900, written just two months before he died a lingering and horrible death of suppurative otitis media, he wrote: "A slim brown Egyptian, rather like a handsome bamboo walking-stick, occasionally serves me drinks at the Café d'Égypte, but he does not console me for the loss of the wanton sylvan boy of Italy" (*L*, 834).

When Wilde left prison, his worst expectations of public rejection were fulfilled. Although he had adopted a pseudonym to avoid detection, the name he chose, Sebastian Melmoth, reveals that he expected or invited harassment: Sebastian is the saint who was pierced with arrows, and Melmoth is the name of the unlucky wandering Jew in the novel *Melmoth the Wanderer*, which Wilde's great-uncle had written. The curse affected the fate not only of Wilde but of his unhappy family as well. In 1895 his estranged wife, Constance, who had fled to Glion on Lake Geneva with her two young sons, was recognized by the proprietor of her hotel. In no uncertain terms he told her to leave, at which point she decided to change her name, as well as her sons', to Holland.[43]

Wilde was shunned in the streets even by old friends like George Alexander, who had acted the lead role of Ernest in *The Importance of Being Earnest*. In the summer of 1897 even Aubrey Beardsley failed to show up for dinner when Wilde invited him. It is true that not all Oscar's old friends deserted him, but he was often humiliated. There were, however, occasional humanitarian gestures. A woman writer whose novel Wilde had mocked saw him being snubbed by some English people one day. She went over to him, took his arm, and said loudly: "Oscar, take me to tea."[44] Such small kindnesses could not save him from his increased isolation, poverty, tendency to drink absinthe (or anything else in sight), public promenades with young boys, and deteriorating health. He was seen in shabby suits in shabby cafés surrounded by shabby male prostitutes.

The one great hope of his life had been to see Bosie again, but their reunion was a disaster. Bosie, who had loved the triumphant, aesthetic, mentally and physically perfumed Wilde, Wilde in the full flush of his success, was disappointed by the flabby, sickly, impoverished jailbird who was always asking for handouts. Wilde became destitute after his wife found out he was seeing Douglas and stopped her allowance to him. Bosie, neither willing nor able to support Wilde, managed occasionally to mobilize some funds, but never enough to be of significant help. Wilde's letters during his last two years show mental, physical, and economic decline: his handwriting steadily deteriorated; he lamented the loss of his once "Greek and gracious" lettering. The proprietor of the Hôtel d'Alsace, in which Wilde spent his last days, said that Wilde used to try to write at night. "Towards the end it became very difficult for him to write, and he used to whip himself up with cognac. A *litre* bottle would hardly see him through the night. And he ate little and took but little exercise. He used to sleep till noon, and then breakfast, and then sleep again till five or six in the evening."[45]

The theme of Wilde's final letters is disease and deterioration. He begs for money and complains of itching red rashes and of what he euphemistically termed "poisoning by mussels" (L, 817). He was treated with arsenic and strychnine, which in the nineteenth century were standard remedies for syphilis. He suffered extreme pain in his head and throat, along with the persistent rash. In the middle of November 1900, in one of his last letters, he complained to Frank Harris that he had "taken so much morphine that it has no more effect on me than water. Chloral and opium are the only things the doctor can think of, as the surgeon declines to allow any subcutaneous injections till the wounds heal up" (L, 840). His ear had been operated on for an infection, but the infection worsened and developed into the attack of meningitis that finally killed him. From 27 September 1900 on he had constant medical care for his rashes and ear infection. After the ear operation on 10 October he was weak, aged, disoriented, and usually bedridden, except when he insisted on going out for an absinthe. For the last week or so of his life he was delirious with a high fever. He died at 2:00 P.M. on 30 November 1900.

The source of the original ear injury is curious. Wilde gave what seems a spurious explanation to Frank Harris—that he had fallen on his ear in the chapel in Wandsworth Prison. "I must have burst the drum of it, or injured it in some way, for all through the winter it has ached and often bleeds a little."[46] The fall by itself does not seem a likely source of such a severe ear injury. Syphilis, though not the source of the final ear infection, cannot have improved his chances for recovering from it. Whatever the medical reality, one should remember that Wilde's father was an otologist and an eye and ear surgeon and that Oscar may have had fantasies connected with the ear. In *Salome*, Jokanaan's first description of Christ is: "When he cometh . . . the eyes of the blind shall see the day, and the ears of the deaf shall be opened" (CW, 554).

Looking back at the end of Oscar Wilde's life, one begins to understand the orphic utterance in *The Ballad of Reading Gaol* and the central theme of his life:

> The man had killed the thing he loved
> And so he had to die. (*CW*, 844)

One suspects several layers of meaning in these words. The end of his days approaching, Oscar holds judgment over himself and pronounces his death sentence: his syphilis has finally eroded the talented, boisterous, yet sensitive personality. He has knowingly disregarded the lives of others and possibly, even probably, infected his wife and his children. He has disappointed his mother and his father. He has disappointed Bosie. But most of all he has disappointed himself as an artist and as a human being full of high aims and ideals. He has been killing those he loves, especially the person he loved the most: Oscar Wilde, the poet, philosopher, and dramatist, who once remarked that "to love oneself is the beginning of a lifelong romance" and who asserted in his trials that "I have never given adoration to anybody but myself."[47] With characteristic Wildean immodesty he becomes Everyman in the *Ballad*:

> And all men kill the thing they love,
>   By all let this be heard,
> Some do it with a bitter look,
>   Some with a flattering word,
> The coward does it with a kiss
>   The brave man with a sword. (*CW*, 860)

The *Ballad*, Wilde's final literary effort, written at Naples between May and July 1897, was, as he said, his *"chant de cygne."* He bids adieu, "sorry to leave with a cry of pain—a song of Marsyas, not a song of Apollo; but Life, that I have loved so much—too much—has torn me like a tiger. . . . [I am] the ruin and wreck of what once was wonderful and brilliant, and terribly improbable" (*L*, 715). Realizing that he was dying and wanting to pull himself together for a last creative effort, he expels a long sigh—one hundred and nine stanzas long—a swan song indeed, though hardly that of a lily-white swan. He was not a man to choose either form or content casually. Deciding on the popular ballad form for his last poem, Wilde emphasizes his fall from the refined height of the life which he had led. The latest of all the Oscar Wildes, the dying soldier of the *Ballad*, is a hero we have not met before in his oeuvre, a common man.

A soldier whom Wilde has seen every day for several weeks is being executed. Wilde immediately puts himself in the soldier's place at the moment of execution:

> And the wild regrets and the bloody sweats
> None knew so well as I. (*CW*, 853)

With "wild" used as the unconscious link between the soldier and Oscar and "bloody sweats" as a vivid image of disease, the syphilis is again at the center of his daily life. Again the oblique self-condemnation: he is accusing himself of being a murderer, of killing the thing he loved, by having given his disease to all the boys whose beds he shared. He feels that he deserves to die for passing it on. The meter of the poem is taken from Thomas Hood's popular poem of 1829, "The Dream of Eugene Aram," about a murderer and the terrible guilt that betrays him. Wilde was drawn to the meter because it stood for the content of Hood's poem and for Wilde's self-accusations.

Much of Wilde's imagery supports this interpretation. He endows a group of phantoms haunting the prison on the night before the execution with vaguely sexual sins:

> Some wheeled in smirking pairs;
> With the mincing step of a demirep
> Some sidled up the stairs.

Just before this, the phantoms warn the prisoners about taking chances, apparently sexual chances:

> *"he does not win who plays with Sin*
> *In the secret House of Shame!"* (CW, 851)

Wilde searches for redemption from his sins when he imagines roses blooming in the corpse of the dead soldier:

> For who can say by what strange way,
>   Christ brings his will to light,
> Since the barren staff the pilgrim bore
>   Bloomed in the great Pope's sight? (CW, 855)

This is a reference to Richard Wagner's *Tannhäuser,* in which the knight who sinned in the Mount of Venus—Venusberg, the mons veneris of female anatomy—is redeemed when his staff blooms in front of the Pope. In Wagner's version, Tannhäuser's redemption is connected with his death. Naturally, Wilde would want to glorify the death he imagined came from syphilis as an adequate penance for his "murders." Indeed, for Wilde, who went back to boys the minute he was out of prison, resurrection was really reerection; that was why he deemed himself unworthy of redemption. He jokes about the unlikeliness of his redemption in a letter of late March 1900, just eight months before his death: "I fear that if I went before the Holy Father with a blossoming rod it would turn into an umbrella or something dreadful of that kind. . . . Only an hour after I . . . had evolved a new evangel of morals, dear

Aleck [Robert Ross's elder brother] passed before the little *café* behind the Madeleine, and saw me with a beautiful boy in gray velvet. . . . His [Aleck's] smile was terrible. . . . I really felt it very much. At luncheon I had been singularly ethical. I am always ethical at the Café de la Paix" (*L,* 819).

All his life Oscar Wilde had planned to straighten out his account with one great act that would gain him redemption or forgiveness. But although he did not receive forgiveness, and indeed his life was not forgivable, we have to forgive him because of all he has given us.

NOTES

INTRODUCTION

1. The Judas kiss, the kiss that kills, was the coup de grace during his trials for indecent acts. When asked in cross-examination whether he had kissed a certain sixteen-year-old servant, Wilde replied, with some hauteur, that he had not, deriding the boy's ugliness. The prosecution took full advantage of this flippant reply, succeeded in bringing Wilde to the verge of tears, and turned the jury against him. H. Montgomery Hyde, ed., *The Trials of Oscar Wilde* (New York: Dover, 1962), 133.

2. Oscar Wilde, *The Letters of Oscar Wilde*, ed. Rupert Hart-Davis (New York: Harcourt, Brace and World, 1962), 373. Hereafter references to this work will be cited in the text as *L*.

3. Oscar Wilde, *A Woman of No Importance*, in *Complete Works of Oscar Wilde*, ed. Vyvyan Holland (London: Collins, 1986), 457. Hereafter references to this work will be cited in the text as *CW*.

4. In his study of Leonardo da Vinci, Freud remarked that biographers "devote their energies to the task of idealization, aimed at enrolling the great man among the class of their infantile models—at reviving in him, perhaps, the child's idea of his father." And if not God the father, then the devil. The result of this approach is an incomplete portrait: a "cold, strange, ideal figure instead of a human being to whom we might feel ourselves distantly related" (Sigmund Freud, "Leonardo Da Vinci and a Memory of His Childhood," in *The Standard Edition of the Complete Psychological Works of Sigmund Freud* [hereafter cited as *SE*], trans. James Strachey [London: Hogarth Press, 1981], 11:130). In *Freud and the Culture of Psychoanalysis* (Boston: George Allen and Unwin, 1984), Steven Marcus quotes Freud's sour remark that "biographical truth does not exist" and comments on the "problematics of biography, even in these advanced times," and on the complications and enrichment of biographic study that have come about as a result of Freud's influence: "As a rule, the great have been idealized by their followers and

contemporaries. In the name of truth and reality they are subsequently, again as a rule, de-idealized. The great now seem less than great and their followers seem absurd. Something's wrong here. It has now become the turn of the de-idealization to be seen as excessive and sometimes false and hence to be itself undone. And so it goes. The great by their self-generated words and autonomous deeds have changed the course of history; every great man is the result of a convergence of cultural-historical forces and an expression of them. Who's on first, what's on second, and both have to be true" (209).

5. Bernard C. Meyer, "Notes on the Uses of Psychoanalysis for Biography," *Psycho-analytic Quarterly* 56 (1987): 288.

6. Richard Ellmann, "Freud and Literary Biography," in *Freud and the Humanities,* ed. Peregrine Horden (New York: St. Martin's Press, 1985), 67, 70, 71.

7. Freud, "Dostoevsky and Parricide," *SE* 21:177.

8. Wilde, K39M3 081 (19—?), typescript (hereafter TS) of Coulson Kernahan, "Oscar Wilde: Some Recollections," William Andrews Clark Memorial Library, University of California, Los Angeles.

9. A. H. Cooper-Prichard, *Conversations with Oscar Wilde* (London: Philip Allan, 1931), 12, in Clark Library.

10. Wilde, MS T951L/S988, autograph letter signed (hereafter ALS), 26 August 1935, Reginald Turner to A. J. A. Symons, in Clark Library.

11. In 1857, three years after Wilde's birth, Thomas De Quincey's essay on Judas Iscariot appeared, an essay that Wilde, who admired De Quincey, probably read. The first two sentences could easily have been written about Wilde: "Everything connected with our ordinary conceptions of this man, of his real purposes . . . apparently is erroneous. Not one thing, but all things, must rank as false which traditionally we accept about him" ("Judas Iscariot," in *Studies on Secret Records, Personal and Historic; With Other Papers* [Edinburgh: James Hogg, 1858], 1). De Quincey argued that Judas was not necessarily a traitor, but a loyal devotee supporting his Lord. The redemption of the traitor as loyal to his Lord appealed to Wilde.

12. In a letter of 16 November 1885, Wilde asked: "Is the world a dust heap or a flower garden? . . . Poisonous, or perfect, or both?" (Wilde, *More Letters of Oscar Wilde,* ed. Rupert Hart-Davis [New York: Vanguard Press, 1985], 59; hereafter references to this work will be cited in the text as *ML*). In another letter he remarks that the basis of literary friendship is "mixing the poisoned bowl."

13. Arthur Ransome, *Oscar Wilde: A Critical Study* (London: Martin Secker, 1912), 199. Critchley's article can be found in the *Encyclopedia Britannica Medical and Health Annual, 1990* (Chicago: Encyclopedia Britannica, 1990).

14. Joris-Karl Huysmans, *Against Nature,* trans. Robert Baldick (London: Penguin, 1982), 98, 101, 102; originally published as *A rebours* (1884).

15. One of many books inspired by Wilde is Claude J. Summers, *Gay Fictions: Wilde to Stonewall; Studies in a Male Homosexual Literary Tradition* (New York: Contin-uum, 1990).

16. See, e.g., Eve Kosofsky Sedgwick, *Epistemology of the Closet* (Berkeley: University of California Press, 1990).

CHAPTER 1: *SALOME*

1. Richard Ellmann writes, "In his criticism and in his work generally, Wilde balanced two ideas which . . . look contradictory. One is that art is disengaged from actual life, the other that it is deeply incriminated with it. . . . That art is sterile, and that it is infectious, are attitudes not beyond reconciliation. Wilde never formulated their union, but he implied something like this: by its creation of beauty art reproaches the world, calling attention to the world's faults through their very omission: so the sterility of art is an affront or parable. Art may also outrage the world by flouting its laws or by picturing indulgently their violation. Or art may seduce the world by making it follow an example which seems bad but is discovered to be better than it seems. In these various ways the artist forces the world towards self-recognition. Yet this ethical or almost ethical view of art coexists in Wilde with its own cancellation" (Ellmann, introduction to *The Artist as Critic: Critical Writings of Oscar Wilde* (New York: Random House, 1969), xxvi–xxvii).

   Hesketh Pearson quotes Wilde as saying, "We are never more true to ourselves than when we are inconsistent" and commented that Wilde "could be as profound as he pretended to be superficial" (Hesketh Pearson, *Oscar Wilde: His Life and Wit* [New York: Harper and Bros., 1946], 126, 176). André Gide wrote, "I still wonder that the climax should have held so little surprise in a life so strangely conscious, a life in which even the fortuitous seemed deliberate" (André Gide, *Oscar Wilde,* trans. Bernard Frechtman [New York: Philosophical Library, 1949], viii). Jorge Luis Borges wrote: "By reading and re-reading Wilde in the course of the years, I have noticed a fact which his panegyrists seem not to have suspected: the simple, easy to verify fact that Wilde was nearly always right. *The Soul of Man Under Socialism* is not only eloquent but fair. His diverse articles in the *Pall Mall Gazette* and the *Speaker* were full of perspicacious observations which went beyond the possibilities of Leslie Stephen and Saintsbury in their best days. He offered to the age that which it craved, emotional comedies for the many, verbal arabesques for the few, and he accomplished these dissimilar tasks with a kind of careless happiness. . . . Wilde, a man who despite being used to evil and misfortune, retained an invulnerable innocence" (Jorge Luis Borges, "About Oscar Wilde," in *Other Inquisitions, 1937–1952,* trans. Ruth L. C. Simms [1946; rpt., New York: Simon and Schuster, 1965], 79–81).

2. W. W. Ward, "Oscar Wilde: An Oxford Reminiscence," appendix in Vyvyan Holland, *Son of Oscar Wilde* (New York: Oxford University Press, 1988), 250. Ward was one of Wilde's closest friends at Oxford.

3. H. Montgomery Hyde, *Oscar Wilde* (New York: Da Capo, 1981), 23–24.

4. Ibid., 137; Wilde's emphasis, as recorded by a stagehand.

5. Pearson, *Oscar Wilde,* 44.

6. Martin Fido, *Oscar Wilde: An Illustrated Biography* (New York: Peter Bedrick, 1985), 6.

7. Gide, *Oscar Wilde,* 16.

8. Hyde, *The Trials of Oscar Wilde,* 9.

9. Ibid., 152.

10. Pearson, *Oscar Wilde,* 255.

11. George Bernard Shaw, "My Memories of Oscar Wilde," in Frank Harris, *Oscar Wilde: His Life and Confessions* (New York: Covici, Friede, 1930), 393–94. Shaw writes: "You know that there is a disease called gigantism, caused by 'a certain morbid process in the sphenoid bone of the skull—viz., an excessive development of the anterior lobe of the pituitary body' (this is from the nearest encyclopedia). 'When this condition does not become active until after the age of twenty-five, by which time the long bones are consolidated, the result is acromegaly, which chiefly manifests itself in an enlargement of the hands and feet.' I never saw Lady Wilde's feet, but her hands were enormous, and never went straight to their aim when they grasped anything, but minced about, feeling for it. And the gigantic splaying of her palm was reproduced in her lumbar region. Now Oscar was an overgrown man, with something not quite normal about his bigness—something that made Lady Colin Campbell, who hated him, describe him as 'that great white caterpillar.' You yourself describe the disagreeable impression he made on you physically, in spite of his fine eyes and style. Well, I have always maintained that Oscar was a giant in the pathological sense, and that this explains a good deal of his weakness."

12. Harry Furniss, *Some Victorian Women* (John Lane, 1923), quoted in Terence de Vere White, *The Parents of Oscar Wilde: Sir William and Lady Wilde* (London: Hodder and Stoughton, 1967), 127.

13. Hyde, *Oscar Wilde,* 4.

14. Shaw, in Harris, *Oscar Wilde,* 388.

15. Harris, *Oscar Wilde,* 13.

16. Vyvyan Holland, *Oscar Wilde: A Pictorial Biography* (New York: Viking, 1960), 8.

17. Shaw, in Harris, *Oscar Wilde,* 388.

18. Pearson, *Oscar Wilde,* 9, 22.

19. White, *The Parents of Oscar Wilde,* 28, and Hyde, *Oscar Wilde,* 6.

20. Robert Kee, *Ireland: A History* (London: Abacus, 1982), 77, 101.

21. White, *The Parents of Oscar Wilde,* 84.

22. TS 559, p. 27, letter, Jane Francesca Elgee Wilde (hereafter JW) to unidentified, 1850; the letters of Lady Wilde, originally in the archives of Elkin Mathews, publisher, are now in the University of Reading Library.

23. TS 559, p. 13, letter, JW to "My kind friend," June 1848, University of Reading Library.

24. TS 559, pp. 48–49, letter, JW to unidentified, November 1852, University of Reading Library.

25. TS 559, p. 40, letter, JW to "My dear friend, enlightener and correspondent," Sunday, 1850, University of Reading Library.

26. In another letter she writes: "Everyone seems walled round with ice and egoism and form. There is no breaking down this barrier. Every day I feel this cold isolation more and more. Life to me is like wandering amid the snowfields of the North Pole. Some human form occasionally rises for a moment above a distant ice pack and then disappears again and I am left lonelier and chillier than ever. How can people weep at Death? To me it is the only happy moment of our miserable, incomprehensible existence. And yet Life can be beautiful" (TS 559, p. 33, letter, JW to unidentified, n.d. [ca. 1850], University of Reading Library).

27. White, *The Parents of Oscar Wilde*, 155.

28. TS, pp. 45–46, letter, JW to unidentified, 1852, University of Reading Library.

29. TS, pp. 47–48, letter, JW to unidentified, November 1852, University of Reading Library.

30. Ibid.

31. Ibid.

32. TS, p. 51, letter, JW to unidentified, 22 November 1854, University of Reading Library.

33. John Lahr, introduction to *The Plays of Oscar Wilde* (New York: Vintage, 1988), xvi.

34. Uncatalogued material, Clark Library.

35. MS Wilde W6712L W6721 (1895?), Clark Library.

36. Robert Harborough Sherard, *The Real Oscar Wilde* (Philadelphia: David McKay, n.d. [ca. 1915]), 177.

37. Horace Wyndham, *Speranza: A Biography of Lady Wilde* (London: Boardman, 1951), 73.

38. Hyde, *Oscar Wilde*, 10.

39. Robert D. Pepper, introduction to *Oscar Wilde, Irish Poets and Poetry of the Nineteenth Century: A Lecture Delivered in Platt's Hall, San Francisco, on Wednesday April Fifth, 1882*, ed. Robert D. Pepper (San Francisco: Book Club of San Francisco, 1972), 16.

40. Wyndham, *Speranza*, 205–06.

41. Wilde, *Irish Poets*, 30.

42. Ibid., 32–33.

43. White, *The Parents of Oscar Wilde*, 18.

44. Freud, "A Childhood Recollection from *Dichtung und Wahrheit*," *SE* 17:156.

45. Uncatalogued material, letter, JW to Oscar Wilde, ca. 1893, Clark Library.

46. White, *The Parents of Oscar Wilde*, 262.

47. Ibid., 35–36, 60, 43–44.

48. Holland, *Son of Oscar Wilde*, 12, and Holland, *Oscar Wilde*, 12.

49. Quoted in Stuart Mason [Christopher Millard], *Bibliography of Oscar Wilde* (London: T. Werner Laurie, 1914), 295.

50. Sherard, *The Real Oscar Wilde*, 250.

51. Thomas Hood, "The Bridge of Sighs," in *The Complete Poetical Works of Thomas Hood,* ed. Walter Jerrold (London: Henry Frowde, 1906), 649–50.

52. Quoted in Mason, *Bibliography of Oscar Wilde,* 295.

53. Ibid., 295–96. The portion of *Parodies of the Works of English and American Authors* quoted is from vol. 6, pt. 64.

54. Emile Zola, *Nana* (Cleveland: Fine Editions Press, 1946), 467.

55. This is suggested in the reflections of Wilde's biographer Boris Brasol: "[It is not] fair to draw parallels between 'Requiescat,' a hymn to innocence, to a darling child, fragrant and chaste as the lily of the valley, and Hood's plea in defense of a 'fallen woman' stained with 'muddy impurity.' Besides, even if it were true that Wilde had been influenced by the *Bridge of Sighs,* this does not in the least rob *Requiescat* of its singular beauty (Boris Brasol, *Oscar Wilde: The Man, The Artist, The Martyr* [New York: Octagon Books, 1975], 82). Actually a number of writers have drawn attention to this curious selection of meter by Wilde; Arthur Ransome wrote in 1912 that it "seems ungracious to remember this poem's indebtedness to Hood" (quoted in Mason, *Bibliography of Oscar Wilde,* 295). In 1914 Bosie contemptuously referred to Wilde's poem as "a flagrant copy of Hood's lines beginning 'Take her up tenderly'" (Lord Alfred Douglas, *Oscar Wilde and Myself* [New York: Duffield, 1914], 204–05). Frances Winwar remarked in 1940 that Wilde had borrowed from Hood "the rhythm of his dirge for Isola, 'Requiescat,' the sole perfect poem of his volume of poems" (Winwar, *Oscar Wilde and the Yellow Nineties* [New York: Blue Ribbon, 1940], 68). Hesketh Pearson in 1946 called the poem derivative (Pearson, *Oscar Wilde,* 99), and H. Montgomery Hyde wrote in 1975 that the poem "owes something at least in metre to Hood" (Hyde, *Oscar Wilde,* 7).

56. Martin Seymour-Smith, *Fallen Women* (London: Thomas Nelson, 1969), 166.

57. Alfred, Lord Tennyson, *In Memoriam* (1850; New York: Norton, 1973), p. 11 (sect. 13, l. 1) and p. 14 (sect. 17, ll. 19–20); p. 63 (sect. 97); p. 20 (sect. 27).

58. Freud, "The Question of Lay Analysis," *SE* 20:186.

59. Hyde, *Oscar Wilde,* 370.

60. Matthew Arnold, "Requiescat," in *Poetry and Criticism of Matthew Arnold,* ed. A. Dwight Culler (Boston: Houghton Mifflin, 1961), 147.

61. TS 559, p. 46, letter, JW to unidentified, 1852, University of Reading Library.

62. White, *The Parents of Oscar Wilde,* 147.

63. Ibid., 152–204.

64. The *Daily News of London* of 19 December 1864 had an editorial that began, "The court of Common Pleas in Dublin was engaged during five days of last week in trying a libel case which the reporters have modestly entitled 'extraordinary,' and which, if there were no Divorce Court on this side of St. George's Channel, we should be disposed in this place to describe as disgusting. It is not, however, the quality of the literature of this trial that boasts an exceptional savour among the garbage of the law courts. It is rather that relative position of the parties to the action that appears 'extraordinary' to those who have not had the advantage of

being present at the trial" (4). The *Times* of London of 20 December 1864 offered this: "To English eyes Lady Wilde's lot will appear to be the hardest, for she had been subjected to annoyances which it was almost impossible to endure, and she had taken what seemed to her the most proper course in writing privately to the father of the lady who gave her cause for complaint. Still some of the expressions in her letter were indefensible. Had Lady Wilde simply called upon Dr. Travers to restrain his daughter from annoying her she could hardly have been blamed, but the actual terms and charges of the letter seem to have been regarded by the Jury as libelous. . . . We can only think it unfortunate that so much scandal was ever allowed to become public" (6–7). Both newspapers are in the National Library of Ireland, Dublin.

65. Hyde, *Oscar Wilde,* 10.
66. Alexander Grinstein alludes to the death of Isola as a significant influence in Wilde's work; see "On Oscar Wilde" (*Annual of Psychoanalysis,* vol. 1, ed. Chicago Institute of Psychoanalysis [New York: Quadrangle, 1973], 345–662) and "Oscar Wilde" (*American Imago* 37, no. 2 [Summer 1980]: 125–79). Karl Beckson also mentions, in "Oscar Wilde and the Masks of Narcissus," the influence of Wilde's sister's death on his work. Observing Wilde's decorations on the envelope in which he kept his sister's hair, Beckson speculates on Wilde's "identification with the lost object" and suggests that "the young Oscar had developed a rescue or revenge fantasy concerning Isola. . . . The envelope containing her hair was a talisman" (*Psychoanalytic Study of Society,* vol. 10, ed. Werner Muensterberger, L. Bryce Boyer, and Simon A. Grolnick [Hillsdale, N.J.: Analytic Press, 1984], 255). Jerome Kavka also cites Wilde's narcissism and guilt for the death of his sister as important elements in *The Picture of Dorian Gray* ("Oscar Wilde's Narcissism," *Annual of Psychoanalysis,* vol. 3 [New York: International Universities Press, 1975], 408).
67. Walter Pater, "The Child in the House," in *Imaginary Portraits,* ed. Eugen J. Bryzenk (New York: Harper and Row, 1964), 27.
68. Samuel Taylor Coleridge, "The Rime of the Ancient Mariner," in *The Portable Coleridge,* ed. I. A. Richards (New York: Viking, 1978), 86.
69. Ibid., 88–89, 94.
70. Douglas, *Oscar Wilde and Myself,* 122–23, 124.
71. Edward Shanks, "Oscar Wilde," in *Oscar Wilde: The Critical Heritage,* ed. Karl Beckson (London: Routledge and Kegan Paul, 1970), 409.
72. Quoted in Hyde, *The Trials of Oscar Wilde,* 39.
73. W. H. Auden, *Forewords and Afterwords* (New York: Random House, 1973), 321.
74. Averil Gardner, "'Literary Petty Larceny': Plagiarism in Oscar Wilde's Early Poetry," *English Studies in Canada* 8, no. 1 (March 1982): 49–61.
75. Quoted in Hyde, *The Trials of Oscar Wilde,* 39–40.
76. T. G. Wilson, *Victorian Doctor* (London: Methuen, 1942), 199. Arthur Ransome writes: "It is said that before Wilde's birth, his mother had hoped for a girl. He was a second son" (Ransome, *Oscar Wilde* [1912], 29).

77. MS 10, 517, letter, Jane Francesca Elgee to unidentified (probably Charles Gavan Duffy, editor of *The Nation*), among "Six Miscellaneous Letters of Figures in the Young Ireland Movement," National Library of Ireland.

78. White, *The Parents of Oscar Wilde,* 104, 105.

79. TS 559, p. 51, letter, JW to unidentified, 22 November 1854, University of Reading Library.

80. Wyndham, *Speranza,* 77, 108.

81. Ibid., 197.

82. "Historic Women," *Woman's World,* January 1888, 97, Clark Library.

83. Max Beerbohm, *Letters to Reggie Turner,* ed. Rupert Hart-Davis (London: Soho Square/Richard Clay, 1964), 37.

84. A recent article summarizes some of the difficulties: Robert M. Friedman, "The Psychoanalytic Model of Male Homosexuality: A Historical and Theoretical Critique," *Psychoanalytic Review* 73, no. 4 (Winter 1986): 79–115.

85. Pearson, *Oscar Wilde,* 9.

86. Beerbohm, *Letters to Reggie Turner,* 63.

87. Freud, "New Introductory Lectures on Psycho-Analysis," *SE* 22:100–01.

88. Sir Edmund Trelawny Backhouse, "The Dead Past" (written in Peking in 1943), MS Eng. misc. d. 1225, pp. 69ff., Bodleian Library, Oxford University.

89. Hyde, *Oscar Wilde,* 187, 393.

90. Hyde, *The Trials of Oscar Wilde,* 254.

91. Freud, *The Interpretation of Dreams, SE* 4:111–12. Regarding the musical aspects of *Salome,* Pater writes in "The School of Giorgione" that "all the arts in common [are] aspiring towards the principle of music; music being the typical, or ideally consummate art, the object of the great *Anders-Streben* of all art, of all that is artistic, or partakes of artistic qualities. *All art constantly aspires towards the condition of music"* (*The Renaissance: Studies in Art and Poetry,* ed. Donald L. Hill [Berkeley: University of California Press], 105–06). Incidentally, when Lord Alfred Douglas reviewed *Salome* for an Oxford undergraduate publication he edited, he seemed quite taken with the comparison of *Salome* to a piece of music: "One thing strikes one very forcibly in the treatment, the musical form of it. Again and again it seems to one that in reading one is listening; listening, not to the author, not the direct unfolding of a plot, but to the tones of different instruments, suggesting, suggesting, always indirectly, till one feels that by shutting one's eyes one can best catch the suggestion" (*The Spirit Lamp: An Aesthetic, Literary and Critical Magazine,* p. 20, Clark Library).

92. W. Graham Robertson, "Of Oscar Wilde," in *Time Was* (London: Hamish Hamilton, 1931), 130–38; rpt. E. H. Mikhail, *Oscar Wilde: Interviews and Recollections,* 2 vols. (London: Macmillan, 1979), 1:212.

93. Freud, "Three Essays on the Theory of Sexuality," *SE* 7:198.

94. Wyndham, *Speranza,* 76–77.

95. Pearson, *Oscar Wilde,* 94.

96. Richard Ellmann, *Oscar Wilde* (London: Hamish Hamilton, 1987), 13.

97. Wyndham, *Speranza,* 70.

98. Sherard, *The Real Oscar Wilde,* 65–66.

99. Wyndham, *Speranza,* 71.

100. William M. Murphy, *Prodigal Father: The Life of John Butler Yeats, 1839–1922* (Ithaca: Cornell University Press, 1978), 551. The senior Yeats wrote to his son, "I wonder what Lady Wilde thought of her husband? I remember the scandalous trial in Dublin when he escaped by the skin of his teeth. On that occasion, Lady Wilde was loyal."

101. Wyndham, *Speranza,* 69, 68, 114–16, 76.

102. Ibid., 87.

103. Freud, *The Interpretation of Dreams, SE* 5:408–09.

104. Theodor Reik, *Listening with the Third Ear* (New York: Farrar, Straus, 1948), 249.

105. Christopher Nassaar, *Into the Demon Universe: A Literary Exploration of Oscar Wilde* (New Haven: Yale University Press, 1974), 99–100.

106. Unsigned review, *Pall Mall Gazette,* 23 February 1893; rpt. Beckson, *Oscar Wilde,* 137; see also 132–43.

107. Backhouse, "The Dead Past," 26ff.

108. André Gide remarked that "indeed Douglas' personality seemed much stronger and much more marked than Wilde's; yes, Douglas' personality was overweening; a sort of fatality swept him along; at times he seemed almost irresponsible; and as he never attempted to resist himself, he would not put up with anyone or anything resisting him either. To tell the truth Bosy [sic] interested me extremely; but 'terrible' he certainly was, and in my opinion it is he who ought to be held responsible for all that was disastrous in Wilde's career. Wilde beside him seemed gentle, wavering, and weak-willed. Douglas was possessed by the perverse instinct that drives a child to break his finest toy; nothing ever satisfied him; he always wanted to go one better." Gide, *If It Die . . .* (London: Secker and Warburg, 1950), 274, in Clark Library.

109. Richard Ellmann, "A Late Victorian Love Affair," in *Oscar Wilde: Two Approaches* (Los Angeles: William Andrews Clark Memorial Library, University of California, 1977), 10; Backhouse, "The Dead Past," sect. 3, entitled "Supplement: Oscar Wilde and Others," 53.

110. Beerbohm, *Letters to Reggie Turner,* 38–39.

111. Mary Hyde, introduction to *Bernard Shaw and Alfred Douglas: A Correspondence,* ed. Mary Hyde (New York: Ticknor and Fields, 1982), xxxix.

112. Douglas, *Oscar Wilde and Myself,* 28–29.

113. Hyde, *Oscar Wilde,* 142.

114. Alvin Redman, ed., *The Wit and Humor of Oscar Wilde* (New York: Dover, 1959), 130. This is the only source I have yet found for this remark, but I deem it genuine.

115. Lady Wilde, "The American Irish," rpt. Wyndham, *Speranza,* 222.

116. Hyde, *The Trials of Oscar Wilde,* 201, 133.

117. Pearson, *Oscar Wilde,* 271, 270.

118. Incidentally, Willie Wilde in a letter of the late 1880s (not precisely dated; Ms Wilde 6722L W6721, Clark Library) apparently refers to the Irish political interests embodied in this play and his brother's other early drama, *The Duchess of Padua:* "Well Oscar old dear . . . You are working bravely. . . . Say if you would like par [journalist's slang for a paragraph puffing something] about Vera or the Duchess of Bally Padua."
119. Redman, *The Wit and Humor of Oscar Wilde,* 118.
120. Beerbohm, *Letters to Reggie Turner,* 37.
121. Pearson, *Oscar Wilde,* 170–71.
122. Mikhail, *Oscar Wilde,* 2:450–51.

CHAPTER 2: DISEASE AND INSPIRATION

1. Richard Ellmann, "The Critic as Artist as Wilde," in *Golden Codgers* (New York: Oxford University Press, 1973), 70. According to Ellmann in his recent biography of Wilde, Wilde said to Reggie Turner, "Who do you think seduced me? Little Robbie" (*Oscar Wilde,* 261, 570). (He is referring to Robert Ross, then seventeen, who became a lifelong friend.) Ellmann therefore concludes that Wilde, until that seduction in 1886, had "managed not to commit himself about physical as once about spiritual things"—a reference to Wilde's indecisiveness about joining the Roman Catholic church. Ellmann's sources for this information are unpublished letters of A. J. A. Symons and Reggie Turner, as well as Arthur Ransome's biography of Wilde.
2. In a long letter to A. J. A. Symons (part of which I have quoted in the Introduction), Wilde's old friend Reginald Turner tells all he remembers about Oscar's early life and developing sexual inclinations. The letter reads, in part: "I never heard about his Oxford friends. . . . In his Irish school, Portora [boarding school] . . . Oscar was a contemporary of Edward Carson [later the prosecutor at his trial] & he told me they used to walk about the playing fields arms linked or around their necks—schoolboy-fashion. As to his abnormal inclinations & practices I don't think that he ever developed them till much later. He never hinted at any such early relationships or episodes. Instead [Indeed?] he asked me not long before he died to guess who it was who had seduced him, though he said he was conscious of impending fate before that. . . . He then told me. It was one of his great friends—he is no longer alive but I wont put his name on paper though I would tell you it when we meet for your private ear. When I told the person in question some time after Oscar's death he said it was not true but an invention of Oscar's, though he had no unusual objections to the fact, though he did not wish then to be saddled with any responsibility in a step which led to ruin or responsibility" (Wilde, MS T951L, ALS, 26 August 1935, Reginald Turner to A. J. A. Symons, Clark Library). Symons then apparently wrote back to Turner, having guessed correctly that the name in question was that of Robert Ross. Turner replied: "That was the name which I avoid mentioning. Certainly Oscar told me in

all seriousness but when I told Robbie he absolutely denied it & said Oscar was 'romancing.' However after what you say about Millard that settles it. R. no doubt had his reasons for denying it to me, especially as it was when his feud with Bosie was [growing?] hot, but as he *did* say it I never felt sure what was the truth? One knows that it [?] matters except as something [handwriting almost illegible] Oscar himself did not set much importance by it but told it to me as a matter of interest & not in any way of fixing any blame on anybody. He was too wise for that." There is another letter from one Cecil Georges Bazil to Christopher Millard, which reads in part: "May I ask you on what grounds or from what source, you can write, as Ransome has also written that Oscar's unlucky habits dated from 1886. Of course, when you wish it, I shall keep any detail secret" (Wilde B363L M645, 10 October 1925, Clark Library).

3. Wilfrid Hugh Chesson, "A Reminiscence of 1898," in *More Letters of Oscar Wilde,* ed. Hart-Davis, 204.

4. Wilde's sexual inclinations seem to have been known, at least to himself, long before 1886; from 1879 to 1881 he lived with Frank Miles, a homosexual, and both were close friends of another homosexual, Lord Ronald Gower (see Hyde, *Oscar Wilde,* 19, 25, 26, 35, 121, 185; see also Rupert Croft-Cooke, *Feasting with Panthers* [London: W. H. Allen, 1967]), 124, 171, 193–97, 203, 231). On 21 August 1881 Frank Miles's father wrote to Wilde to tell him that his wife had sliced out of the book entitled *Poems* one of Wilde's recently published poems. Very much the concerned father, he added, "As to morality, I can't help saying Frank ought to be clear—he has, I believe, often argued with you. Our first thought of course must be of him and his good name and his profession. If in sadness I advise a separation for a time it is not because we do not believe you in character to be very different to what you suggest in your poetry, but it is because you do not see the risks we see in a published poem that . . . makes all who read it say to themselves, 'this is outside the province of poetry,' 'it is licentious and may do a great harm to any soul that reads it'" (Ellmann, *Oscar Wilde,* 141–42, 146). According to Ellmann, Miles senior also wrote to his son, enjoining him to separate from Wilde, so perhaps there is some truth in Frank Harris's report that Miles's father insisted his son "should not be contaminated!" and had to part with Wilde (Frank Harris, *My Life and Loves,* ed. John F. Gallagher [New York: Grove Press, 1963], 414–17).

5. Wilde S551L/S988, ALS, Robert Sherard to A. J. A. Symons, 24 April 1935, Clark Library.

6. Uncatalogued materials, ALS, Robert Sherard to William Douglas Gray, 3 December 1933, Clark Library (the letter is in a pale green binder marked "Sherard, Robert Harborough, 1861–1943"). The sentence I quote occurs in a lengthy postscript defending Wilde against André Gide's claim that Wilde had slept with an under-age Arab boy: "I ought to issue a P.S. to *André Gide's Wicked Lies* [a pamphlet written by Sherard]. I ought to have pointed out the enormity of the charge agst [sic] Oscar considering the fact that he knew himself to be syphilitic and so,

supposing he had committed the outrage with which Gide (and Renier) charge him it would mean that in debauching an Arab child he would wilfully have exposed his victim to a terrible infection and disease. Kind, humane Oscar Wilde." But by that time—Wilde went to Algiers in 1895—he may no longer have been so kind and humane. Paresis destroys these qualities. ALS, Robert Sherard to A. J. A. Symons, May 1937, Clark Library.

7. Brasol, *Oscar Wilde,* 384.

8. Ellmann, *Oscar Wilde,* 86, 91.

9. William Allen Pusey, *The History and Epidemiology of Syphilis* (Springfield, Ill.: Charles C. Thomas, 1933), 59; John Thorne Crissey, M.D., and Lawrence Charles Parish, M.D., *The Dermatology and Syphilology of the Nineteenth Century* (New York: Praeger, 1981), 80–90, 94.

10. E. C. Tramont, "Treponema Pallidum" (Syphilis), in *Principles and Practice of Infectious Diseases,* ed. G. L. Mandell, R. G. Douglas, Jr., and J. E. Bennett (New York: John Wiley, 1990), 1794–1807; and telephone conversations during September–November 1993 with Neal H. Steigbigel, M.D., head, Division of Infectious Diseases, Montefiore Medical Center, professor of medicine, Albert Einstein College of Medicine, Bronx, New York. For a layperson's description of the course of the disease, see Sigmund Stephen Miller, ed., *Symptoms* (London: Pan/Macmillan, 1979), 366–68.

11. Tramont, "Treponema Pallidum," 1325.

12. Jonathan Hutchinson, F.R.S., LL.D., *Syphilis* (Philadelphia: Lea Bros., n.d. [ca. 1887]), 494. Hutchinson writes: "As a rule . . . to which there are very few exceptions, I think that we may hold that, after two years have elapsed, there is no risk of hereditary transmission. I am speaking of patients who have been under careful mercurial treatment. Most of my own patients have taken mercury in small doses for six or eight months continuously in the first instance, and often for several short periods subsequently. Many patients who were wishful to marry as early as possible, I have advised to continue mercury as a precaution through the whole of the two years. Although, however, I have myself had but few opportunities for observation in cases not treated by mercury, yet I am quite prepared to believe that the mere lapse of time is, in most cases, a very efficient cure for syphilis so far as its contagious properties are concerned. The virus appears to die out, although, as daily recurring facts prove, the individual's own liability to suffer from tertiary symptoms is by no means passed."

13. Ellmann, *Oscar Wilde,* 89–91, 99.

14. Crissey and Parish, *Dermatology and Syphilology,* 366.

15. Wilde MS H736L S988, letter, Otho Holland Lloyd to A. J. A. Symons, 22 May 1937, Clark Library.

16. ALS, Robert Sherard to A. J. A. Symons, 13 May 1937, Clark Library. For an account of Constance Wilde's illness and death, see Anne Clark Amor, *Mrs. Oscar Wilde: A Woman of Some Importance* (London: Sidgwick and Jackson, 1983), 155, 192, 212–14, 221, 224. I gratefully acknowledge permission to cite Constance

Wilde's unpublished love letters, the source for which must remain unidentified.

17. Unpublished letter from Robert Sherard to A. J. A. Symons, 13 May 1937, Clark Library.

18. Robert Sherard, *The Life of Oscar Wilde* (London: T. Werner Laurie, 1906), 334–39. Sherard writes: "He was ever a man fond of the pleasures of the table, of wines and spirits, and the use of the narcotic, tobacco. Till that point in his career [1892, when he reaped large financial rewards from his first comedy] absence of means had put a certain check upon extravagant indulgence. After his accession to prosperity this check was removed, and for many months, indeed, for the period of three years, he was overstimulating his body and poisoning his nerve-centres. . . . A very distinguished lady who has made a life study of the question of nutrition on the mental state of man recently expressed in a letter her conviction that it was to his irregular mode of life that much of Oscar Wilde's downfall could be attributed. . . . 'My belief is,' she wrote . . . 'that had he had some really true friend who could have kept all alcohol and meat and high living away from him he would have returned to his poor wife, and all would have been different.' Alcohol was sheer poison to him. All the extraordinary acts which he committed, the acts of sheer insanity, were committed, not when he was drunk, for he never was drunk, but when alcohol had developed an epileptic crisis in his brain."

19. Wilfrid Scawen Blunt, *My Diaries, Being a Personal Narrative of Events, 1888–1914* (London: Martin Secker, 1932), pt. 1, 145–46; rpt. Mikhail, *Oscar Wilde,* 1:237.

20. W. Graham Robertson, *Time Was* (London: Hamish Hamilton, 1931), 130–138; rpt. Mikhail, *Oscar Wilde,* 1:209–10.

21. Robert Ross, unfinished and unpublished preface (MS in Clark Library) to his projected collection of Wilde's letters to him (*L,* 564).

22. Doctor's report, Paris, 27 November 1900, quoted in Ellmann, *Oscar Wilde,* 547. One medical authority claims that his symptoms could have resulted from "an intercranial complication of suppurative otitis media, unrelated to syphilis." Terence Cawthorne, "The Last Illness of Oscar Wilde," *Proceedings of the Royal Society of Medicine* (London), 52 (February 1959): 123–27.

23. See Richard Ellmann's discussion of Wilde and syphilis in *Oscar Wilde,* 88–91; and see my Introduction, where I discuss the full history of Wilde's syphilis and his cause of death.

24. Backhouse, "Memoirs," 88.

25. Facsimile of letter written by Constance Wilde (Sherard, *The Real Oscar Wilde,* 173).

26. See Christopher Nassaar, *Into the Demon Universe: A Literary Exploration of Oscar Wilde* (New Haven: Yale University Press, 1974), 1.

27. Ellmann, *Oscar Wilde,* 90–91.

28. Unsigned interview, *St. James Gazette,* 18 January 1895 (*ML,* 196). Hart-Davis deduces from one of Wilde's letters (ca. January 1895) that the author of the interview was Robert Ross (*ML,* 128n).

29. Pearson, *Oscar Wilde,* 281, 330.

30. *The Letters of Oscar Wilde*, 848. See also Pearson, *Oscar Wilde*, 331; and Ellmann, *Oscar Wilde*, 545. According to Ellmann, Wilde complained to Alice Rothenstein, "I can't even afford to die."

31. Ellmann, *Oscar Wilde*, 546.

32. Freud, "Humour," *SE* 21:162.

33. William Sharp, untitled review, *Academy*, 5 September 1891, xl, 194; rpt. Beckson, *Oscar Wilde*, 108–09; and W. B. Yeats, "Oscar Wilde's Last Book," *United Ireland* 26 (September 1891): 5; rpt. Beckson, *Oscar Wilde*, 111.

34. Oscar Wilde, "Impressions of America," in Ellmann, *The Artist as Critic*, 6.

35. Eugen Bleuler, *Textbook of Psychiatry*, trans. A. A. Brill (New York: Dover, 1951), 252.

36. Pierre Champion, *Marcel Schwob et son temps* (Paris: n.p., 1927), 99; Vincent O'Sullivan, *Aspects of Wilde* (London: Constable, 1936), 75–76; both quoted in Ellmann, *Oscar Wilde*, 327.

37. Lillie Langtry, *The Days I Knew* (London: Hutchinson, 1925), 86–97; rpt. Mikhail, *Oscar Wilde*, 2:257.

38. Gide, *Oscar Wilde*, 20.

39. Pusey, *The History and Epidemiology of Syphilis*, 37.

40. William J. Brown, James F. Donoghue, Norman W. Axnick, Joseph H. Blount, Neal H. Ewen, and Oscar G. Jones, *Syphilis and Other Venereal Diseases* (Cambridge: Harvard University Press, 1970), 14.

41. Gide, *Oscar Wilde*, 14–15.

42. J. D. Rolleston, "The Folk-lore of Venereal Disease," *British Journal of Venereal Diseases* 18 (1942): 2–3, 5.

43. Jane Francesca Elgee Wilde, *Ancient Legends, Mystic Charms, and Superstitions of Ireland* (Boston: Ticknor, 1888), 199, 222–23.

44. Michael Grant and John Hazel, *Gods and Mortals in Classical Mythology* (Springfield, Mass.: Merriam, 1973), 365.

45. W. B. Yeats, *The Trembling of the Veil* (New York: Macmillan, 1927), 197.

46. Harris, *Oscar Wilde*, 337–38.

47. Nassaar, *Into the Demon Universe*, 7.

48. From 1888 to 1891 he produced two books of fairy tales, much literary criticism, a novel, and a drama, *Salome*. Since his children, Cyril and Vyvyan, were two and three in 1888, Wilde's first collection of fairy tales, *The Happy Prince and Other Tales*, may have been written for them. In the previous year, Wilde's mother had published her compilation of folklore, *Ancient Legends, Mystic Charms, and Superstitions of Ireland*, and in 1852, two years before Oscar was born, his father's study of Irish myths, *Irish Popular Superstitions*, had appeared; fairy tales were apparently a long-standing family interest, particularly because Oscar's father was interested in the archaeology and anthropology of ancient Ireland.

49. Unsigned review, *Pall Mall Gazette*, 30 November 1891, 3; unsigned review, *Athenaeum*, 6 February 1892, 177; unsigned review, *Theatre*, 1 June 1891, xvii, 295; rpt. Beckson, *Oscar Wilde*, 113, 117, 81.

50. Freud, *Delusions and Dreams in Jensen's Gradiva*, *SE* 9:35.

CHAPTER 3: WILDE IN HIS LETTERS

1. The personality revealed in the *Letters*—which were my first source for biographical facts and conclusions about Wilde—has led many critics to claim that in his
letters Wilde creates his greatest work of art. A typical comment came from Harry
T. Moore: "After [*The Importance of Being Earnest*] these letters may well prove to
be Wilde's most impressive achievement. . . . They exhibit [him] at his worst and
best, forgivable even in some of his most outrageous faking, and always magnet-
ically human" ("Correspondence De Profundis," *Saturday Review,* 20 October
1962, 26). In the *Spectator,* Constantine Fitzgibbon wrote that "the charming,
amusing, thoughtful, apparently imperious but fundamentally humble Oscar
Wilde who is revealed to us is far more interesting than the character of wit and
scandal and tragedy we have known from the partial and sometimes mendacious
biographies. . . . For here it is his own voice that we hear, and with so many
intonations and over so many years that after some 900 pages Oscar Wilde lives"
("The Fallacy of Reading Gaol," *Spectator,* 29 June 1962, 861). A. Dwight Culler
wrote in the *Yale Review,* "His letters are the documentary form in which [his life
as a work of art] has come down to us" ("Correspondents with Posterity," *Yale
Review* 52, no. 2 [December 1962]: 289).

   Wilde apparently inspired great letters in addition to writing them. The exuber-
ant missives from American dramatist Clyde Fitch (1865–1909), quoted below,
reveal what seems to have been a wonderful affair—with Wilde's writings as well
as with the man himself. Hints of *Salome*—specifically, the part imitating the Song
of Songs—and a fascination with Dorian and Mr. W. H. are evident.

You precious maddening man:
   Your letters are more than you—because they come and you *don't.* Last night
when I came home I flung myself in the best evening clothes and all with my
Blackwood. "I will just look at it" I thought. But I could not leave it. I read,
unconscious of the uncomfortability of my position and of the fact that one arm
and two legs were asleep, fast.
   Oh! Oscar!
   The story is *great*—and—fine!
   I believe in Willie Hughes: I don't care if the whole thing is out of your amazing
beautiful brain. I don't care for the laughter, I only know I am convinced and I *will.*
   I *will* believe in Willie H.
   Sometime, if the Gods are kind I shall *send you* a picture of Mr. W. H., it may be
another forgery—but that won't make any difference, will it?
   What?
   More! Only that isn't the word *Adoration!*
   Invent me a language of love. *You* could do it.
Bewilderedly, All yours

Clyde

[Wilde/F544L/W6721 (1889?), Clark Library]

Nobody loves you as *I* do. When you are here I dream. When you are away I awake. I and the chiming clock we have our secrets.

The book is here and I can hardly wait to read it. I am so proud of you, you great *great* man. Make me what you will only keep me yours forever.

Clyde
[Wilde/F544L/W6721/(189-?) a]

It is 3. And you are not coming. I've looked out of the window many, many times. The brown is blurred, quite colorless, and the silver heart is leaden.

---------I have not slept. I have only dreamt, and thought. I don't know where I stand, nor why. I don't care I only want to be *there. There.* You were right. Away with knowledge. It is only grievous to know. I will only wonder & love.

Passionately yrs

am I

Its [illeg., possibly "dawn"]
Clyde

[overleaf]

nor you—nor a line "is it for this that I have given away—"

[Wilde/F544L/W6721/(189-?) b]

Perfect. *Perfect . . . Perfect!* . . .

It is the most delicate, the most exquisite, the most complete idyl I have ever read. Oh! you adorable creature. You *are* a great genius and Oh! such a sweet one. Never was a genius so sweet so adorable. Plod thro' yr history you will find no other.

And I—wee I—i—am allowed to loose the latchet of your shoe . . . Am bidden tie it up—and I do, in a *lover's knot!*

You are my poetry—my painting—my music—You are my sight—and sound, and touch.

Your love is the fragrance of a rose—the sky of a summer—the wing of an angel. The cymbal of a cherubim.

You are always with me that [though?] I have not seen you since Time—it stopped when you left. All, always, in every weather

Gloriously, absorbingly
Yours
Clyde
[Wilde/F544L/W7621/(189-?) c]

My dear Oscar:

I *am* so glad to come to you tonight—my last night in London.

You have dyed all that I have done and am this summer in Angleterre. You have been the sun that has glorified my horizon, and if night came on, and the sun set in a sad splendor, the morning came with its own golden halo and shone sweetly into the thicket where the brown eyed Fawn lay in his grass green bed, with a strangely shaped wound—like this—[draws little valentine heart] in his side. A hunter in snaring his shadow had wounded his heart. But the Brown eyed Fawn was happy. "He has my heart", he sang. "But the *wound,* the wound is mine—and no one can take it from me!"

Clyde

[overleaf]

Note: George Power wishes me to ask you to come to a *quiet little* party at his rooms tonight. I have promised to go for a little when I have Tite St. & G. P. wishes you to come—if you will—I fancy there is to be some music, probably, a song or two.

> So I shall come *"dressed"*
> > A part of a song
>
> Day with no sun, & night without a moon
> Is life love has not sweetened with a kiss
> > A bud which wantons with its spring too soon,
> And so I long for sorrow, with its bliss!

[Wilde/F544L/W6721/(189-?) d]

2. Samuel Taylor Coleridge, "Hamlet," in *The Portable Coleridge,* ed. I. A. Richards (New York: Penguin, 1985), 426.
3. P. Frogatt, "Sir William Wilde, 1815–1876," *Proceedings of the Royal Irish Academy, Section C—Archaeology, Celtic Studies, History, Linguistics, Literature,* 77, no. 10 (1977): 261.
4. TS 559, p. 46, letter, JW to unindentified, 1852, University of Reading Library.
5. Robert Harborough Sherard, *The Real Oscar Wilde* (Philadelphia: David McKay, n.d. [ca. 1915]), 177–78.
6. A less complete version of the letter is in *The Letters of Oscar Wilde,* 3. Richard Ellmann prints the most complete version available, which I quote here, from the Stetson sale catalogue, 1920 (Ellmann, *Oscar Wilde,* 3). The letter, dated 8 September 1868 (Oscar was almost fourteen) and sent from Portora, the boarding school in Enniskillen that he and his brother, Willie, attended, reads: "Darling Mama, The hamper came today, and I never got such a jolly surprise, many thanks for it, it was more than kind of you to think of it. Don't please forget to send me the *National Review. . . .* The flannel shirts you sent in the hamper are both Willie's, mine are one quite scarlet and the other lilac but it is too hot to wear them yet. You never told me anything about the publisher in Glasgow, what does he say? And have you written to Aunt Warren on the green note paper?" Ellmann records that "the rest of the letter is said to have referred to a cricket win over a regimental side, and to 'that horrid regatta.' Accompanying the letter was a sketch, now lost, captioned 'ye delight of ye boys at ye hamper and ye sorrow of ye hamperless boy.'"
7. Hart-Davis records that although Wilde's letter requesting any early verses she might have written has disappeared, the Queen's Minute was preserved and reads: "Really what will people not say and invent. Never cd the Queen in her whole life

write *one line* of *poetry* or make *a Rhyme* even. This is therefore all *invention* & a *myth*" (*L*, 215n).

8. See Casey Miller and Kate Swift, *The Handbook of Nonsexist Writing* (New York: Barnes and Noble, 1980), 73–77: "Honorary epithets like *first lady* and *leading lady* reflect esteem, but when incorporated in a job title, *lady* usually implies a lesser valuation. . . . Obviously *woman* is the most useful all-around word for referring to adult female people. . . . Used as a noun, *woman* connotes independence, competence, and seriousness of purpose as well as sexual maturity. Because these qualities in women are often seen as threatening, some people shy away from the very word, as if it were taboo, and use alternatives like *lady, girl,* and *gal* as euphemism."

9. This quotation appears in several places in the uncatalogued Clark material. I first found it on a page torn from a catalogue dated 15 June 1926, advertising the sale of items from Wilde's "Phrases and Philosophies for the Use of the Young."

10. Steven Marcus, "He Resisted Everything except Temptation," *New York Times Book Review,* 17 November 1985, 7.

11. *New York World,* 3 January 1882, 1; rpt. Mikhail, *Oscar Wilde,* 1:36.

12. Oscar Wilde, "The English Renaissance," in *The Writings of Oscar Wilde,* 14 vols. (New York: Lamb, 1909), 9:104.

13. As Lionel Trilling wrote of Keats, "The fact is . . . that because of the letters it is impossible to think of Keats only as a poet. Once they have come into our possession, we inevitably think of him as something even more interesting than a poet, we think of him as a man, and as a certain kind of man, a hero." Introduction to *The Selected Letters of John Keats* (New York: Farrar, Straus and Young, 1951), 3.

14. Lloyd Lewis and Henry Justin Smith, *Oscar Wilde Discovers America, 1882* (New York: Harcourt, Brace, 1936), 55.

15. Ibid., 57.

16. Indeed, Robert Sherard said of Wilde's effusive letters to him that Wilde was "in the habit of writing extravagant letters, which those who received them took for exactly what they were, effusions partly humorous, partly pathetic, but obviously insincere, and written as literary essays in epistolary style" (Sherard, *The Real Oscar Wilde,* 27).

17. His mother, a flamboyant letter writer who admired anyone with an epistolary flair, probably instigated his interest in epistolary style. In 1850, as a young woman, Speranza exults over a letter from a friend identified as "The Athenian," who she says "sent me a glorious letter of six sheets. It was like one of St. Paul's" (TS 559, p. 27, letter, JW to unidentified, 1850, University of Reading Library). One of her husband's few surviving letters suggests a sardonic twist that made him fit that category well. In a letter of December 1854 he wrote to a friend about research: "Doctor King had written to say that you do not know where the 'annals of the city of Galway' are. Perhaps when you have a moment you would tell me where they were when you quoted from them in your 'History of Galway'" (MS h/12N20/302, Royal Irish Academy). In a letter of 1848 she forwarded to a friend

some love letters an older married man had sent her and commented: "I sent you [his] letters just as a correspondent of Shakespeare might send one of his as a matter of literary interest" (TS 559, pp. 7–8, letter, JW to "My kind friend," June 1848, University of Reading Library). In a move not surprising for a mother whose son paraded a love affair in the Café Royale, she goes on to indicate an interest in publicizing these letters. Affecting to disclaim any sensationalism, she insists: "I consider them only in a literary point of view and not personal." In another letter she confides, "He writes to me weekly and I have told him that I certainly will publish all his letters. Write a word and introduce them" (TS 559, p. 16, letter, JW to unidentified, January 1849, University of Reading Library). Wilde was well aware of famous literary correspondences, especially those of the eighteenth century; he would certainly have known of Jonathan Swift, especially since his father wrote a book on Swift's final illness; Horace Walpole, Thomas Gray, Charles Lamb, Prosper Mérimée, and William Cowper were, judging by Wilde's professed fascination with the egotism of letter writers, familiar to him. Most of these writers were known as witty conversationalists, a quality that certainly would have appealed to Wilde.

18. Thomas Moore, *The Life of Lord Byron: With His Letters and Journals* (Philadelphia: Gihon, 1851), 180. Byron wrote: "This morning I *swam* from *Sesos* to Abydos. The immediate distance is not above a mile, but the current renders it hazardous;—so much so that I doubt whether Leander's conjugal affection must not have been a little chilled in his passage to Paradise. I attempted it a week ago, and failed. . . . But, this morning being calmer, I succeeded, and crossed the 'broad Hellespont' in an hour and ten minutes." Moore writes that Byron worked to build his physical strength and avoid becoming fat: "The fear of becoming, what he naturally inclined to be, enormously fat, had induced him, from his first entrance at Cambridge, to adopt, for the purpose of reducing himself, a system of violent exercise and abstinence, together with the frequent use of warm baths. But the embittering circumstance of his life—that which haunted him like a curse . . . was . . . the trifling deformity of his foot" (77).

19. John Keats, *Life and Letters of John Keats,* intro. Robert Lynd, ed. Richard Monckton Milnes, Lord Houghton (1848; rpt. London: J. M. Dent, 1959), 62, 118.

20. Pearson, *Oscar Wilde,* 329–30. See also Ellmann, *Oscar Wilde,* 545. Ellmann's version of the quip is slightly different: "I will never outlive the century. The English people would not stand for it." Another version of this remark is in a letter from Robert Ross to More Adey in *The Letters of Oscar Wilde,* 848.

21. Moore, *The Life of Lord Byron,* 70.

22. Jane Francesca Elgee Wilde, *Notes on Men, Women, and Books* (London: Ward and Downey, 1891).

23. Moore, *The Life of Lord Byron,* 59.

24. G. W. Knight, *The Christian Renaissance* (New York: Norton, 1962); rpt. Harold Bloom, ed., *Oscar Wilde: Modern Critical Views* (New York: Chelsea House, 1985), 35.

25. Quoted in Hyde, *Oscar Wilde,* 38.

26. Matthew Arnold, "John Keats," in *The English Poets,* ed. Thomas Humphrey Ward (London: Macmillan, 1888), 4:428, 433.

27. Wilde, *The Annotated Oscar Wilde,* ed. H. Montgomery Hyde (London: Orbis, 1982), 48.

28. John Keats, *Letters to Fanny Brawne,* ed. J. B. Forman (London: Reeves and Turner, 1888), 36.

29. TS 559, p. 66, letter, JW to unidentified, ca. 1854, University of Reading Library.

30. Speranza's sudden, unembarrassed shifts between revolutionary enthusiasm and snobbery go a long way toward explaining the uncertainties of Oscar's audiences and friends alike about how "sincere" he was. He was as sincere as she was; he was consistently inconsistent. Robert Ross wrote that Wilde "was never quite sure himself where and when he was serious" (*L,* 859). Wilde admits the same in *An Ideal Husband:* when Lord Goring's father complains, "Humph! Never know when you are serious or not," Lord Goring quips, "Neither do I, father" (*CW,* 538). Wilde was never comfortable with his stance as a fighter, nor with his private, contemplative life. Given Wilde's identification with Byron, Edmund Wilson's characterization of Byron might have been written of Wilde: "I cannot accept the opinion . . . that Byron was a 'blackguard' and a 'cad.' This is . . . to assume that . . . he is sincere in his cynicism but not in his warmth of emotion. It is to assume that one cannot take a personal relation with cynicism and seriousness at the same time. . . . The truth is that Byron . . . never knew where he stood nor what he really wanted. He was a force of enormous energy, running amuck through a world in which he could not find peace" (Edmund Wilson, "Byron in the 'Twenties,'" in *The Shores of Light* (New York: Farrar, Straus, 1952); rpt. Paul West, ed., *Byron: A Collection of Critical Essays* (Englewood Cliffs, N.J.: Prentice-Hall,1963), 138.

31. Keats, *Life and Letters of John Keats,* 76–77.

32. TS 559, p. 27, letter, JW to unidentified, 1850, University of Reading Library.

33. Beerbohm, *Letters to Reggie Turner,* 87.

34. Lord Alfred Douglas, *The Autobiography of Lord Alfred Douglas* (London: Martin Secker, 1929), 238–39, 2. Bosie proudly confessed: "I have been twice convicted for libel at the Old Bailey, once for libelling my father-in-law, Colonel Custance, by accusing him of defrauding his daughter, and once for libelling Winston Churchill, by accusing him of writing a deliberately false account of the battle of Jutland with the object of enabling a group of Jews to make a financial *coup* on the American stock markets."

35. Keats, *Life and Letters of John Keats,* 76–77.

36. Edward Shanks, "Oscar Wilde," *London Mercury,* July 1924; rpt. Beckson, *Oscar Wilde: The Critical Heritage,* 407.

37. Matthew Arnold, "Essay on Byron," in *Poetry and Criticism of Matthew Arnold,* ed. A. Dwight Culler (Boston: Houghton Mifflin, 1961), 358–62.

38. *The Letters of Oscar Wilde,* 594–95. Sporus was the ultimate in debased, epicene

masochism. As Suetonius recounts, "Having tried to turn the boy Sporus into a girl by castration, he [Nero] went through a wedding ceremony with him—dowry, bridal veil and all—which the whole Court attended; then brought him home, and treated him as a wife. He dressed Sporus in the fine clothes normally worn by an Empress and took him in his own litter not only to every Greek assize and fair, but actually through the Street of Images at Rome, kissing him amorously now and then. A rather amusing joke is still going the rounds: the world would have been a happier place had Nero's father Domitius married that sort of wife" (Suetonius, *The Twelve Caesars,* trans. Robert Graves [Baltimore: Penguin, 1957], 223).

39. Ellmann, *Oscar Wilde,* 440. Ellmann writes: "A Jewish businessman of [Harris's] acquaintance happened to mention owning a yacht, and Harris asked him if he would rent it for a month. The man was willing, and asked what Harris planned to do. On impulse Harris told him exactly what he wanted it for, and the yachtsman then said, 'In that case you can have it for nothing.' He too wanted Wilde to escape. Harris now made his proposal to Wilde. The yacht was at Erith, he said, and they could leave at once. Much skepticism has been shown about this yacht, yet both Yeats and Ada Leverson [an old and loyal friend of Wilde's] knew of the plan, and it seems to have been available even if it was not waiting at Erith with steam up, as Harris dramatically pictured it. Wilde however refused to go." Ellmann's sources for this story are W. B. Yeats, *Autobiography* (New York: Macmillan, 1927), 191; Harris, *Oscar Wilde,* 203–08; Ada Leverson, *Letters to the Sphinx from Oscar Wilde and Reminiscences of the Author* (London, 1930), 41; and *Reynolds's News,* 2 June 1895.

40. One might speculate that the vision of himself as Sporus, and the shame and gratification he experienced in that role, show that his unconscious purpose in taking his mother as a model (and in constantly posing as a warrior) was to achieve his father's love. The source of the violent masochistic vision of the sexual act that Wilde desired was probably not only innate masochism but also the child's perception of the sexual act as a violent aggression.

41. H. Montgomery Hyde, *Lord Alfred Douglas* (New York: Dodd, Mead, 1985), 126.

42. TS 559, p. 25, letter from JW, October 1848, University of Reading Library.

43. TS 559, pp. 27–28, letter from JW, 1850, University of Reading Library.

CHAPTER 4: THE DIALECTICS OF *THE IMPORTANCE OF BEING EARNEST*

1. On the eve of Lady Wilde's editor's trial for sedition in June 1848, after his lawyer told her that it was possible to defend all but the inflammatory article she had written, she denounced herself as the author to the solicitor general and wrote to a friend: "I think this piece of Heroism will make a good scene when I write my Life, but . . . I shall never write sedition again" (TS, p. 13, letter, JW to "My Kind Friend," June 1848, University of Reading Library). Soon thereafter she leapt to

her feet in the courtroom to shout out her authorship of her article, wrongly attributed to her editor, an act that may have saved him from a harsh sentence.

2. Ellmann, *Oscar Wilde*, 439. Ellmann's sources are William M. Murphy, *Prodigal Father: The Life of John Butler Yeats, 1839–1922* (Ithaca: Cornell University Press, 1978), 192–93; Harris, *Oscar Wilde*, 200; Sherard, *The Life of Oscar Wilde*, 366, and *Oscar Wilde: Story of an Unhappy Friendship* (London: T. Werner Laurie, 1902), 170; and Ada Leverson, *Letters to the Sphinx*, 148–53.

3. To Frank Harris, Bosie wrote, "I was fascinated by Wilde. . . . I really in the long run adored and was 'crazy' about him" (Hyde, *Lord Alfred Douglas*, 28). Wilde tried again and again to get away from Bosie and was always driven, without understanding why, to return to him. In *De Profundis* he wrote: "I blame myself for the entire ethical degradation I allowed you to bring on me. . . . I remember, as I was in the railway carriage whirling up to Paris, thinking what an impossible, terrible, utterly wrong state my life had got into, when I, a man of world-wide reputation, was actually forced to run away from England, in order to try and get rid of a friendship that was entirely destructive of everything fine in me from the intellectual or ethical point of view" (*L*, 429–33). Douglas, *Autobiography*, 76.

4. Harris, *Oscar Wilde*, 104.

5. Douglas, *Autobiography*, 64.

6. MS Eng. misc. d. 1225, Backhouse, "Last Memories of Lélian and Other Common Friends," in "Memoirs."

7. "H. F.," *New York Times*, 17 February 1895; rpt. Beckson, *Oscar Wilde*, 188.

8. Shaw's most surprising remark about the play, in a letter appended to Frank Harris's 1916 biography of Wilde, is that although he found the play "extremely funny," he thought it was "essentially hateful." In his review of 23 February 1895 he wrote: "I cannot say that I greatly cared for *The Importance of Being Earnest*. It amused me, of course; but unless comedy touches me as well as amuses me, it leaves me with a sense of having wasted my evening. I go to the theatre to be moved to laughter, not to be tickled or bustled into it; and that is why, though I laugh as much as anybody at a farcical comedy, I am out of spirits before the end of the second act, and out of temper before the end of the third, my miserable, mechanical laughter intensifying these symptoms at every outburst. If the public ever becomes intelligent enough to know when it is really enjoying itself and when it is not, there will be an end of farcical comedy" (Shaw, review signed G. B. S., *Saturday Review*, 23 February 1895, lxxix, 249–50; rpt. Beckson, *Oscar Wilde*, 194–95).

9. Ada Leverson, "The Last First Night," *New Criterion* (London), January 1926, 148–53; rpt. Mikhail, *Oscar Wilde*, 2:268.

10. Ellmann, *Oscar Wilde*, 361.

11. Henry James, *The Portrait of a Lady* (New York: Penguin, 1986), 65. In "The Decay of Lying," Wilde wrote: "Mr. Henry James writes fiction as if it were a painful duty, and wastes upon mean motives and imperceptible 'points of view' his felicitous phrases, his swift and caustic satire" (*CW*, 973).

12. The only source I have been able to find for this remark is Redman, *The Wit and Humor of Oscar Wilde*, 74.

13. In a letter of 28 February 1895, to Robert Ross, Wilde wrote: "Bosie's father has left a card at my club with hideous words on it [it read: "For Oscar Wilde, posing somdomite (*sic*)"]. I don't see anything now but a criminal prosecution. My whole life seems ruined by this man. The tower of ivory is assailed by the foul thing. On the sand is my life spilt. I don't know what to do" (*L*, 384).

14. Ellmann, *Oscar Wilde*, 394.

15. His letters reveal a curious fascination with Bosie's father. He writes ca. 17 February 1895: "The Scarlet Marquis make a plot to address the audience on the first night of my play! . . . He left a grotesque bouquet of vegetables for me! This of course makes his conduct idiotic, robs it of dignity. He arrived with a prize-fighter!! I had all Scotland Yard—twenty police—to guard the theatre. He prowled about for three hours, then left chattering like a monstrous ape" (*L*, 383).

16. "Mr. Oscar Wilde on Mr. Oscar Wilde," *St. James Gazette*, 18 January 1895; rpt. Wilde, *More Letters of Oscar Wilde*, 196. Hart-Davis feels that the interview was probably conducted by Robert Ross, because one of Wilde's letters to Ross, dated approximately 25 January 1895, includes the remark "Thank you so much. The interview is most brilliant and delightful" (*ML*, 128).

17. Michel de Montaigne, *The Complete Essays of Montaigne*, trans. Donald M. Frame (Stanford: Stanford University Press, 1965), 221.

18. Solemnization of Matrimony, *Book of Common Prayer*, 56:11.

19. Actually, Wilde was well aware of and sympathetic to the beginnings of the feminist movement in England. When he became editor of *Woman's World*, he sought to shift its focus from fashion to intellect, to marshal the literary talents of prominent women, to keep up with news from women's colleges of Oxford and Cambridge, and to create a forum for the opinions of informed women (*L*, 194–96). He often declared his disgust for the double standard and asked in several of his plays, "Why should there be one law for women and another for men?" His lifetime coincided with those of several prominent feminists, notably Emmeline and Richard Pankhurst. His mother and wife were also involved in the movement, his mother as an avowed revolutionary and his wife in various capacities. An active speaker, Constance addressed the Women's Committee of the International Arbitration and Peace Association, supported Lady Sandhurst's campaign on a feminist platform for a seat on the London County Council, and edited the *Rational Dress Society Gazette* (Amor, *Mrs. Oscar Wilde*, 70, 72, 75).

20. John Gielgud, who acted Ernest, Algernon's friend and the antihero of the play, remarked: "The scene with the muffins [in act 2, when two gentlemen are having an extreme difference of opinion] should be played deliberately and with great seriousness. . . . If [the actors] snatch and shout and talk with their mouths full, the decorum, the deadly importance of the triviality is lost. . . . They are greedy, determined, but still exasperatedly polite" (John Gielgud, *Stage Directions* [New York: Random House, 1963], 81). Gielgud caught Wilde's intention of revealing

that the British forms of utmost politeness and perfect manners are capable of expressing a complete and coarse lack of common courtesy. When Dame Edith Evans first read aloud the role for which she became famous, Lady Bracknell, she remarked, "I know these sort of women. They ring the bell and ask you to put a lump of coal on the fire" (John Gielgud, *An Actor and His Time* [New York: Potter, 1979], 72).

21. The source of this letter is apparently the trial transcript, and the words replaced by brackets were, according to Hart-Davis, "apparently thought too shocking or too obscure to be read out in court" but are inferred from *De Profundis*, in which Wilde quotes them (*L*, 457). The insertion in brackets is from Hart-Davis. The term *renter*—British slang for a male homosexual prostitute—still survives as *rent boy*.

22. Extortion also becomes the contrived motivation of the final scene, when Jack refuses to allow Algy to marry Cecily until Lady Bracknell allows him to marry Gwendolen.

23. Harris, *Oscar Wilde,* 102–03.

24. Brian de Breffny, "The Paternal Ancestry of Oscar Wilde," *Irish Ancestor* 5, no. 2 (1972): 94–103. Although uncertainty about one's origins can, as Freud showed, be kindled in almost every child, circumstances that make for actual uncertainty can easily develop into powerful obsessions, as, in recent history, the cases of Richard Wagner and Adolf Hitler have proven. In both cases, the mere possibility of having a Jewish father seems to have fostered the development of anti-Semitic defenses.

25. In book 19 of the *Odyssey,* Odysseus returns home incognito and is recognized only by his old nurse. While she is washing his feet, she notices the scar Odysseus received when gored by a boar during a hunt (ll. 390–475). For a thorough discussion of the scene, see Erich Auerbach's essay "Odysseus' Scar," in *Mimesis* (Princeton: Princeton University Press, 1953), 3–23. Wilde seems to parody the recognition scene when he shows Miss Prism identifying all the bumps and scrapes on her long-absent handbag: "Yes, here is the injury it received through the upsetting of a Gower Street omnibus in younger and happier days. Here is the stain on the lining caused by the explosion of a temperance beverage" (*CW*, 379).

26. Gide, *Oscar Wilde,* 15–17.

27. Anna, Comtesse de Brémont, *Oscar Wilde and His Mother: A Memoir* (London: Everett, 1911; rpt. New York: Haskell House, 1972), 176–88; rpt. Mikhail, *Oscar Wilde,* 2:450.

28. Oscar Sternbach translated the phrase from Freud's "On Humour." The German word *schön* can also mean "beautiful" or "pleasant" in this context. James Strachey, translator of the *Standard Edition,* rendered the phrase this way: "Well, the week's beginning nicely." Freud, "Humour," *SE* 21:161, 162.

CHAPTER 5: *DE PROFUNDIS*

1. According to Richard Ellmann, E. V. Lucas, an author and the editor of a collection of Wilde's reviews, claims to have suggested this title to Ross (*Oscar Wilde,* 581).
2. Johann Wolfgang von Goethe, *Faust,* pt. 1, trans. Peter Salm (New York: Bantam, 1988), 85, ll. 1349–50.
3. Thomas Martin, "The Poet in Prison," in Mikhail, *Oscar Wilde,* 2:332.
4. Uncatalogued material, letter, TS, Robert Ross to More Adey, Clark Library.
5. Letter, George Bernard Shaw, 23 April 1905, *Neue Freie Presse;* rpt. Beckson, *Oscar Wilde,* 243.
6. In "The Critic as Artist" Wilde remarks, "Ah! it is so easy to convert others. It is so difficult to convert oneself" (*CW,* 1047).
7. Most critics see the letter as the inchoate outpouring of a king who had thrown himself into exile. Gide complained: "[It] can hardly be considered as a book; it is . . . the sobbing of a wounded man who is struggling." Yet he grudgingly confesses: "I was unable to listen to it without tears" (Gide, *Oscar Wilde,* 35). Edouard Roditi observes that it "constantly shifts from the very intimate whisper of the private confessional to the more oratorical tone of a public testament such as *The Confessions of an English Opium Eater* or Cardinal Newman's *Apologia*" (Edouard Roditi, *Oscar Wilde* [Norfolk, Conn.: New Directions, 1947], 10). H. Montgomery Hyde described it as "a curious . . . mixture of apology, self-abasement, and violent recrimination" (Hyde, *Oscar Wilde,* 318).
8. Ellmann, *Oscar Wilde,* 479.
9. See Rupert Hart-Davis's lengthy footnote on pp. 423–24 of his edition of Wilde's *Letters.*
10. In 1939 Bosie remarked during a dinner conversation that he "was personally with Wilde, staying with him and in and out of his study all the time he was writing *The Importance of Being Earnest;* that they talked and laughed about it and a number of the jokes were the repartée Lord Alfred had made himself to Wilde and which were worked up and incorporated in the play" (Hyde, *Lord Alfred Douglas,* 309–10).
11. Harris, *Oscar Wilde,* 229; Ellmann, *Oscar Wilde,* 477–79. Wilde characterized Isaacson as a man who was "not . . . able to enjoy his breakfast unless some one was punished before he ate it" (Wilfrid Hugh Chesson, "A Reminiscence of 1898," *The Bookman* [New York] 34 [December 1911]: 389–94; rpt. Mikhail, *Oscar Wilde,* 2:376).
12. Ellmann, *Oscar Wilde,* 479.
13. Robert Sherard reports Wilde's bitter words after prison: "The fact is that when a man has had two years hard labour, people quite naturally treat him as a pariah dog—this is a social truth that I realise every day. I don't complain about it. There is no use complaining about facts" (Sherard, *The Real Oscar Wilde,* 161).

14. I mention here the writers who appear to have had the largest impact on Wilde. Others whose work is typical of the genre are Edmund Gosse and William Hale White (whose pseudonym was Mark Rutherford).

15. M. H. Abrams first isolated the genre that he terms the "crisis autobiography" in *Natural Supernaturalism: Tradition and Revolution in Romantic Literature* (New York: Norton, 1971). He traces the influence of Augustine's style of autobiography on English, and particularly Victorian, autobiographies. The idea of the auto-biographer playing "a special role in a providential plot" whose design is clear only to his mature self, after a period of great crisis and spiritual transformation, is characteristic of the genre. (See his chapter 2, "Wordsworth's 'Prelude' and the Crisis-Autobiography.") Jerome Buckley, in a similar vein, discusses the importance of the idea of conversion to the Victorian imagination. In *The Victorian Temper: A Study in Literary Culture* (Cambridge: Harvard University Press, 1951), he discerns a "general pattern of nineteenth-century conversion" in fiction, poetry, and autobiography, a charting of "the soul's growth from unshadowed hope through the denial of life itself towards the final conquest of doubt and despair" (87). A number of recent studies have built on the ideas of Abrams and Buckley. In *The Apprenticeship of Beatrice Webb* (Ithaca: Cornell University Press, 1985), Deborah Nord locates Beatrice Webb in the tradition of spiritual crisis autobiographies. Two recent studies trace the use of Christian typology in Victorian autobiographies. In *Victorian Autobiography: The Tradition of Self-Interpretation* (New Haven: Yale University Press, 1986), Linda Peterson discusses Carlyle, Ruskin, Newman, Martineau, and Gosse; in *The Victorian Self: Autobiography and Biblical Narrative* (Ithaca: Cornell University Press, 1989), Heather Henderson treats Newman, Ruskin, and Gosse. In *Figures of Autobiography: The Language of Self-Writing in Victorian and Modern England* (Berkeley: University of California Press, 1983), Avrom Fleishman examines a number of Christian influences on autobiography and considers *De Profundis* to be "part of the late Victorian movement toward secular versions of Christianity" (286–93).

16. John Stuart Mill's experience is typical. Suddenly he saw that he would not be happy even if all his objects in life were realized and that therefore "the whole foundation on which my life was constructed fell down. . . . I frequently asked myself . . . if I could, or was bound to go on living, when life must be passed in this manner. I generally answered to myself, that I did not think I could possibly bear it beyond a year" (John Stuart Mill, *Autobiography,* ed. Jack Stillinger [1873; rpt. Boston: Houghton Mifflin, 1969], 81–85). Reading Marmontel's *Memoirs* and the poetry of Wordsworth and Coleridge, he discovers that feeling is not dead in him. This is the beginning of the gradual death of his Benthamite self—the relinquishing of the Utilitarian philosophy in which he was raised—and the rebirth of a new self in what he called the "culture of the individual"—the belief in the importance of feeling and expressing emotions, which Mill derived from his readings of Wordsworth's poetry.

17. Thomas Carlyle, *Sartor Resartus: The Life and Opinions of Herr Teufelsdrockh,* ed.

Charles Frederick Harrold (New York: Odyssey, 1937), 157, 169, 183. Even the title of Carlyle's autobiographical treatise, *Sartor Resartus* (The Tailor Retailored), suggests a remodeling of the entire personality.

18. John Henry Cardinal Newman, *Apologia pro Vita Sua,* ed. David J. DeLaura (New York: Norton, 1968), 121. For instance, describing the moment of his own conversion, when he ceases to believe in the Anglican idea of the *Via Media,* Newman writes: "The words of St. Augustine . . . struck me with a power which I never had felt from any words before. To take a familiar instance, they were like the 'Turn again Whittington' of the chime, or, to take a more serious one, they were like the 'Tolle, lege,—Tolle, lege,' of the child, which converted St. Augustine himself. 'Securus judicat orbis terrarum!' By those great words of the ancient Father, interpreting and summing up the long and varied course of ecclesiastical history, the theory of the *Via Media* was absolutely pulverized" (98–99).

19. Ellmann, *Oscar Wilde,* 479.

20. O'Sullivan, *Aspects of Wilde,* 36. Lucien Chardon de Rubempré is a central figure in several works of Balzac's *Comédie humaine.* Julien Sorel is the quasi-suicidal hero of Stendhal's *Le Rouge et le noir.*

21. By July 1896, he had sufficient writing material and nearly all the books he wanted (see Hyde, *Trials of Oscar Wilde,* 296; Ellmann, *Oscar Wilde,* 464, 476).

22. Newman appears in Wilde's letters fairly frequently. In July 1876, while still an undergraduate at Oxford, Wilde wrote: "About Newman I think that his higher emotions revolted against Rome but that he was swept on by Logic to accept it as the only rational form of Christianity. His life is a terrible tragedy. I fear he is a very unhappy man. I bought a lot of his books before leaving Oxford" (*L,* 20). In early March 1877, still full of conflict about whether he should embrace Catholicism, he writes: "I have dreams of a visit to Newman, of the holy sacrament in a new Church, and of a quiet and peace afterwards in my soul" (*L,* 31). About two weeks later he writes: "I am going . . . to see Newman at Birmingham to burn my fingers a little more" (*L,* 33). (Hart-Davis comments: "There is no evidence that this visit ever took place" [*L,* 33n].)

23. The letter reads: "Do you remember young Wise [an undergraduate in Wilde's college] of this place? He is awfully caught with the wiles of the Scarlet Woman and wrote to Newman about several things: and received the most charming letters back and invitations to come and see him: I am awfully keen for an interview, not of course to argue, but merely to be in the presence of that divine man. . . . I will send you a long account of it: but perhaps my courage will fail, as I could hardly resist Newman I am afraid" (*L,* 33).

24. Newman, *Apologia pro Vita Sua,* 79.

25. Ibid., 184. In a letter of 1 May 1897, Wilde wrote: "I do want to be rid of the endless doubt, distress, and anxiety. I can bear any certainty at all" (*L,* 533).

26. By finding in Old Testament figures "anticipations" or "foreshadowings" or "types" of Christ, the redeemer, typology imposes an expected pattern on human development, whose end is redemption or salvation through Christ. Northrop

Frye comments, "Typology relates to the future, and is consequently related primarily to faith, hope, and vision. When we want what the funeral service calls the comfort of a reasonable religion, we may deliberately attach a typological belief to some causal process, and say that the latter provides evidence for the former" (Northrop Frye, *The Great Code: The Bible and Literature* [New York: Harcourt, 1982], 82).

27. Fleishman, *Figures of Autobiography,* 201, 286–87. He quotes Wilde's remark in *De Profundis:* "Sorrow is the ultimate type both in life and art; . . . of course all this [interpretation of experience] is foreshadowed and prefigured in my art."

28. Frye, *The Great Code,* 80–81.

29. Newman was, as Heather Henderson has demonstrated, "anxious to show that his conversion [to Catholicism] was not an abrupt, discontinuous change, a betrayal of friends, follower, and church, but rather a natural, almost organic process." She claims that he saw typology as "a form of annunciation: through typology God communicates his truths to man in a partial form, adapted for their understanding. . . . Typology . . . would appear to offer Newman just the organic, developmental model of both sacred and individual history he needs to account for his own conversion as a natural process" (Henderson, *The Victorian Self,* 21–22). Henderson points out that to this end Newman discovers analogies between his own life and the life of Moses, who was traditionally considered a type of Christ the redeemer. Moses led the Israelites out of slavery in Egypt and through the wilderness, and Newman wanted to see himself as the savior leading the English church out of liberalism. In a sermon delivered 15 April 1832, entitled "Moses the Type of Christ," Newman said that "before Christ came, Moses alone saw God face to face. . . . [Only] Christ really saw, and ever saw, the face of God" (Henderson, *The Victorian Self,* 59: Newman, *Parochial and Plain Sermons,* 7:122, 124).

30. By the time Wilde wrote *De Profundis,* struggles with his own divided self had led him to the interest in psychology that permeates his work. In his earliest surviving essay, "The Rise of Historical Criticism," which he wrote as an undergraduate, he remarks: "The one scientific base on which the true philosophy of history must rest is the complete knowledge of human nature in all its wants, its aspirations, its power, and its tendencies" (*CW,* 1124). This brings him close to the Freudian concept of psychodynamics. Recognizing that these psychodynamics are a general characteristic of human nature, he adds: "The method by which the fool arrives at his folly was as dear to him as the ultimate wisdom of the wise. So much, indeed, did the subtle *mechanisms of mind* fascinate him" (*CW,* 1012, my emphasis). Heather Henderson remarks in *The Victorian Self:* "Typology . . . depends upon the perception of a similarity between two events, and the assumption that the latter in some sense repeats the former. . . . [Typology] is linked to the past through repetition, and to the future thought chronological progression towards salvation" (69–70). "Salvation" is a redemption from conflicts.

31. On at least two occasions in *De Profundis* Wilde remarks that Bosie will always be seen as a sort of "Infant Samuel," while "in the lowest mire of Malebolge I sit

between Gilles de Retz and the Marquis de Sade" (*L*, 431, 465). Samuel was chosen by God to be a prophet and announced that David would be king, so as Avrom Fleishman has pointed out, Wilde is "[directing] us to the biblical book in which David's tale is begun" (Fleishman, *Figures of Autobiography*, 287). A great deal of work has been done on the use of typology by Victorian novelists, poets, and autobiographers. G. P. Landow, in *Victorian Types, Victorian Shadows: Biblical Typology in Victorian Literature, Art, and Thought* (Boston: Routledge and Kegan Paul, 1980), remarks, "I was originally . . . quite skeptical about the importance of this mode of biblical symbolism to any Victorian writer but John Ruskin, whom I considered an anomaly. I have since realized that typology helps us to understand other major figures in both Victorian literature and art" (ix). He suggests that "many men and women retained habits of mind associated with typology long after its initial religious basis had changed or vanished" (56). Heather Henderson writes in *The Victorian Self* that "The Christian autobiographer acts . . . as an antitype, or fulfillment, of Christ, and the autobiographical subject becomes a potential type for all men, a pattern for their redemption" (9).

32. Indeed, the lines that Wilde quotes in *De Profundis* from the "servant songs" in the Old Testament book of Isaiah are those best known as a typological foreshadowing of Christ: "He is despised and rejected of men, a man of sorrows and acquainted with grief: and we hid as it were our faces from him" (Isa. 53:3). Wilde himself points out in *De Profundis* that these lines "had seemed to [Christ] to be a prefiguring of himself" (*L*, 481). Typological interpreters of Scripture chose to perceive the similarities in the two entirely different and unrelated lives of Isaiah and Christ—particularly in the idea that both take upon themselves the sins of others—as evidence of a mystical connection between them. Wilde, employing typological thinking because it gave him a chance to imagine a divine purpose in the crisis of his life, could not avoid his critical and self-critical spirit: his intellect exposed the wish fulfillment in Newman's and other writers' typological formulations. John Freccero has incidentally shown that in the prologue to the *Inferno*, Dante was quite self-consciously imitating the stages of Augustine's spiritual journey. See chapter 1, "The Prologue Scene," in John Freccero, *The Poetics of Conversion* (Cambridge: Harvard University Press, 1986), 1–28.

33. Robert Sherard writes, "I was told that the man who first recognised the prisoner shouted 'By God, that is Oscar Wilde,' and spat on him" (Sherard, *The Real Oscar Wilde*, 280).

34. Fleishman, *Figures of Autobiography*, 289.

35. He complains of Bosie's rages; during one of them, Wilde, fearing that Bosie was going to pull out a knife or brandish a pistol, fled for his life. Trying to dignify cowardice, Wilde asserts: "It was not the first time I had been obliged to save you from yourself" (*L*, 467). He remarks, "There were times, even in those dark days . . . when I actually longed to console you. So sure was I that at last you realised what you had done" (*L*, 453). At the end of the letter he sees himself as one "chosen" to teach Bosie "the meaning of Sorrow, and its beauty."

36. With all that, Wilde has glimmers of genuine insight in the midst of all these artificial attempts to find a resonance of his "saved" self in his earlier "fallen self": "The real fool . . . is he who does not know himself. I was such a one too long. . . . Everything that is realised is right" (*CW*, 425). "My Art was to me . . . the great primal note by which I revealed, first myself to myself, and then myself to the world" (*CW*, 447). "Everything must come to one out of one's own nature. There is no use in telling a person a thing that they don't feel and can't understand" (*CW*, 448). "The fact of my having been the common prisoner of a common gaol I must frankly accept, and . . . one of the things I shall have to teach myself is not to be ashamed of it" (*CW*, 469–70). "I ruined myself: and . . . nobody, great or small, can be ruined except by his own hand" (*CW*, 465). "A sentimentalist is simply one who desires to have the luxury of an emotion without paying for it" (*CW*, 501).

37. Ellmann included this photograph in *Oscar Wilde*, facing p. 371. Wilde is wearing a long curly wig, an elaborate headdress of apparently Bedouin-inspired silver-work, serpentine arm bands, a glittering, tightly fitting top that might have been the envy of Gypsy Rose Lee and that gives him the illusion of having plump breasts, a long skirt with a jewel-encrusted belt, and numerous rings.

38. Thomas Wentworth Higginson, "Unmanly Manhood," *Woman's Journal* (Boston), 4 February 1882, xiii, 33; rpt. Beckson, *Oscar Wilde*, 51.

39. Unsigned review, *Pall Mall Gazette*, 12 May 1891, 3; rpt. Beckson, *Oscar Wilde*, 92.

40. Beerbohm, *Letters to Reggie Turner*, 36.

41. Max Beerbohm, "A Lord of Language," *Vanity Fair*, 2 March 1905, cxxiii, 309; rpt. Beckson, *Oscar Wilde*, 249.

42. Letter, Frank Harris to George Bernard Shaw, 27 November 1900, in George Bernard Shaw, *Bernard Shaw: Collected Letters, 1898–1910*, ed. Dan H. Laurence (New York: Dodd, Mead, 1972), 2:196.

43. Amor, *Mrs. Oscar Wilde*, 189.

44. Ellmann, *Oscar Wilde*, 505.

45. Sherard, *The Real Oscar Wilde*, 410.

46. Harris, *Oscar Wilde*, 234.

47. Hyde, *The Trials of Oscar Wilde*, 112.

SELECTED BIBLIOGRAPHY

MANUSCRIPT SOURCES

The Bodleian Library, Oxford University, Oxford

MS Eng. misc. d. 1225 and MS Res. d. 332: "Memoirs of Sir Edmund Trelawny Backhouse," particularly "The Dead Past." Backhouse knew Wilde and his circle and was intimately acquainted with Lord Alfred Douglas's brother. Portions of the memoirs correspond to testimony given at Wilde's trials and reveal aspects of his personality that are highly relevant to his writing.

The British Library, London

Add. MSS 37,942–37,948: manuscripts of Wilde's poem "The Sphinx"; his four comedies, *Lady Windemere's Fan, A Woman of No Importance, An Ideal Husband,* and *The Importance of Being Earnest;* and *De Profundis.*

Jane Francesca Elgee Wilde, *Social Studies.* Out-of-print work revealing her ideas about personality and self-presentation.

National Library of Ireland, Dublin

MSS 5756–5757: letters to Charles Gavan Duffy from persons prominent in literary and political affairs, 1840–54. Duffy was Lady Wilde's editor in her radical days; also includes letters written by her.

MS 7544: Larcom papers; includes condolence letter from Wilde's mother to Lady Larcom.

MS 905: Hamilton letters and papers. Sir William Rowan Hamilton, a colleague of Sir William Wilde, Oscar's father, was also a close friend of Lady Wilde.

MS 10,517: miscellaneous letters from members of the radical Young Ireland movement, including a letter from Wilde's mother to her editor.

MS 15,281: letter regarding family matters from Wilde's mother to Mrs. Olivecrona, a Swedish woman whose husband was a colleague of Sir William Wilde.

MS 13,987: letters of Sir William Wilde to four colleagues regarding matters connected with the Royal Irish Academy.

Royal Irish Academy, Dublin

MS h/12N20/302: letter of Sir William Wilde to a friend regarding research; revealing of Wilde's father's personality and its influence on Oscar.

University of Reading Library, Reading

Letters of Jane Francesca Elgee Wilde, formerly in the archives of Elkin Mathews, publisher: series of letters from Oscar's mother from the time of her days in the Young Ireland movement until Oscar was about two years old; revealing of her hopes, dreams, and aspirations for him.

William Andrews Clark Memorial Library, University of California, Los Angeles

Personal and family correspondence, literary manuscripts of Oscar Wilde and his circle, 1870–1957; illuminates the relationship between Oscar and his brother, William.

NEWSPAPERS

Daily News (London), December 1864.
Dublin Evening Post, December 1864.
Freeman's Journal, February 1849, December 1864.
Irish Times, December 1864.
The Nation, February 1849, December 1864.
Northern Whig, February 1849, December 1864.
Saunder's Newsletter, December 1864.
The Times (London), December 1864.

PUBLISHED SOURCES

Abrams, M. H. *Natural Supernaturalism: Tradition and Revolution in Romantic Literature.* New York: Norton, 1971.

Ackroyd, Peter. *The Last Testament of Oscar Wilde.* New York: Perennial Library, 1985.

Allan, Clifford. "Homosexuality and Oscar Wilde: A Psychological Study." *International Journal of Sexology* 11, no. 4 (May 1949): 205–21.

Amor, Anne Clark. *Mrs. Oscar Wilde: A Woman of Some Importance.* London: Sidgwick and Jackson, 1983.

Arnold, Matthew. "John Keats." In *The English Poets,* edited by Thomas Humphrey Ward. Vol. 4. London: Macmillan, 1888.

———. *Poetry and Criticism of Matthew Arnold.* Edited by A. Dwight Culler. Boston: Houghton Mifflin, 1961.

Auden, W. H. *Forewords and Afterwords.* New York: Random House, 1973.

Beerbohm, Max. *Letters to Reggie Turner.* Edited by Rupert Hart-Davis. London: Soho Square/Richard Clay, 1964.

Beckson, Karl. "The Importance of Being Angry: The Mutual Antagonism of Oscar and Willie Wilde." In *Blood Brothers,* edited by Norman Kiell. New York: International Universities Press, 1983.

———. "Oscar Wilde and the Masks of Narcissus." In *The Psychoanalytic Study of Society,* edited by Werner Muensterberger, L. Bryce Boyer, and Simon A. Grolnick. Vol. 10. Hillsdale, N.J.: Analytic Press, 1984.

Beckson, Karl, ed. *Oscar Wilde: The Critical Heritage.* London: Routledge and Kegan Paul, 1970.

Bergler, Edmund. "Salome: The Turning Point in the Life of Oscar Wilde." *Psychoanalytic Review* 43 (1956): 97–103.

Bleuler, Eugen. *Textbook of Psychiatry.* Translated by A. A. Brill. New York: Dover, 1951.

Bloom, Harold, ed. *Oscar Wilde: Modern Critical Views.* New York: Chelsea House, 1985.

Bonaparte, Marie. *Edgar Allan Poe.* 2 vols. Paris: Editions Denoël et Steel, 1933.

Borges, Jorge Luis. "About Oscar Wilde." In *Other Inquisitions, 1937–52.* Translated by Ruth L. C. Simms. 1946. Reprint, New York: Simon and Schuster, 1965.

Borland, Maureen. *Wilde's Devoted Friend: A Life of Robert Ross, 1869–1918.* Oxford: Lennard, 1990.

Brasol, Boris. *Oscar Wilde: The Man, the Artist, the Martyr.* New York: Octagon, 1975.

Breffny, Brian de. "The Paternal Ancestry of Oscar Wilde." *Irish Ancestor* 5, no. 2 (1972): 94–103.

Brown, William J., James F. Donoghue, Norman W. Axnick, Joseph H. Blount, Neal H. Ewen, and Oscar G. Jones. *Syphilis and Other Venereal Diseases.* Cambridge: Harvard University Press, 1970.

Buckley, Jerome. *The Victorian Temper: A Study in Literary Culture.* Cambridge: Harvard University Press, 1951.

Byron, George Gordon, Lord. *Lord Byron: Selected Letters and Journals.* Edited by Leslie Marchand. Cambridge: Belknap Press, Harvard University, 1982.

Carlyle, Thomas. *Sartor Resartus: The Life and Opinions of Herr Teufelsdrockh.* Edited by Charles Frederick Herrold. 1833–34. Reprint, New York: Odyssey Press, 1937.

Cawthorne, Terence. "The Last Illness of Oscar Wilde." *Proceedings of the Royal Society of Medicine* (London) 52 (February 1959): 123–27.

Charney, Maurice, and Joseph Reppen. *The Psychoanalytic Study of Literature.* Hillsdale, N.J.: Analytic Press, 1985.

Chasseguet-Smirgal, Janine. "Loss of Reality in Perversions—with Special Reference to Fetishism." *Journal of the American Psychoanalytic Association* 18 (1981): 511–34.

Coleridge, Samuel Taylor. *The Portable Coleridge.* Edited by I. A. Richards. New York: Viking, 1978.

Coriat, Isidor H. "The Sadism in Oscar Wilde's 'Salome.'" *Psychoanalytic Review* 1 (1914): 257–59.

Crissey, John Thorne, M.D., and Lawrence Charles Parish, M.D. *The Dermatology and Syphilology of the Nineteenth Century.* New York: Praeger, 1981.

Croft-Cooke, Rupert. *Feasting with Panthers.* London: W. H. Allen, 1967.

Culler, A. Dwight. "Correspondents with Posterity." *Yale Review* 52, no. 2 (December 1962): 283–90.

Dawson, Terence. "Fear of the Feminine in *The Picture of Dorian Gray.*" *Psychoanalytic Review* 77, no. 2 (Summer 1990): 263–80.

De Quincey, Thomas. *Studies on Secret Records, Personal and Historic: With Other Papers.* Edinburgh: James Hogg, 1858.

Douglas, Lord Alfred. *The Autobiography of Lord Alfred Douglas.* London: Martin Secker, 1929.

———. *Oscar Wilde and Myself.* New York: Duffield, 1914.

Eagleton, Terry. *St. Oscar.* Great Britain: Field Day, 1989.

Eder, Doris. "The Idea of the Double." *Psychoanalytic Review* 65 (1978): 579–614.

Ellmann, Richard. "Freud and Literary Biography." In *Freud and the Humanities,* edited by Peregrine Horden. New York: St. Martin's Press, 1985.

———. *Golden Codgers.* New York: Oxford University Press, 1973.

———. "A Late Victorian Love Affair." In *Oscar Wilde: Two Approaches.* Los Angeles: William Andrews Clark Memorial Library, University of California, 1977.

———. *Oscar Wilde.* London: Hamish Hamilton, 1987.

Ellmann, Richard, ed. *The Artist as Critic: Critical Writings of Oscar Wilde.* New York: Random House, 1969.

Fido, Martin. *Oscar Wilde: An Illustrated Biography.* New York: Peter Bedrick, 1985.

Fitzgibbon, Constantine. "The Fallacy of Reading Gaol." *Spectator,* 29 June 1962, 861–62.

Fleishman, Avrom. *Figures of Autobiography: The Language of Self-Writing in Victorian and Modern England.* Berkeley: University of California Press, 1983.

Freccero, John. *The Poetics of Conversion.* Cambridge: Harvard University Press, 1986.

Freud, Sigmund. "A Childhood Recollection from *Dichtung und Wahrheit.*" In *The Standard Edition of the Complete Psychological Works of Sigmund Freud.* Vol. 17. Translated by James Strachey. London: Hogarth Press, 1981.

———. *Delusions and Dreams in Jensen's* Gradiva. *SE* 9.

———. "Dostoevsky and Parricide." *SE* 21.

———. "On Humour." *SE* 21.

———. *The Interpretation of Dreams. SE* 5.

———. "Leonardo Da Vinci and a Memory of His Childhood." *SE* 11.

———. *New Introductory Lectures on Psychoanalysis. SE* 22.

———. "The Question of Lay Analysis." *SE* 20.

———. "Three Essays on Sexuality." *SE* 7.

Friedman, Robert M. "The Psychoanalytic Model of Male Homosexuality: A Historical and Theoretical Critique." *Psychoanalytic Review* 73, no. 4 (Winter 1986): 483–519.

Frogatt, P. "Sir William Wilde, 1815–1876." *Proceedings of the Royal Irish Academy, Section C—Archaeology, Celtic Studies, History, Linguistics, Literature* 77, no. 10 (1977): 261–79.

Frye, Northrop. *The Great Code: The Bible and Literature.* New York: Harcourt, 1982.

Gagnier, Regenia. *Idylls of the Marketplace: Oscar Wilde and the Victorian Public.* Stanford: Stanford University Press, 1986.

Gardner, Averil. "'Literary Petty Larceny': Plagiarism in Oscar Wilde's Early Poetry." *English Studies in Canada* 8, no. 1 (March 1982): 49–61.

Gide, André. *Oscar Wilde.* Translated by Bernard Frechtman. New York: Philosophical Library, 1949.

Gielgud, John. *An Actor and His Time.* New York: Clarkson N. Potter, 1979.

———. *Stage Directions.* New York: Random House, 1963.

Goethe, Johann Wolfgang von. *Faust,* pt. 1. Translated by Peter Salm. New York: Bantam, 1988.

Gold, Stanley. "Frankenstein and Other Monsters: An Examination of the Concepts of Destructive Narcissism, and Perverse Relationships between Parts of the Self as Seen in the Gothic Novel." *International Review of Psycho-Analysis* 12 (1985): 101–08.

Grant, Michael, and John Hazel. *Gods and Mortals in Classical Mythology.* Springfield, Mass.: Merriam, 1973.

Green, Bernard A. "The Effects of Distortions of the Self: A Study of *The Picture of Dorian Gray.*" In *The Annual of Psychoanalysis,* edited by George H. Pollack, M.D., et al. Vol. 7. New York: International Universities Press, 1979.

Greenacre, Phyllis. *Swift and Carroll: A Psychoanalytic Study of Two Lives.* New York: International Universities Press, 1955.

Grinstein, Alexander. "On Oscar Wilde." In *The Annual of Psychoanalysis,* edited by Chicago Institute of Psychoanalysis. Vol. 1. New York: Quadrangle/Times, 1973.

———. "Oscar Wilde." *American Imago* 37, no. 2 (Summer 1980): 125–79.

Gunn, Daniel. *Psychoanalysis and Fiction: An Exploration of Literary and Psychoanalytic Borders.* New York: Cambridge University Press, 1988.

Harris, Frank. *My Life and Loves.* Edited by John F. Gallagher. New York: Grove Press, 1963.

———. *Oscar Wilde: His Life and Confessions.* New York: Covici, Friede, 1930.

Henderson, Heather. *The Victorian Self: Autobiography and Biblical Narrative.* Ithaca: Cornell University Press, 1989.

Holland, Vyvyan. *Oscar Wilde: A Pictorial Biography.* New York: Viking, 1960.

———. *Son of Oscar Wilde.* New York: Oxford University Press, 1988.

Hood, Thomas. *The Complete Poetical Works of Thomas Hood.* Edited by Walter Jerrold. London: Henry Frowde, 1906.

Hutchinson, Jonathan, F.R.S., L.L.D. *Syphilis.* Philadelphia: Lea Bros., n.d. (ca.1887).

Hyde, H. Montgomery. *Lord Alfred Douglas: A Biography.* New York: Dodd, Mead, 1985.

———. *Oscar Wilde.* New York: Da Capo, 1981.

Hyde, H. Montgomery, ed. *The Trials of Oscar Wilde.* New York: Dover, 1962.

Hyde, Mary, ed. *Bernard Shaw and Alfred Douglas: A Correspondence.* New York: Ticknor and Fields, 1982.

James, Henry. *The Portrait of a Lady.* New York: Penguin, 1986.

Jullian, Philippe. *Oscar Wilde.* London: Paladin Grafton, 1986.

Kaplan, Leo. "Analysis of 'The Picture of Dorian Gray.'" *Psyche and Eros* 3 (1922): 8–21.

Kavka, Jerome. "Oscar Wilde's Narcissism." *The Annual of Psychoanalysis.* Vol. 3. New York: International Universities Press, 1975.

Keats, John. *Letters to Fanny Brawne.* Edited by J. B. Forman. London: Reeves and Turner, 1888.

———. *Life and Letters of John Keats.* Edited by Richard Monckton Milnes, Lord Houghton. London: J. M. Dent, 1867.

———. *The Selected Letters of John Keats.* Edited by Lionel Trilling. New York: Farrar, Straus and Young, 1951.

Kee, Robert. *Ireland: A History.* London: Abacus, 1982.

Kohl, Norbert. *Oscar Wilde: The Works of a Conformist Rebel.* Translated by David Henry Wilson. New York: Cambridge University Press, 1989.

Landow, G. P. *Victorian Types, Victorian Shadows: Biblical Typology in Victorian Literature, Art, and Thought.* Boston: Routledge and Kegan Paul, 1980.

Lewis, Lloyd, and Henry Justin Smith. *Oscar Wilde Discovers America, 1882.* New York: Harcourt, Brace, 1936.

Lichtenberg, Joseph, ed. *Empathy.* Vol. 1. Hillsdale, N.J.: Analytic Press, 1984.

Lieberman, E. James. *Acts of Will: The Life and Work of Otto Rank.* New York: Free Press, 1985.

McGinnis, Robert M. "The Image of 'La Belle Dame sans Merci' in Wilde's Plays." *Literature and Psychology* 18 (1968): 123–34.

Mahler, Margaret S., Fred Pine, and Anni Bergman. *The Psychological Birth of the Human Infant: Symbiosis and Individuation.* New York: Basic, 1975.

Mandell, G. L., R. G. Douglas, Jr., and J. E. Bennett, eds. *Principles and Practice of Infectious Diseases.* New York: Wiley, 1990.

Marcus, Steven. *Dickens from Pickwick to Dombey.* New York: Clarion, 1965.

———. *Freud and the Culture of Psychoanalysis.* Boston: George Allen and Unwin, 1984.

———. "He Resisted Everything except Temptation." *New York Times Book Review,* 17 November 1985, 7, 9.

———. *The Other Victorians: A Study of Sexuality and Pornography in Mid-Nineteenth-Century England.* New York: Meridian, 1974.

Mason, Stuart [Christopher Millard]. *Bibliography of Oscar Wilde.* London: T. Werner Laurie, 1914.

Meyer, Bernard C. "Notes on the Uses of Psychoanalysis for Biography." *Psychoanalytic Quarterly* 56 (1987): 287–316.

Mikhail, E. H., ed. *Oscar Wilde: Interviews and Recollections*. 2 vols. London: Macmillan, 1979.

Mill, John Stuart. *Autobiography*. Edited by Jack Stillinger. 1873. Reprint, Boston: Houghton Mifflin, 1969.

Miller, Casey, and Kate Swift. *The Handbook of Nonsexist Writing*. New York: Barnes and Noble, 1980.

Miller, Sigmund Stephen, ed. *Symptoms*. London: Pan/Macmillan, 1979.

Montaigne, Michel de. *The Complete Essays of Montaigne*. Translated by Donald M. Frame. Stanford: Stanford University Press, 1965.

Moore, Harry T. "Correspondence *De Profundis.*" *Saturday Review*, 20 October 1962, 26.

Moore, Thomas. *The Life of Lord Byron: With His Letters and Journals*. 2 vols. Philadelphia: Gihon, 1851.

Murphy, William M. *Prodigal Father: The Life of John Butler Yeats, 1839–1922*. Ithaca: Cornell University Press, 1978.

Nassaar, Christopher. *Into the Demon Universe: A Literary Exploration of Oscar Wilde*. New Haven: Yale University Press, 1974.

Newman, John Henry, Cardinal. *Apologia pro Vita Sua*. Edited by David J. DeLaura. New York: Norton, 1968.

Niederland, William G. "Psychoanalytic Approaches to Artistic Creativity." *Psychoanalytic Quarterly* 45, no. 2 (1976): 185–212.

Nord, Deborah. *The Apprenticeship of Beatrice Webb*. Ithaca: Cornell University Press, 1985.

O'Sullivan, Vincent. *Aspects of Wilde*. London: Constable, 1936.

Pater, Walter. *Imaginary Portraits*. Edited by Eugen J. Bryzenk. New York: Harper and Row, 1964.

————. *The Renaissance: Studies in Art and Poetry*. Edited by Donald L. Hill. Berkeley: University of California Press, 1980.

Pearson, Hesketh. *Oscar Wilde: His Life and Wit*. New York: Harper and Bros., 1946.

Pepper, Robert D., ed. *Oscar Wilde, Irish Poets and Poetry of the Nineteenth Century: A Lecture Delivered in Platt's Hall, San Francisco, on Wednesday, April Fifth, 1882*. San Francisco: Book Club of San Franciso, 1972.

Peterson, Linda. *Victorian Autobiography: The Tradition of Self-Interpretation*. New Haven: Yale University Press, 1986.

Pierloot, Roland A. "Impersonal Objects in Morbid Jealousy." *International Review of Psycho-Analysis* 15 (1988): 293–305.

Pusey, William Allen. *The History and Epidemiology of Syphilis*. Springfield, Ill.: Charles C. Thomas, 1933.

Raby, Peter. *Oscar Wilde*. New York: Cambridge University Press, 1988.

Ragland-Sullivan, Ellie. "The Phenomenon of Aging in Oscar Wilde's *Picture of Dorian Gray*: A Lacanian View." In *Memory and Desire: Aging—Literature—*

Psychoanalysis, edited by Kathleen Woodward and Murray M. Schwartz. Bloomington: Indiana University Press, 1986.

Rank, Otto. *Will Therapy.* New York: Norton, 1978.

Ransome, Arthur. *Oscar Wilde: A Critical Study.* London: Martin Secker, 1912.

Rascovsky, Matilde Wencelblat de, and Arnold Raskovsky. "On Consummated Incest." *International Journal of Psychoanalysis* 31, pts. 1 and 2 (1950): 42–47.

Redman, Alvin. *The Wit and Humor of Oscar Wilde.* New York: Dover, 1959.

Reik, Theodor. *Listening with the Third Ear.* New York: Farrar, Straus, 1948.

Reilly, Robert. *The God of Mirrors.* Boston: Atlantic Monthly Press, 1986.

Roazen, Paul. *Helene Deutsch: A Psychoanalyst's Life.* New York: Meridian, 1985.

Roditi, Edouard. *Oscar Wilde.* Norfolk, Conn.: New Directions, 1947.

Rogers, Robert. *A Psychoanalytic Study of the Double in Literature.* Detroit: Wayne State University Press, 1970.

Rolleston, J. D. "The Folk-lore of Venereal Disease." *British Journal of Venereal Disease* 18 (1942): 1–12.

Runyan, William. *Life Histories and Psychobiography: Explorations in Theory and Method.* New York: Oxford University Press, 1985.

Sedgwick, Eve Kosofsky. *Epistemology of the Closet.* Berkeley: University of California Press, 1990.

Seymour-Smith, Martin. *Fallen Women.* London: Thomas Nelson, 1969.

Shaw, George Bernard. *Bernard Shaw: Collected Letters, 1898–1910.* Edited by Dan H. Laurence. New York: Dodd, Mead, 1972.

Sherard, Robert. *The Life of Oscar Wilde.* London: T. Werner Laurie, 1906.

———. *The Real Oscar Wilde.* Philadelphia: David McKay, n.d. (ca. 1915).

———. *Oscar Wilde: The Story of an Unhappy Friendship.* London: T. Werner Laurie, 1902.

Skura, Meredith Anne. *The Literary Use of the Psychoanalytic Process.* New Haven: Yale University Press, 1981.

Smith, Philip E., and Michael S. Helfand. *Oscar Wilde's Oxford Notebooks: A Portrait of Mind in the Making.* New York: Oxford University Press, 1989.

Summers, Claude J. *Gay Fictions: Wilde to Stonewall; Studies in a Male Homosexual Literary Tradition.* New York: Continuum, 1990.

Tennyson, Alfred, Lord. *In Memoriam.* Edited by Robert H. Ross. 1850. Reprint, New York: Norton, 1973.

Trosman, Harry. *Freud and the Imaginative World.* Hillsdale, N.J.: Analytic Press, 1985.

Weiss, Daniel. *The Critic Agonistes: Psychology, Myth, and the Art of Fiction.* Edited by Eric Solomon and Stephen Arkin. Seattle: University of Washington Press, 1985.

Weil, Edmund. "The Origins and Vicissitudes of the Self-Image." *Psychoanalysis* 6, no. 1 (1958): 3–19.

West, Paul, ed. *Byron: A Collection of Critical Essays.* Englewood Cliffs, N.J.: Prentice-Hall, 1963.

White, Terence de Vere. *The Parents of Oscar Wilde: Sir William and Lady Wilde.* London: Hodder and Stoughton, 1967.

Wilde, Jane Francesca Elgee. *Ancient Legends, Mystic Charms, and Superstitions of Ireland.* Boston: Ticknor, 1888.

Wilde, Oscar. *The Annotated Oscar Wilde.* Edited by H. Montgomery Hyde. London: Orbis, 1982.

———. *Complete Works of Oscar Wilde.* Edited by Vyvyan Holland. London: Collins, 1986.

———. *The Writings of Oscar Wilde.* 14 vols. New York: Lamb, 1909.

———. *The Letters of Oscar Wilde.* Edited by Rupert Hart-Davis. New York: Harcourt, Brace and World, 1962.

———. *More Letters of Oscar Wilde.* Edited by Rupert Hart-Davis. New York: Vanguard Press, 1985.

Wilson, T. G. *Victorian Doctor.* London: Methuen, 1942.

Winwar, Frances. *Oscar Wilde and the Yellow Nineties.* New York: Blue Ribbon, 1940.

Wright, Elizabeth. *Psychoanalytic Criticism: Theory in Practice.* New York: Methuen, 1984.

Wyndham, Horace. *Speranza: A Biography of Lady Wilde.* London:T. V. Boardman, 1951.

Yeats, W. B. *Autobiography.* New York: Macmillan, 1927.

Young-Bruehl, Elizabeth. *Anna Freud: A Biography.* New York: Summit, 1988.

———. "Psychoanalysis and Biography." In *The Psychoanalytic Study of the Child,* edited by Albert J. Solnit, Ruth S. Eissler, and Peter B. Neubauer. Vol. 40. New Haven: Yale University Press, 1985.

Zola, Emile. *Nana.* Cleveland: Fine Editions Press, 1946.

INDEX

of, 92, 96, 159nn13, 14; social isolation resulting from, 118, 120, 132;
reading in prison, 121–22
—works: "The Critic as Artist," xiii,
xiv–xv, 24, 74, 114, 115, 117, 123;
"The Portrait of Mr. W. H.," xv, xviii;
Salome, xvi, xvii–xviii, 24, 25–33,
34, 66, 127, 144n91; De Profundis,
xviii, xix, 66, 69–70, 71, 108, 110–
25, 126–30, 131; The Ballad of Reading Gaol, xx, 16–17, 18–19, 57, 87–
88, 131, 133–35; The Picture of Dorian Gray, xx, 22, 23, 39, 48–49, 60,
62–63, 69, 81; Lady Windermere's
Fan, 2, 3, 27, 36, 94; An Ideal Husband, 3, 19, 27, 99, 156n30; The Importance of Being Earnest, 3, 47, 93,
94–96, 97, 98, 99–107, 108–9, 130–
31, 158n8; "Requiescat," 9–11, 12,
13, 15, 53, 142n55; "The Harlot's
House," 11–13, 16; "Ballade de Marguerite," 13; A Woman of No Importance, 19, 22, 73, 93, 94, 95, 101;
Vera, or the Nihilists, 35, 36–37; "The
Decay of Lying," 36, 47, 114,
158n11; "The Soul of Man under Socialism," 36, 62, 82; "Charmides,"
40; "Endymion," 40; "Wasted Days,"
40; "Pen, Pencil and Poison," 46;
"The Canterville Ghost," 50–52,
53–54, 55; "Lord Arthur Savile's
Crime," 53, 55–56, 57, 58, 59–60;

"The Young King," 60–61, 62,
127; "The Birthday of the Infanta,"
61; "The Happy Prince," 64–65, 127;
"The Selfish Giant," 65–66; "The
Star Child," 66–67; "Ravenna," 76;
"On the Sale by Auction of Keats's
Love Letters," 78; "The Grave of
Keats," 79–80; "The Truth of
Masks," 100; "The Master," 125–26;
"The Remarkable Rocket," 126; "The
Rise of Historical Criticism," 164n30
Wilde, Sir William (father), 22, 71; re-
lationship with wife, 4, 6, 14; knight-
hood, 4, 7; as physician, 4, 9, 70;
influence on Wilde, 9, 55, 70, 97; af-
fair with Mary Travers, 14–15, 29,
97; death of, 97
Wilde, Willie (brother), 5, 6–7, 8–9,
22, 30, 35
Wilson, Edmund, 156n30
Woman of No Importance, A, 19, 22, 73,
93, 94, 95, 101
Woman's World, 21, 72–73, 159n19
Wordsworth, William, xi, 61

Yeats, John Butler, 28, 145n100
Yeats, William Butler, 50, 58, 157n39
Young Ireland movement, 5, 6, 35
"Young King, The," 60–61, 62, 127

Zola, Emile, 10